Botanical WATERCOLOR PAINTING FOR BEGINNERS

A Step-by-Step Guide
to Create Beautiful Floral Artwork

Cara Rosalie Olsen

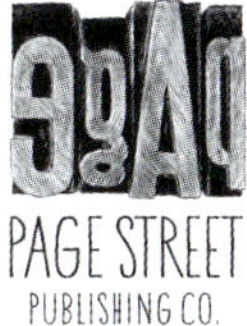

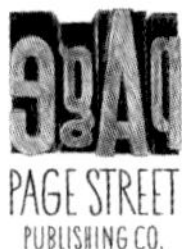

First published in 2022 by
Page Street Publishing Co.
27 Congress Street, Suite 1511
Salem, MA 01970
www.pagestreetpublishing.com

Distributed by Macmillan, sales in Canada by The Canadian Manda Group.

26 27 26 25 24 4 5 6 7 8

ISBN-13: 978-1-64567-592-1
ISBN-10: 1-64567-592-0

Library of Congress Control Number: 2021944913

Cover and book design by Rosie Stewart for Page Street Publishing Co.
Photography by Cara Rosalie Olsen

Printed and bound in China

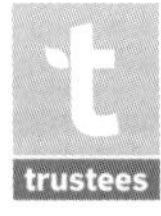

Page Street Publishing protects our planet by donating to nonprofits like The Trustees, which focuses on local land conservation.

For the creative souls and lovers of beauty, most especially flowers, this book is for you.

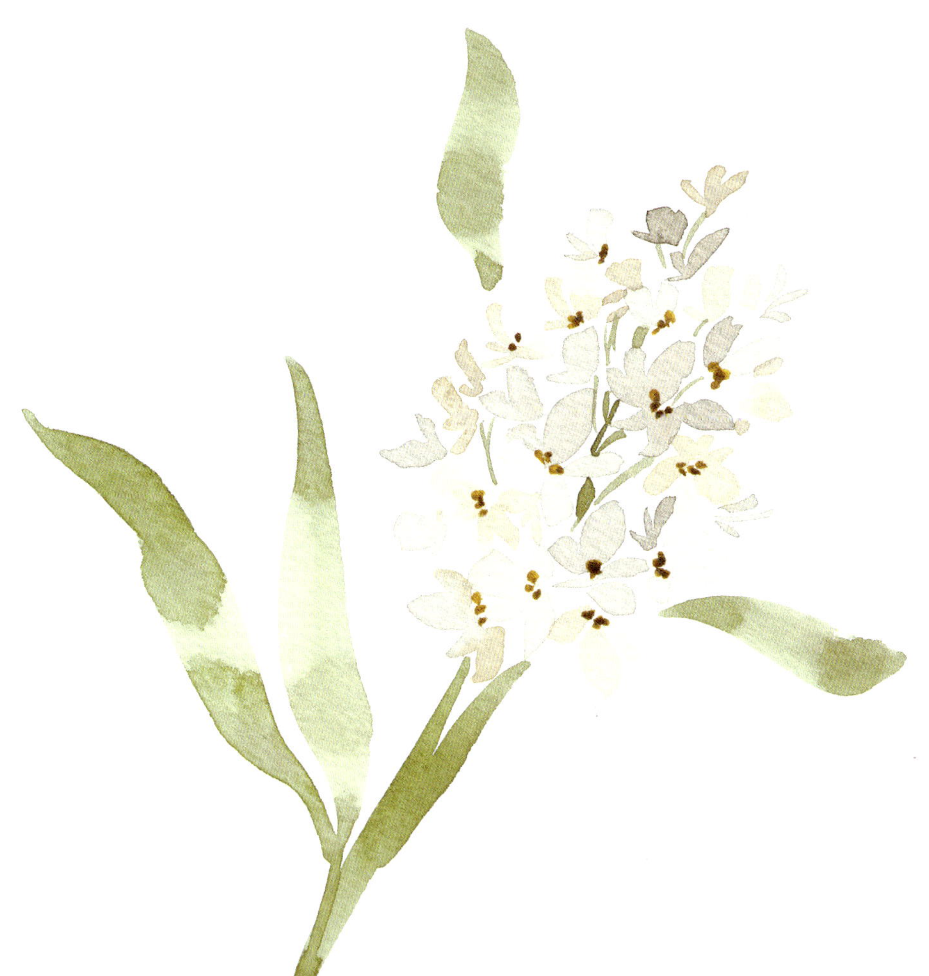

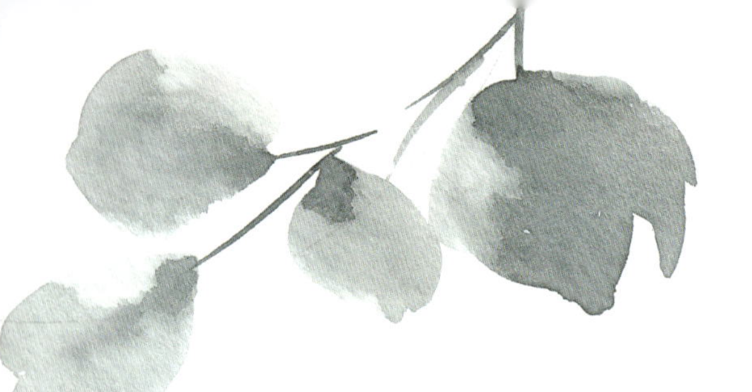

Contents

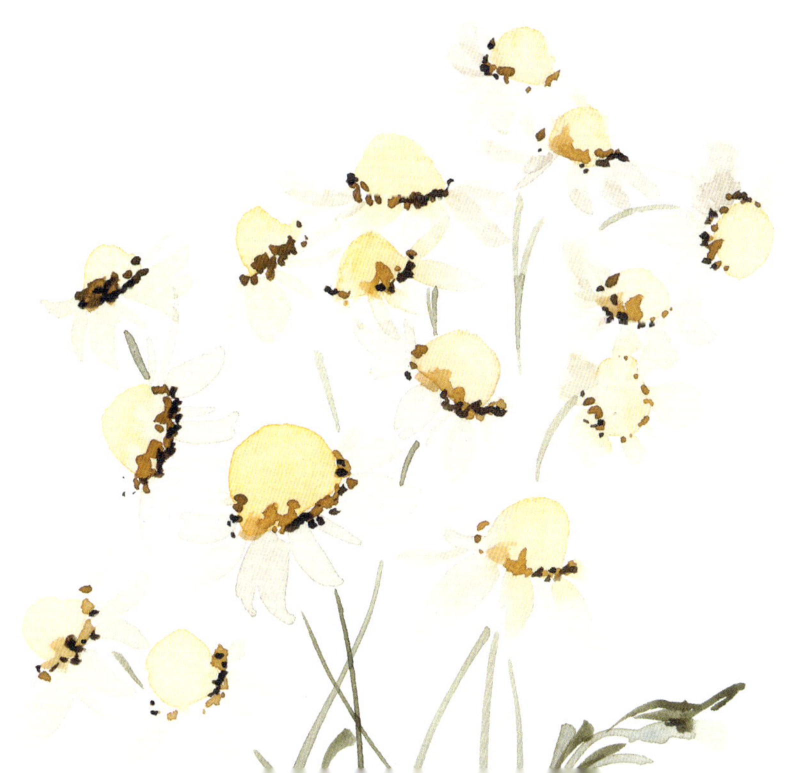

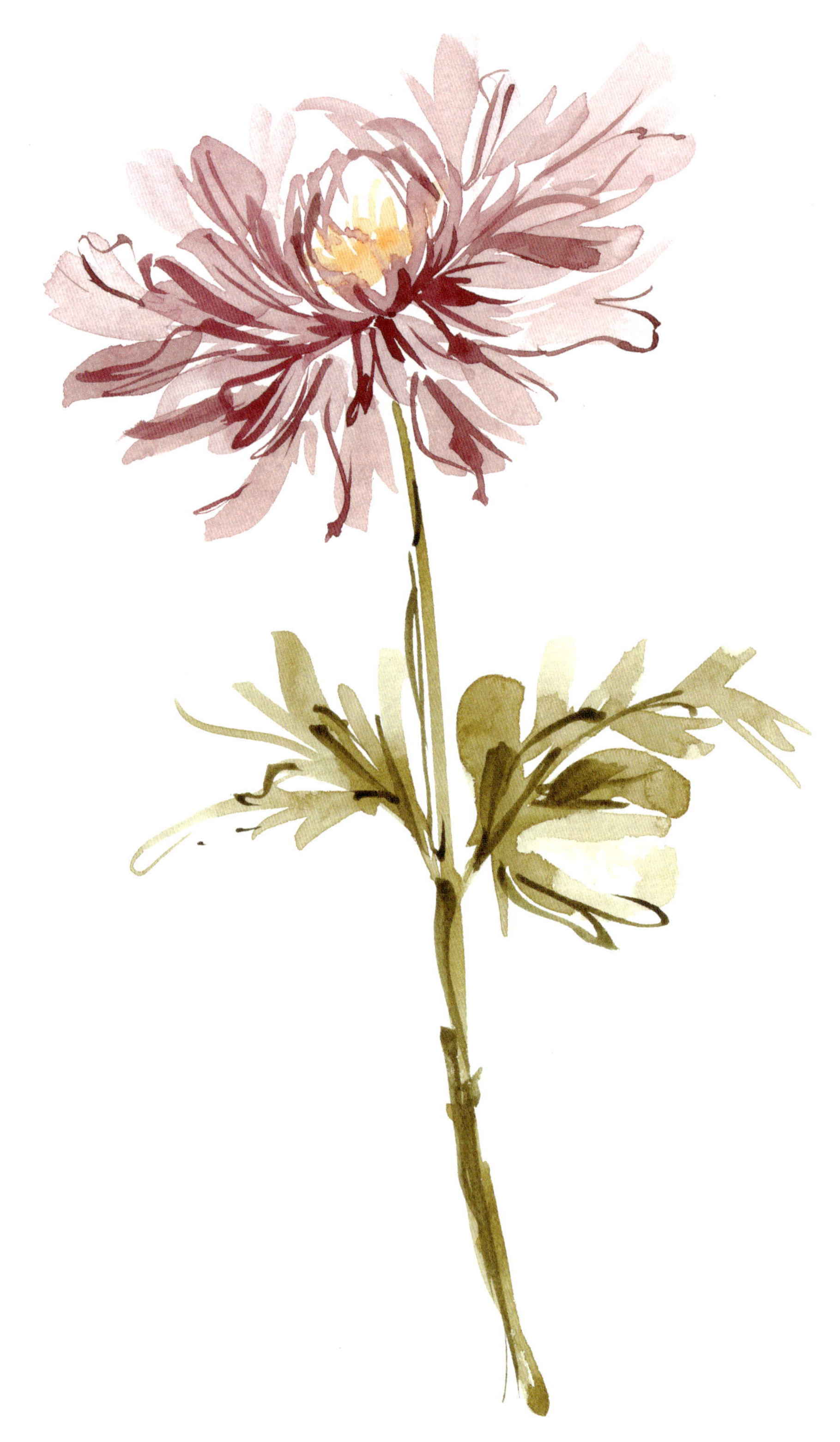

Introduction

Well, hello, and *welcome*, my friend.

The first thing I want to say is that I am *really* glad you're here. For years now, it's been a goal of mine to gather the knowledge and experience I've accumulated on my watercolor journey and give it a home—a home I could hold in my hands and share with you and thousands of others who have fallen for this medium as I have.

The second thing I'd like to mention is that a new book can sometimes feel like a hotel room. You open the door and although everything is clean (let's hope!) and inviting, it doesn't quite feel like *yours*. Not yet, anyway. So, please consider this my personal invitation to throw open your metaphorical suitcase and begin marking up, highlighting and coffee-staining these pages; and more than anything else, make this book *your own*.

I'd also like to take a moment, if you don't mind, to talk about *why* art? *Why* a creative life?

For me, art was quite literally a lifesaver.

In a season of life when I was newly diagnosed with two autoimmune conditions leaving me nearly bedridden, creating was the only thing capable of distracting me from debilitating pain and giving me a reason to get up each day. Creating gave me *purpose*, filled my days with beauty and meaning, and is truly how I came to heal. Whether purely for pleasure or as a means to survival, it is my belief that everyone can benefit from having a creative outlet. The projects in this book are designed to immerse you in the beautiful world of botanical watercolor, showing you exactly how I went from someone with no formal training or experience to a full-time professional artist.

It matters not at all if you've never picked up a brush. As someone who knew nothing about watercolor prior to my career, I know *exactly* what needs to be understood at each stage and *how* to do it. Let me assure you, I made all the mistakes and pitfalls so you won't have to! Although it took me years to learn (and unlearn—oops!) best practices and techniques, I will be guiding you from a place of experience. We will start at the beginning, the very beginning, where I will walk you through each stage of the budding artist and get you creating in *hours*.

The most important tenet for you to remember is that art is not a gift, it is a skill. Never let anyone tell you differently. I am no more gifted than the next person; I couldn't draw a gumdrop when I picked up a pencil for the first time.

What I am is persistent. And although I spend much of my day chasing after two little ones, I have acquired the skills that have landed me collaborations with Laura Ashley and gotten my artwork displayed in stores across the country, the foundation of which I am sharing *in this book*.

If you are ready to unlock your creative spirit, I am ready to teach you all that you will need to know to begin a hobby or a career in fine art. It would be my *honor* to be this person for you. I ask only one thing: Whenever and however long you are learning here with me, I ask you to bring all of you and, very important—when those voices begin hissing in your ear that "you can't" and "you're not good enough," you answer them back: *I absolutely can and am.*

That is my only request. That you fight for you.

Because you have *a story to tell*, a creative one. And you are the *only* one capable of telling it.

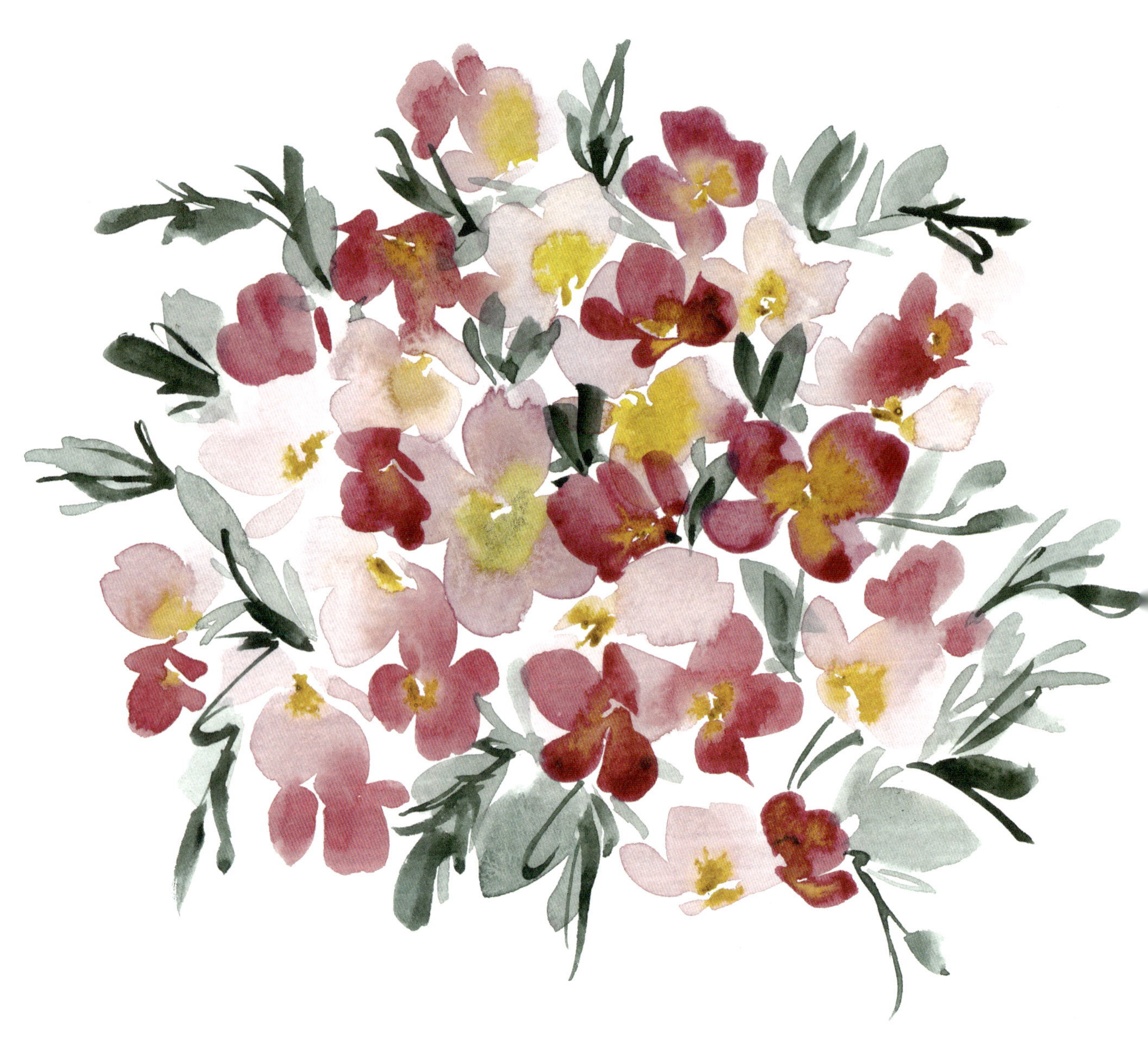

What Is Loose Art?

Before we wade much deeper into the literal water of watercolor study, I'd like to talk with you for a moment about something we will be revisiting again and again throughout this book: loose art.

For the sake of clarity, we should define the word *loose*, as it means different things to everyone. For some, "loose," when applied to watercolor painting, could mean something abstract: highly gestural strokes with a goal to cast only the faintest mirage of something definitive. Or "loose" could mean a structure that plays with the boundaries of what is real and what could be if left to the imagination. If I were to label my own style, I'd say I'm more the latter—someone who feels highly inspired by the shapes and movement of nature, but genuinely longs to tell her own story.

In this book, you will find that each lesson is merely a nod to the subject we are studying, never to be an exact facsimile. You aren't trying to replicate a photo of an African violet, you're trying to convey an African violet as you perceive and feel it. This is intentional. Having studied botanical art for three years, it wasn't until I began allowing myself to break the rules that I found true joy in the process. Joy I want to share with *you*.

Art, any art, should be a representation of the one yielding the medium. It should look and feel like *you*.

Loose art is that for me. I see myself in indistinct shapes, not quite comfortable fitting inside boxes. I see myself in the tangle of leaves as an imperfect structure willing to share the beauty she has to offer. I choose to keep my art loose as a living testimony to the relentless beauty found in the odd and irregular.

A huge misconception about loose art is that it's easier than more structured art, which is simply not true.

If anything, most will agree loose art can be more challenging because there is no right answer. There is a desired end result when botanically approaching a flower that doesn't exist in loose art. There are limitless ways to paint a rose, and whether they are "good" is highly subjective.

None of this is said to dissuade you, but rather to encourage you in continuing to explore the boundaries of your expression. Loose art is innately forgiving, meaning that even when you make a "mistake," there is still room to make beauty with it. *This* is why I choose and teach this art form—for its capacity to offer grace to the artist every step of the way. There are no closed doors, only open windows.

I've chosen to highlight loose art in this book for the freedom it provides, inviting you to be guided and inspired by nature, rather than her prisoner. Art *should* be forgiving. It should make you feel both powerful and vulnerable. It shouldn't be something that leaves you feeling you didn't hit the mark.

More than anything, I would like you to lean in to the mess. I promise to teach you all you need to know about the foundation of botanical watercolor painting, using "loose art" as the backbone to our projects, and in return I ask that you give yourself permission to take risks, even if they don't pan out. By this, you discover your process, and process is GOLD. Process is the reason we keep coming back, why we hunger to keep creating, keep learning. Contrary to belief, art isn't the finished result—it's everything that led up to it.

So, are we ready to do this?

Then, brushes raised . . . cheers to the mess and the magic! It's going to be beautiful, my friend.

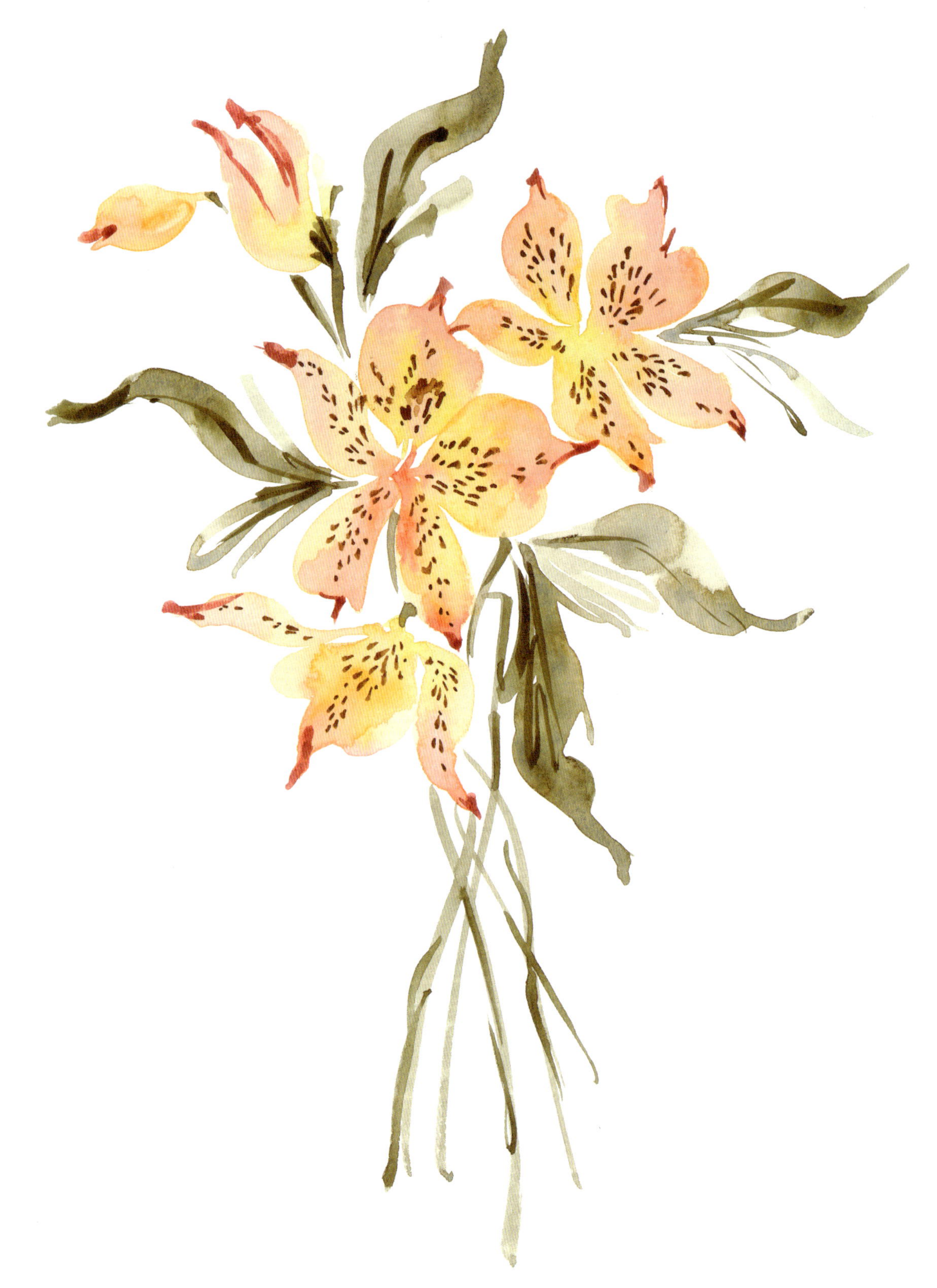

The Artist's Toolbox:

Gathering Your Supplies

Myth: *You need the most expensive supplies to produce quality work.*

I have not found this to be true in my own creative process. While quality products can certainly aid and elevate your craft, skill and technique are by far more important aspects to focus on when you are just starting out. My suggestion (especially for beginners) is to build up your toolbox *slowly*, starting with a few key mid-quality supplies. This is because, if your supplies aren't up to snuff, you won't really know what you're capable of creating. If your supplies are too expensive, you'll be too consumed with not messing up to discover anything worth learning.

Hear me: Mistakes are a critical and necessary part of the learning process, thoroughly necessary for overall growth, and later on, honing your signature style. To alleviate this fear, it's integral we practice with paint and paper that encourages exploration. In just a moment, I'll elaborate on this.

The week I decided I wanted to learn watercolor, I figured I should probably buy some supplies, which seemed like an easy enough thing to do. I got in the car, drove a few miles to get to my local arts and crafts store, and went inside. I estimated it would probably take me fifteen minutes or so to get everything I needed and I'd be home in time to paint a painting—or two!

Cue me, three hours later, weary and slightly dehydrated, making my 87th rotation around the store, approximately zero things in my cart.

How was I *ever* going to be a master painter if I couldn't even pick out brushes?! I'm happy to report this is not where the story ends. I'm helping save you from my initial struggle by sharing all the insight I've gained over the years, so *you* can create in as little time and money as possible!

Watercolor Supplies

An artist's supplies are no different than a carpenter's tools. The ones they choose are absolutely essential for articulating her craft. Through these vessels is how she will communicate all she wishes to say with her art. Furthermore, they are an extension of her creative spirit.

That said . . . quality supplies should be a *lifelong* investment—not something accumulated overnight. One of the very first resources I created for my students was something I desperately wished I had when I was beginning: a comprehensive Watercolor Supply Guide. In it, I talk through my favorite brands, the pros and cons and, most importantly, why I chose them over others. You'll find this resource on my website at RosalieGwenPaperie.com, along with countless other resources to keep your creativity flowing.

If you're just starting your watercolor journey, beyond a cup of water, a paper towel and a small workspace, there are only three things you absolutely *need* to begin: brushes, paper and paint.

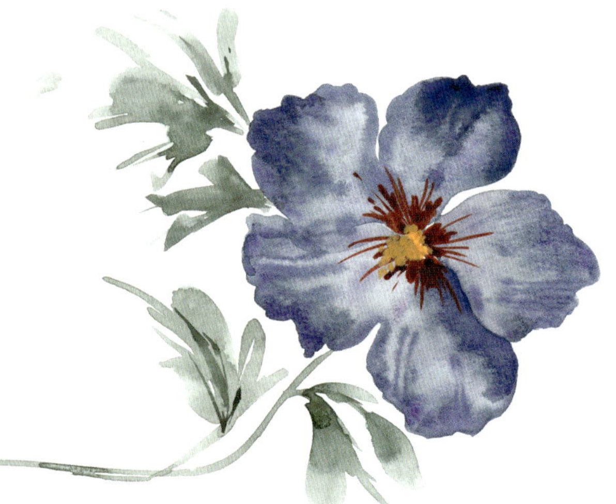

For my projects, I recommend using:

Brushes: Princeton Brush round brushes in sizes 2, 4, 6, 8 and 10 and filbert brush in size 4

Paper: Canson 140-pound (300-gsm) cold-press watercolor pad

Paint: Winsor & Newton Cotman Series Watercolors (with an emphasis on primary colors)

Palette: Or in my case, a salad plate. 'Tis true. If you're not quite ready to splurge on a palette, consider stealing one of your salad plates. I discovered (after numerous attempts working with plastic palettes and loathing how fresh paint would bead when activated with water) that porcelain provides the perfect surface for mixing paint. Be assured watercolor will not stain the plate and that it can be restored to its previous purpose at any time—although I still use plates more than I do fancy-schmancy palettes.

That's it! If you have these items, you are ready to go. Out the door, you should spend no more than $50 to $70. Supporting small local craft stores is lovely and recommended; however, if the upcharge is unrealistic or if the store's inventory is limited, I definitely recommend shopping at Blick.com or JerrysArtarama.com.

Now, let's move a little deeper into our toolbox.

Something else that quickly overwhelmed me when I was very new to watercolor was the abstruse terminology surrounding this medium. Words like *hot-press, cold-press, gsm, loose leaf* and *watercolor block* swooped high over my head and left me spinning in confusion. Because I'm the type of person that wants to have mastered her craft yesterday, I spent more time and energy than I should have learning these terms and how they applied to my pursuit of watercolor. Honestly, it was more of a roadblock than a stepping-stone. When I should have been completely devoted to putting paint on the page and improving my skills, instead I was distracted by making sure I *sounded* like a serious artist.

In this book, I've included the essentials: everything you'll need to know to move through these pages with confidence and complete all 25 beautiful lessons!

Brushes

As mentioned earlier, I use a variety of round brushes in my work, and these are all you will need for all 25 projects, with the addition of one filbert brush. My preferred brand of brush is Princeton Brush; in my opinion, this company makes both an affordable and high-quality brush that lasts quite a while if taken care of properly. In full disclosure, I represent this company as a brand ambassador and have been nothing short of continuously pleased.

Brush Care

Brushes should be cleaned within an hour of use, never left to sit in cups of water, and gently shaped back into position and laid flat to dry or hanging in a brush holder, bristles down. No need to use soap; fresh water works great.

Paper

When you pick up a piece of watercolor paper, one of the things you may notice is the texture upon it. What determines if paper is hot-press, cold-press or rough is merely the way it's been processed. A hot-press paper will be essentially smooth, bearing little to no texture (a.k.a. "tooth" in swanky watercolor circles). Cold-press paper—and results will vary between brands—will have a mid-grain, meaning a mild texture. Rough paper will have the most texture.

I mainly use hot-press and cold-press paper in my floral work because I appreciate the slight differences in effect. For more of a loose effect and less definitive result, hot-press is capable of creating stunning results. If you love those hard, crystallized edges and dramatic bleeds, you may find yourself drawn to cold-press.

Canson makes a wonderful middle-of-the-road paper I use in nearly all my watercolor classes. It's also highly affordable, which as I've mentioned already is a boon to new watercolorists. You won't worry so much about trying (and inevitably failing) if you're not concerned about the money you're "wasting" on good paper.

Additional papers I have worked with and can vouch for:

- Legion
- Arches
- Fabriano
- Strathmore

Please note that for *all* our projects, I will be using a 9 x 12–inch (23 x 30.5–cm) piece of paper. This will help you scale as I make size references and suggested proportions.

Paint

We've reached the final portion of our toolbox—paint!

Before we go into brands, you must first decide whether you are going to use a pan or tubes of watercolors or a blend of both.

A "pan" is a predetermined variety of colors that have been formed into squares or rectangles and come in a travel case. Pans are a wonderful way to explore paint, especially if you're hoping to paint *en plein air* (a.k.a. outdoors).

I prefer to work with tubes of paint, which I daub on a porcelain salad plate and moisten with water. The paint then dries and reactivates with water.

I tend to feel that tubes of paint are more cost effective because there are naturally colors in pans I don't ever use, whereas with tubes, I can purchase exactly what color I want. I also prefer them for color consistency. It can be challenging to execute the same color when working with a pan because you are required to first activate them with water. Using tubes, you are able to achieve the same color each time. They are also marvelous for blending colors, something we'll be discussing in vivid detail in the following chapter.

I've worked with several brands of paint over the years, and I attest that whichever brand below you decide to go with, they all perform remarkably. I've ranked them in order of preference.

- Daniel Smith (this is definitely a splurge)
- Winsor & Newton (the Cotman Series is wonderful and affordable!)
- Sennelier
- Maimeri Blu

Additional Supplies

Pencils: I stand by my earlier statement that paper, brushes, a palette and paper are all you need to begin. That said, it wouldn't be unwise to invest in a set of drawing pencils to keep on hand for sketching purposes. I like Faber-Castell for its range of leads. We will use an HB pencil for two lessons.

Dust-free eraser: A kneadable dust-free eraser comes in handy at the conclusion of a painting when you've used a pencil to sketch out your composition. As long as you've sketched lightly, you should be able to remove all signs of pencil without lifting the color from the paper. I like Faber-Castell.

Wrapping Up

After discussing supplies, I hope, at the very least, I have provided you a bit of clarity, but more important, a sense of ease about beginning exactly where you are at. Repeating myself: *Go slowly*. Build your toolbox little by little. Start with a few brushes and then fill in the gaps as you need to and move forward. Every once in a while, reward progress with the gift of a quality paint or paper, all the while knowing that a true artist isn't limited by a lack of supplies, but rather inspired to get *more* creative about how to express themself.

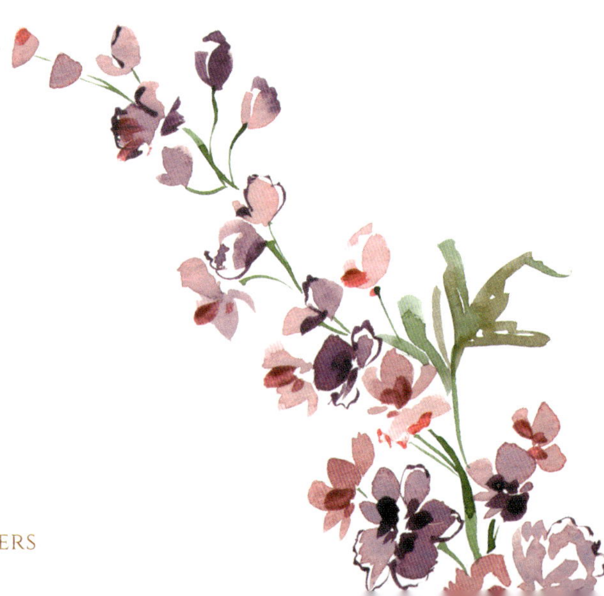

What to Do Before You Paint

Gathering Inspiration

As we move from lesson to lesson, some flowers are going to be more familiar to you than others. At times you might feel as though you understand a certain flower well enough to simply begin the material; however, I encourage you to spend even just a few moments on the Internet finding a few photos to serve as inspiration and reference while painting. It isn't mandatory, as I'll be walking you through my painting step by step; however, you can only benefit from taking a moment to just observe. I promise you it has served me well over the years. My paintings are almost *always* stronger and better for having spent a bit of time looking closely at my subject, and occasionally sketching it out prior to painting. Oddly enough, this helps me break away from the "correct" structure to create something of my own, which is what fuels my creativity.

As you do this for the flowers we'll be learning, try to select photos that are not alike. Meaning, try to have one of the photos showing petals only, another showing petals and a stem, another from a different perspective. The idea is to get a really good look at the flower. Observe the details that feel most *special*. This will vary from artist to artist, and it's truly that simple ritual of noticing and retaining that makes each of us capable of telling a unique story with the same subject matter. Screenshot or save these images to your phone, or pin them on a Pinterest board.

Water-to-Paint Ratios

This section could very well be the most important part of your entire watercolor foundation, so I'm going to do my best to take great care with it.

By a landslide, the most common frustration I see among new artists is their lack of understanding the proper water-to-paint ratios. When I teach online, this is typically where I spend a great deal of time, zooming in on my palette so students can see exactly what the puddle should look like preceding the actual painting portion of study. For our purposes here, I will be using swatches to show you what your color mixes should look like as you add more water.

Additionally, so that we are all on the same page, I am going to be using common analogies to explain consistency.

When paint is expelled from a tube onto a palette, its consistency resembles something akin to mud. It's in its thickest and darkest form, essentially unusable (with the exception of implementing the dry brushstroke technique) and must be decreased in value before it can be applied to paper. We use the term *value* to represent a color's range—darkest being the highest in value, lightest being the lowest in value. You'll learn more about color value on page 21. For now, all you need to know is that paint is decreased in value when it's activated by adding more water.

The easiest way I've found to explain ratios is to imagine that we are working with a scale of 100; when I say I want you to use 90 percent paint and 10 percent water, you can easily wrap your mind around what that would look like. If we were to continue in that way, moving on to 80 percent paint and 20 percent water and working our way toward 10 percent paint and 90 percent water, you would understand that your color would eventually become very light as it is gradually diluted with more water.

For our purposes, I will be using four main consistencies:

80% paint/20% water = horseradish—abbreviation HRC

50% paint/50% water = cough syrup—abbreviation CSC

20% paint/80% water = broth—abbreviation BC

5% paint/95% water = lightest consistency—abbreviation LC

STRAIGHT
FROM TUBE

HORSERADISH
80% PAINT
20% WATER

COUGH SYRUP
50% PAINT
50% WATER

BROTH
20% PAINT
80% WATER

Obviously, perfecting these ratios will take some practice. When we move on to color value, we will do an exercise to help secure this understanding. You will also be provided with example swatches for each project lesson. To keep things succinct and flowing, please be advised I'll be using the abbreviations I have listed here. Note that "LC" is for when we decrease broth consistency even further by adding more water.

Priming Your Brush

Water to a brush is like serum to the skin.

I tend to be on the liberal end of the creative process when it comes to the "Rules of Watercolor," preferring to understand them and then figure out how to break them; however, there are a few codes by which I live and breathe, and will pass on to you.

The first: It is of paramount importance that your brush be properly wetted, a.k.a. primed, before a single bristle is ever laid on the page.

By priming your brush, you are essentially preparing it for paint, the same way you would prepare your skin to accept a moisturizer. To do this, you'll need to soak your brush in a cup of clean water for a few seconds, then swirl it around several times before gently dragging the side of the brush along the rim of the cup to remove excess water. Have a look at the bristles to determine whether your brush is ready to accept paint. The bristles should shine and glisten, without dripping water. This process may need to be repeated a few times before success is achieved.

Because it's difficult to capture exactly how much water is needed on a brush prior to painting, I've opted to use a light purple to show "not enough water," "too much water" and "just right." As you can see, the first example results in a dry brush-stroke, which *can* be a beautiful effect; however, it should be intentional.

The second example shows a very watery stroke without much consistency of color and water. Although we are dedicated to keeping our work loose, and literally going with the flow of things, it's important to be able to apply an even stroke when we want to.

The final example shows a stroke that embodies both the necessary consistency and the gradual transition from light to dark as the paper absorbs the paint and water.

To get a feel for this, grab a piece of paper and a size 8 or 10 brush. Mix any color to cough syrup consistency (CSC) and practice making even, horizontal or vertical strokes.

Tip: *Don't rush things that are mistakenly considered time-wasters or unimportant. Knowing your tools and how they should appear prior to painting is priceless information when it comes to them serving you on the page.*

Prepping Your Palette

Whether you decide to utilize a porcelain palette or a salad plate, or go with a plastic palette is entirely up to you.

The more familiar you become with your paints, the more comfortable you'll be breaking the rules. Initially, however, organization and simplicity are helpful so you don't become overwhelmed. I find that having a fresh palette with a variety of paints I may or may not use to complete a piece is the best way to begin. If I can make one strong suggestion, it would be that you choose a palette with plenty of mixing space. Again, a salad plate works great and is roughly the size you would need to mix three to five colors to their proper consistency.

We'll be talking much more about this in the next chapter, but for now, let's focus on the next step.

Fresh Paint vs Dried Paint

When beginning a project, you can choose either to work with fresh paint from the tube or to activate dried paint that was previously used. If working with fresh paint, you'll find the consistency will require a few brushfuls of water before it can be used.

Dried paint will need a little more work, though not much in my experience. Although it's been hardened to a state of disuse, you'll discover it's very receptive to a bit of water, a.k.a. activation. You'll need to spend a few moments gently agitating the dried paint with a water-saturated brush, taking care to use only the sides of the brush, never the tip. Gradually, the paint will soften and apply itself to the bristles.

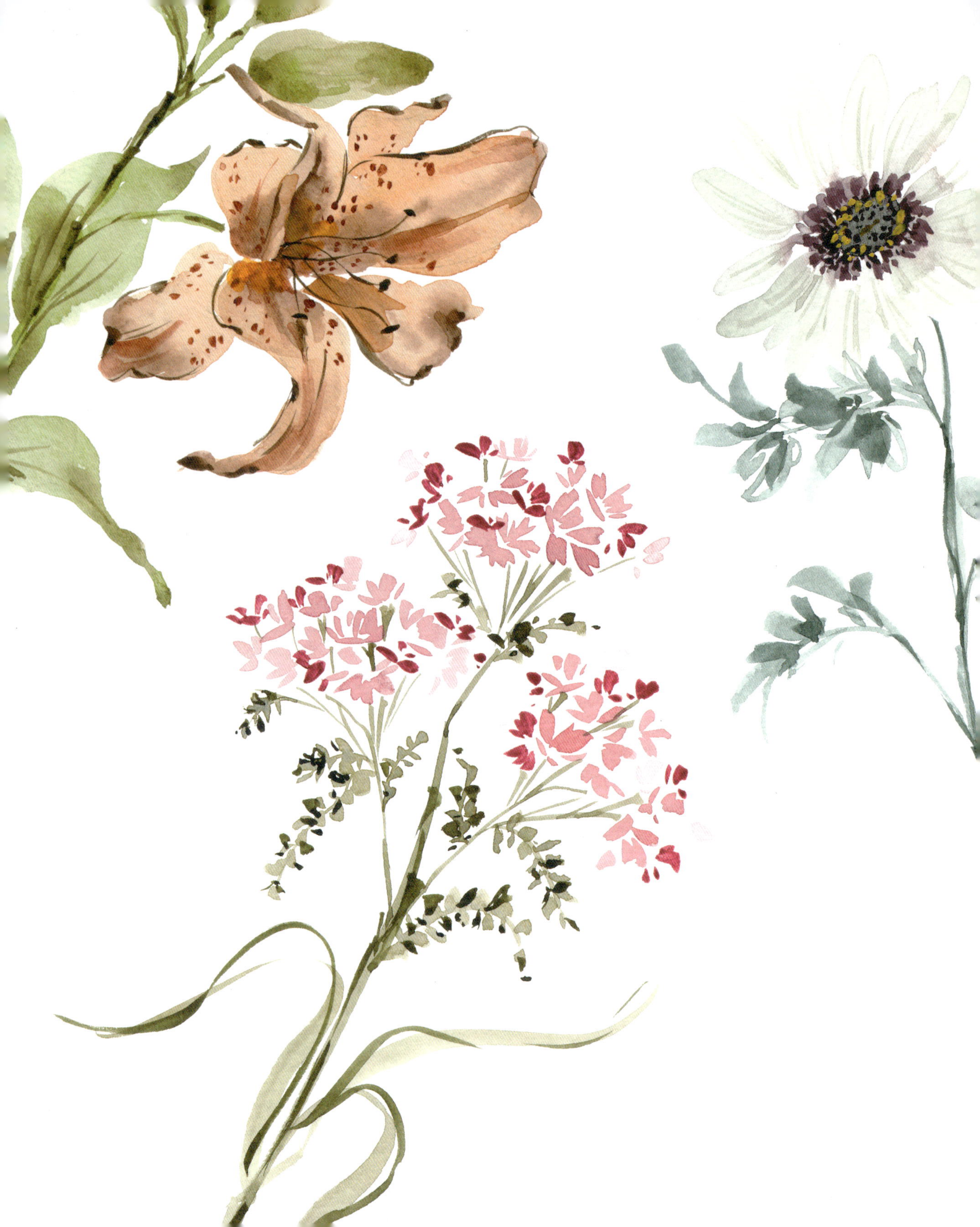

Color:

Exploring Pigment and Understanding Watercolor Techniques

Now that we've thoroughly covered supplies, let's jump into learning how to paint by exploring the techniques that will enable you to be successful in your projects! I know it can be tempting to launch ahead; however, I encourage you to spend a bit of time here. This chapter will prepare you for everything that's ahead and includes fun practice exercises to begin building those painting muscles.

All About Color

The Color Wheel

You likely have seen a color wheel and know the colors of which it's comprised. Just to be safe, we'll review them briefly.

Primary colors: red, yellow, blue

Secondary colors: orange, purple, green. These colors are created when two primary colors are blended together.

Tertiary colors: violet, turquoise, chartreuse, magenta. These colors are achieved by mixing equal parts primary and secondary color.

I like to think of these blends of color as a chord: multiple notes played simultaneously to create a range of sound. Although a musical composition technically can be created using only a single or a couple of notes, it will lack "interest," the quality that encourages the listener to keep listening. The same can be said for a painting. It's in variety—color, shape and movement—that the piece becomes a true masterpiece.

Exercise: Consider putting together your own color wheel now by beginning with the primary colors—red, yellow and blue—and gradually working in all the other colors. You'll need your prepared palette

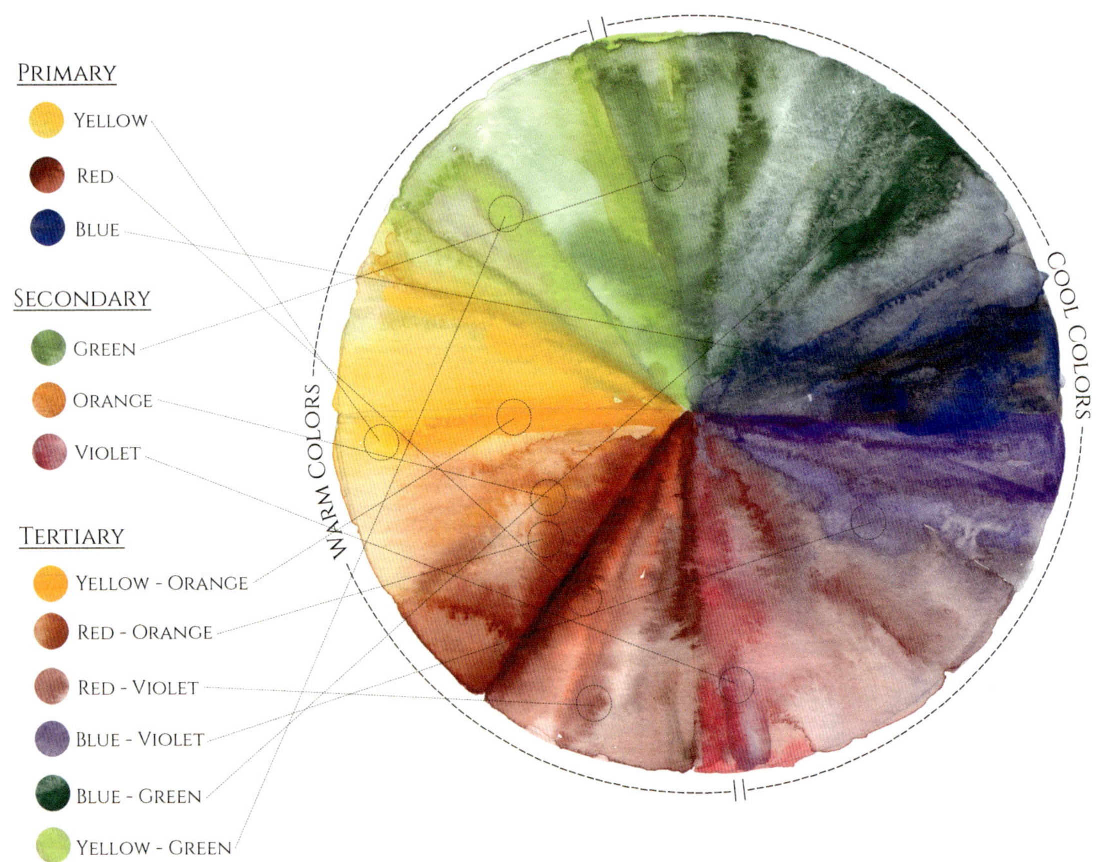

containing the primary colors, a cup of water, a piece of Canson 140-lb (300-gsm) paper (or a watercolor block) and three round brushes. The size of the brush is not so important here, but you want it to be large enough to collect the paint on the bristles. I suggest a size 8 or higher.

Color Value

You may have heard this term used in certain art circles without a clear understanding of what it is, so we'll review this as well. I do this because I personally struggled keeping up with watercolor vernacular when I was just starting, and even if you never use it, it's still nice to know. I'll continue to do my best to clarify these things as we work through our lessons.

If you were to dab a bit of paint on your palette and give it a tiny bit of water, just enough to make it useable, this color would be at its highest value. You cannot make it darker. You can, however, make it lighter by decreasing its value, which would simply be to progressively lighten the hue with water. Here is an exercise that allows you to see exactly how this theory works. Sometimes it's helpful for new watercolorists to spend ten minutes studying a single color by becoming familiar with its highest and lowest value. This information is valuable because you'll know exactly what a single hue is capable of within a given composition. While painting leaves, you may want a level 3 Sap Green or a level 7, with a 3 being the third swatch and a 7 being the seventh. Refer to the diagram below for further clarification.

Knowing the differences, slight as they may be, is key to nuance, which is the backbone of a strong painting.

I've used both a cool color (Ultramarine Blue) and a warm color (Yellow Ochre) to demonstrate how we decrease the color's value. I begin with the darkest version of the color, adding only a few drops of water, and gradually add more water for different versions of the same color. You'll notice in the second example, I'm able to successfully retrieve only five colors before the paint fades to a very pale yellow. With the ultramarine, I'm able to pull out nine unique colors before the paint fades.

Practice this exercise on your own, using a warm and cool color. See how many versions of the same color you're able to make by gradually adding more water to your paint puddle. Each time you lessen the value, you'll need to blot your brush on the paper towel lightly and pick up fresh water from your cup.

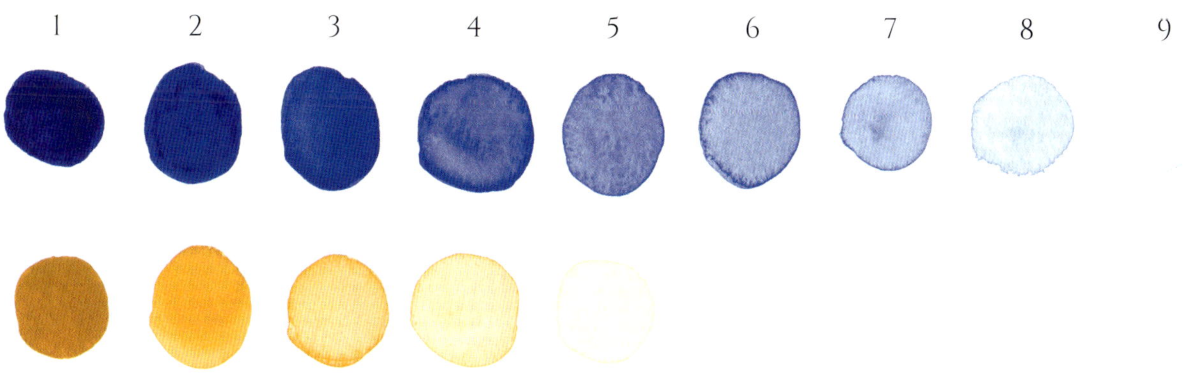

Saturation

When artists talk about saturation of color, they are usually referring to its brightness or intensity of color. Traditionally vibrant colors are thought of as having high saturation, whereas dull colors, grays and browns, are thought of as having low saturation. You can also decrease the saturation of a color by adding water to a painted area, which increases transparency by allowing the paper to show through the paint.

Warm and Cool Colors

Warm colors include: yellow, yellow-orange, orange, red-orange, red, red-violet

Cool colors include: yellow-green, green, blue-green, blue, blue-violet, violet

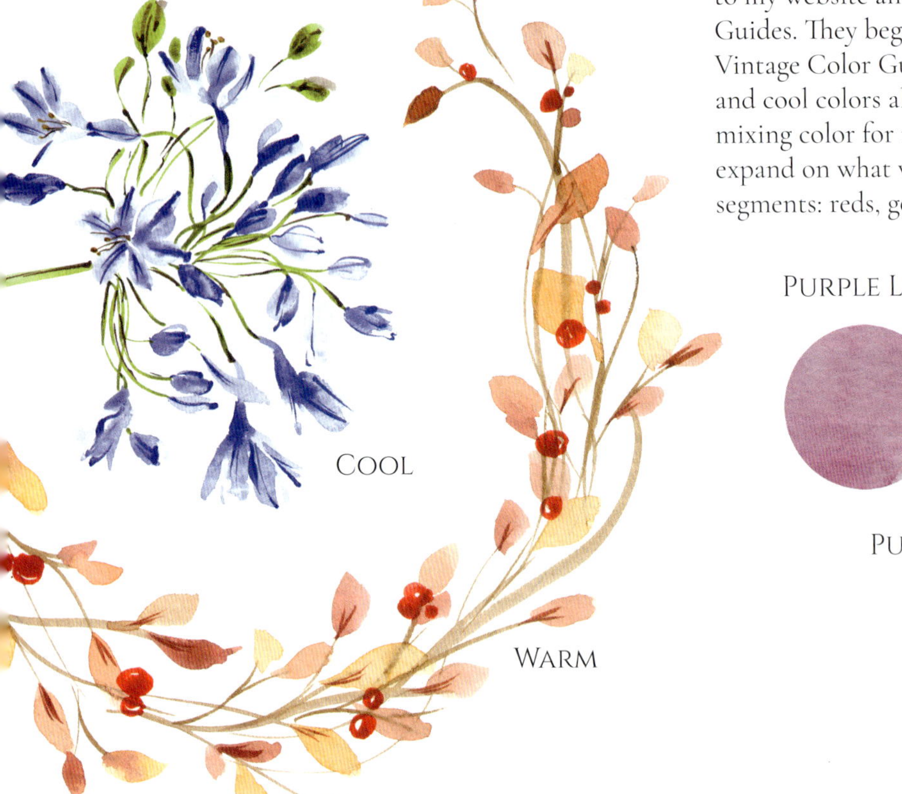

Muddy or Muted Colors

We've come to a section of this book that I am very excited to discuss with you! If there is one thing for which I am known in my community, it's my passion for color and color potential. So much so, in fact, that I spent the better part of a year entirely devoted to creating color recipes for my students and fellow artists to study.

A "color recipe" is simply two or more colors mixed together to achieve a new color. To "mute" a color is to lessen the brightness and vibrancy by adding a neutral hue, such as brown, gray or Yellow Ochre. Several of our projects will involve a muted palette, which will give you a good taste of how we can go beyond store-bought tubes to make our own beautiful creations!

If you find yourself curious about color and desire to go beyond the color wheel, I invite you to head to my website and have a look at my line of Color Guides. They begin with the first installment, the Vintage Color Guide, which is a mix of both warm and cool colors along with the education behind mixing color for muted tones. From there, we expand on what we learned and explore color in segments: reds, golds, greens, blues and whites.

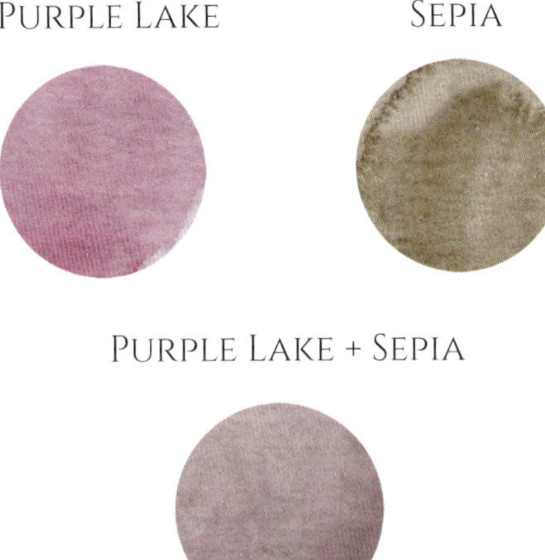

Essential Watercolor Techniques

As we head into the techniques chapter of the book, I'd like you to keep in mind that these are the techniques with which I personally find success and joy when creating. I mean to pass on my knowledge and experience, providing options you may not have already considered; however, if you've already found a different method that works for you, that's okay, too! Different doesn't necessarily mean wrong. We'll keep a sharp eye out for how a certain technique might be limiting you and examine ways we might adjust a bit to put you back on the right path.

Rest assured I will be guiding you step by step and providing helpful tips as we learn each technique, making sure you feel both comfortable and confident prior to beginning the projects!

Loading Your Brush

To "load" your brush simply means to prepare it for painting. You do this essentially the same way you would prime your brush (which is to prepare it for paint): by examining your brush for a glistening sheen and sweeping it across your daub of paint. This is another area you'll need to fiddle with before it becomes familiar, and don't be discouraged if your strokes are too dry or too watery. Eventually you'll begin to notice how the brush should feel and look as you lean into the canvas. When loading the brush, be sure to twirl your brushes gently in 180-degree rotations. You want to make sure you're applying paint to all the bristles.

Brush Posture

When understanding brush posture, the most important aspect is wrist mobility. Because so much of watercolor deals with the magic of timing, you want to be able to bend, flex, curve and nod your wrist with little resistance. If, when holding your brush, you find that you are limited in how you can move, this might be a good time to experiment with other positions. Think of yourself as an orchestral conductor. Your brush is the baton, guiding the flow of music (paint) across the canvas.

The other thing to consider is comfort. If you find that after 30 minutes or an hour, your fingers are swollen or cramped, this could be a clue that the posture isn't doing you any favors in the long run. If you have yet to settle on a position, I invite you now to pick up your brush and begin experimenting with holds. YouTube is always a great place to visit if you want to have a look at options. At some point, grab some scrap paper and leftover paint, and just begin painting. Keep it loose and simple, switching pressure and fingers, and generally exploring different holds. You'll feel it when it's right.

You'll also need to gauge where on the brush you feel most in control. Some artists like to hold their brush just a bit behind the bristles, which can allow for tighter strokes but can be somewhat limiting. Too far back on the handle, and you'll forfeit precision. My happy place is right in the middle, with my index finger on the crimp and my thumb a little farther back for support. Obviously, you'll need to play around to figure out where comfort, control and mobility merge.

The parts of the brush are as follows: toe, belly, ferrule, crimp and handle.

Toe refers to the very tip of the brush. The *belly* is where you're able to make your largest strokes, accessing the widest part of the brush. The *ferrule* and *crimp* are more esoteric terms that refer to the architecture of the brush, specifically the long metal piece between the bristles and handle, and the smaller piece of "crimped" metal, respectively.

Pressure

Just after brush posture, one of the most important aspects to master is proper pressure. Think of pressure as a dance between you and your brush. You're partners, and although you are leading the dance, the entire performance will feel off if you're not there to support your partner.

This is one of those topics where I am only able to take you so far without actual experience of the page. It's something you'll need to *feel* to understand, and will take time before it becomes second nature.

Simplified, pressure comes down to accessing the different areas of the brush.

If your goal is to make fine lines, you'll want to come up on the tippy toe of the brush, applying only the lightest pressure. I call this grazing. For slightly wider strokes, you'll use the same technique, applying mid-pressure. I call this balancing, as it is equal parts you and the brush. Lastly, to yield the widest strokes, you'll come down full pressure, utilizing the belly of the brush until the bristles are flattened.

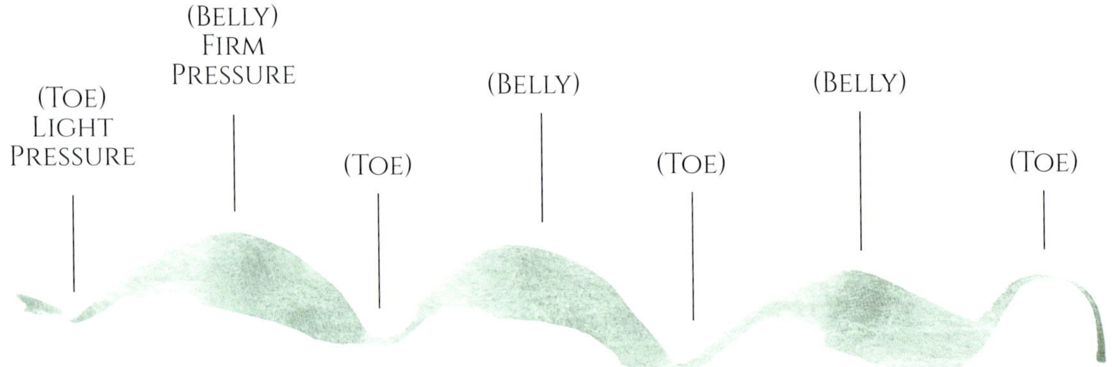

Toe-Belly-Toe Exercise

To get familiar with your brush and what it's capable of, we are going to do a quick exercise executing what I call the toe-belly-toe method. The idea is that we will create alternating thin and thick strokes by coming up on the toe of our brush, and then going full belly for our thickest stroke.

SUPPLIES

One size 10 round brush

Any color paint

Canson 140-lb (300-gsm) cold-press paper

STEP 1.

Use your size 10 brush to mix a puddle of paint to cough syrup consistency (CSC, page 16).

STEP 2.

At a 90-degree angle, apply light pressure to the paper to create a thin line.

STEP 3.

Angling slightly toward the right, apply firmer pressure, gradually flattening the bristles on the paper until they are completely fanned out.

STEP 4.

Gradually lighten pressure as you come back to toe and create another thin line.

STEP 5.

Repeat Steps 1–4 several times until a rhythm is formed.

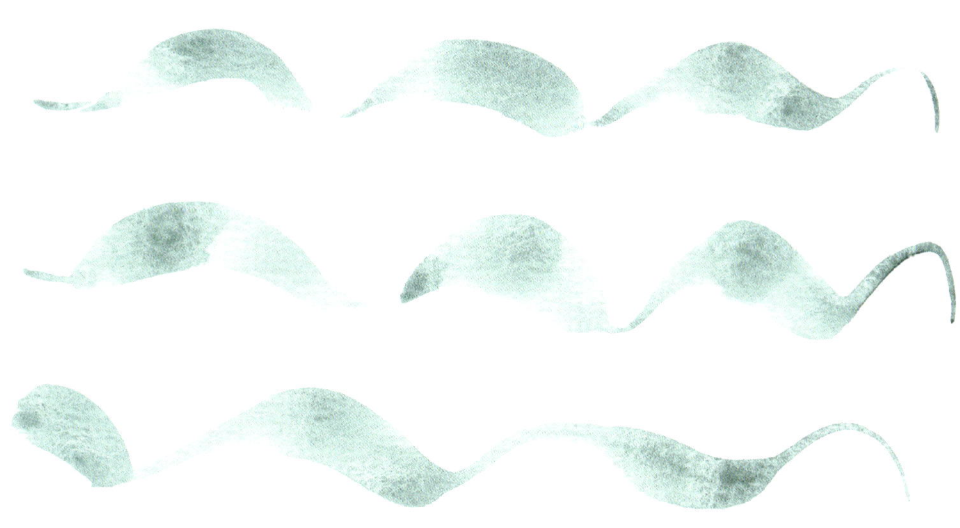

Step 6.

Practice vertical lines, applying the same technique.

Step 7.

Moving horizontally, practice a wavelike rhythm, using the toe of the brush for the summit and the belly for the crest of the wave.

Step 8.

Practice making quick, thin strokes with the toe of the brush, some long, some short.

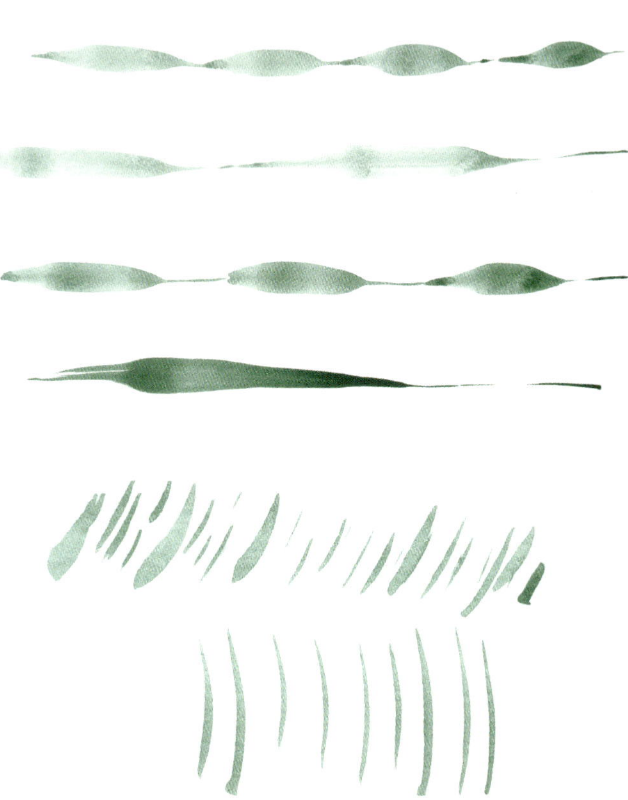

Creating Bleeds

Clouds, water-blooms, fireworks—these are common synonyms you may come across that refer to a *bleed*.

"Bleeding" occurs when excess water is applied to a dry area of the painted paper, causing the color to run and creating sharp, pigmented edges or scalloping. This method doesn't only apply to water, however, as it's also possible to create a bleed by first laying down a light color and then applying a darker and thicker consistency of paint on top of it.

Because my work rests on the side of loose and intuitive, I relish the beauty and spontaneity of bleeds and welcome them happily in my work, and in fact create opportunities to use this technique to my advantage. We will explore this incredibly versatile, not to mention beautiful, technique in the lessons ahead.

Bleed Study Exercise

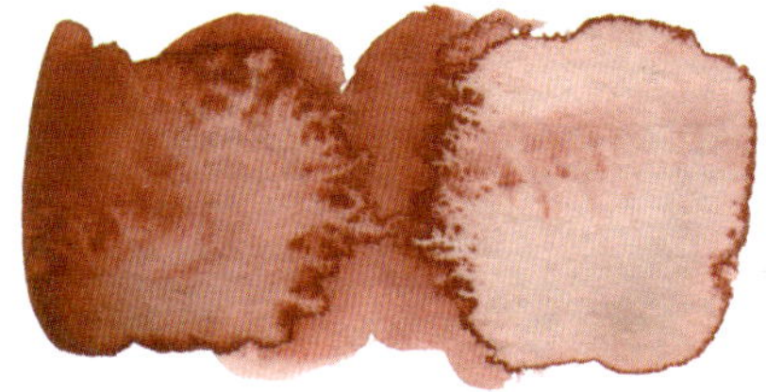

Supplies

Two size 6 round brushes

Winsor & Newton Red Deep (any deep red color will do!)

Canson 140-lb (300-gsm) cold-press paper

Step 1.

Use one size 6 brush to mix a puddle of paint to CSC (page 16).

Step 2.

Paint a swatch or "ribbon" as I have done by moving the brush horizontally in an up-and-down motion. The swatch will naturally lighten in color as you release more paint onto the paper.

Step 3.

Give the paper a chance to soak up the pigment.

Step 4.

Using your second size 6 round brush, dip into your cup of clean water and carefully poke the tip of your brush against the paper. No need to move the brush elsewhere; the water will flow from the bristles into the swatch and the transparent background should appear as you add water.

The bleed may extend all the way to the boundary—the edge of wet media—creating rough edges, or it may only spread a little, leaving a "firework" in the wet media. Mine spread all the way to the edge on the right and made scalloped edges toward the left. No two swatches will ever be exactly alike and this is part of the magic!

Tips:

If nothing happened, your media was too dry. If the colors flood and you aren't able to distinguish lighter and darker area, your media was too wet. Don't fret! This exercise, while simple enough, takes practice before it becomes second nature. If the results aren't to your liking, go for it again until you're satisfied. I encourage this whether you feel you "succeeded" or not. Practice makes progress.

You can also try this exercise in reverse, beginning with broth consistency (page 16) and then adding cough syrup consistency and watching how the dark color creates rough edges.

Softening

For those who wish to lessen the effects of a dark color value, "softening" is a technique in which artists use their brush, slightly moistened, to gently scrub the edges of the media (the swatch, flower, leaf, etc.). You would then need to wipe the excess paint on a paper towel, rewet the brush until it's moist but not sopping wet and repeat. This process may need to be repeated anywhere from two to five times, depending on how much paint you desire to remove. The effect will leave the area much lighter in appearance as though it was partially erased.

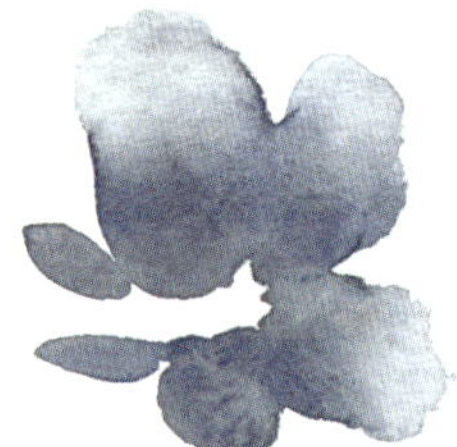

Rewetting or Glazing

This is a simple maneuver achieved by taking a brush containing only clean water and wetting an area that has dried, thus adding a layer of water to it. It's used when an artist wants to darken a previously painted element or to add contrast to an element. You want to make sure you don't actually lift the color, so it's important your brush be properly primed before glazing. You can find more info on priming your brush on page 16.

First Layer

Glazed Layer

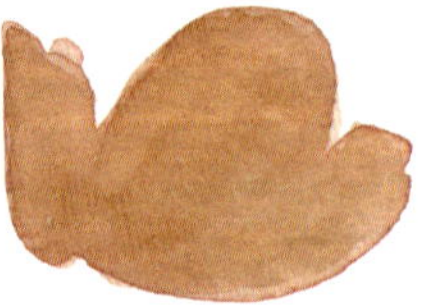

Blending Colors

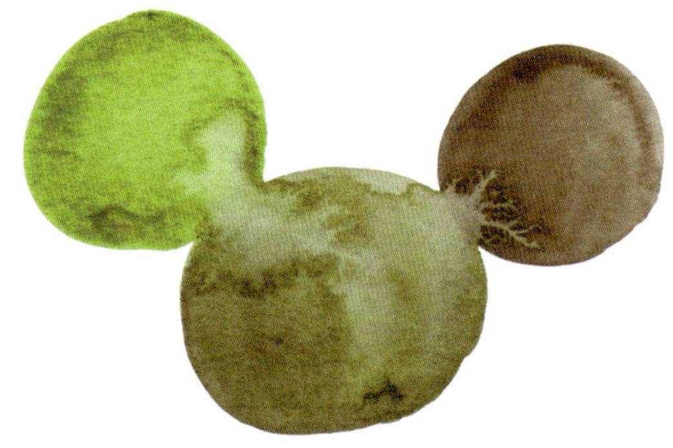

Supplies

Two size 8 round brushes

Sap Green

Sepia

Canson 140-lb (300-gsm) cold-press paper

Step 1.

Prime one size 8 brush and mix one pile, using Sap Green to CSC (page 16).

Step 2.

Prime the other size 8 brush and repeat using Sepia and mix to CSC.

Step 3.

Rinse one of the brushes and blend the two colors together, taking care to mix all the color so you get an even shade.

Step 4.

Make a circle and fill it in to discover what color you've made—it should be an earthy, olive green.

Wet-into-Wet Technique

We cannot talk about the wet-into-wet technique without also talking about boundaries. *"Boundaries" in watercolor refer to the area of paper that has been moistened. When you go to apply pigment, you'll notice it only moves so far as the boundary of water. The most important part of using wet into wet is timing. Just as we discussed earlier while making a "bleed," if your media is too dry, the paint won't spread. If the media is too wet, the paint will turn into a puddle of water. You're searching for that in-between—an even coating of water. The best trick I ever learned was to get down at eye level with the paper and check for an even glistening coat of water. Look for dry pockets and areas where there might be small pools of water. It's worth it to take the time up front to make sure your canvas is ready for action!*

To better understand this technique, let's do a brief exercise, which we will later refer back to for a quick reminder.

Supplies

Three round brushes of the same size (size 8 or 10)

Quinacridone Fuchsia

Yellow Ochre

Canson 140-lb (300-gsm) cold-press paper

Step 1.

With one brush, mix a pile of paint to CSC (page 16), using Quinacridone Fuchsia.

Step 2.

With a second brush, mix a pile of paint to CSC, using Yellow Ochre.

Step 3.

With your third brush, load the brush with clean water and paint a circle.

Step 4.

Using your brush loaded with Quinacridone Fuchsia, start at the left side of the circle and release the paint onto the paper by applying gentle pressure so that it spreads across the circle.

Step 5.

This time, drop Yellow Ochre on the right side of the circle so that it spreads.

You'll see a merging of color toward the middle and likely some bleeding has occurred. This technique is especially lovely for adding a center to wet petals. I purposely used these colors so you could see the effect it would make were we to paint a flower instead of circle.

Stroke Guide: Leaves and Flowers

Before heading into the main lessons, I want to go over the strokes you'll be using in our lessons so you will easily be able to refer to this section while painting. This practice beforehand is essential for strengthening your painting muscles and beginning to secure muscle memory, all of which will help you feel both comfortable and confident in our projects.

Supplies

One size 6 round brush

Canson 140-lb (300-gsm) cold-press paper

Palette

Sap Green

Sepia

Simple Stroke

Step 1.

Begin by mixing Sap Green and Sepia to BC (broth consistency, page 16). This is a focal color we'll be using in many of our lessons, including the first one, so I'd like for you to get familiar with making and using it.

Step 2.

Using your size 6 brush, you will begin by applying the toe of your brush lightly to the paper to create the back end of the leaf.

Step 3.

Follow through by gradually increasing pressure until the bristles are flat at the middle of the leaf, and then begin lifting up and decreasing pressure to return to the toe of your brush for the pointed part of the leaf. You may then need to use the toe of your brush to shape the tip of the leaf—or you can elect to leave it "unshaped" for a looser look. Either is wonderful!

I suggest making a drill out of this stroke and repeating these steps 15 to 30 times until you become comfortable.

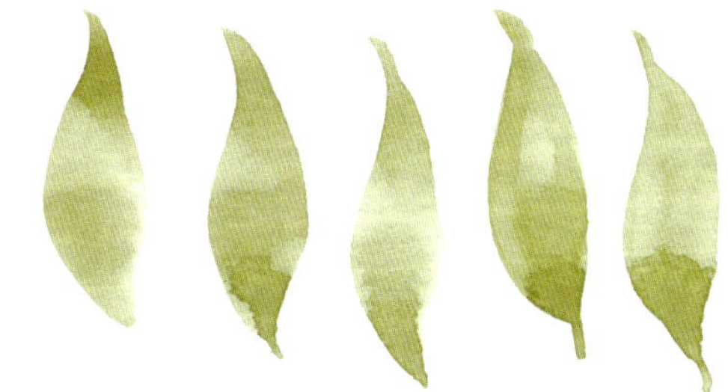

Unshaped Tip Shaped Tip

Compound Stroke

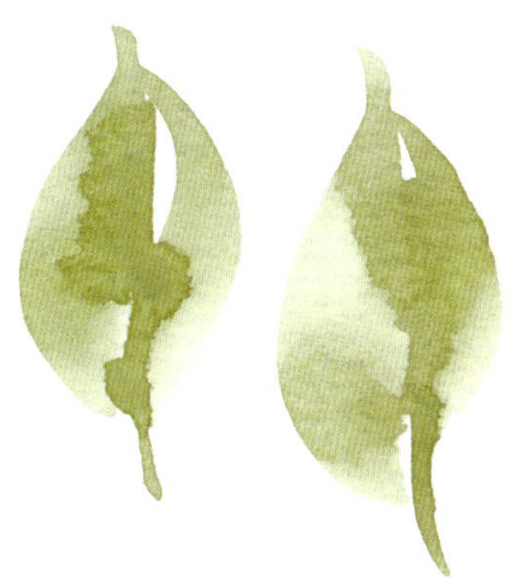

Step 1.

Using the same color mixture and brush as for the simple stroke, repeat the previous three steps; however, this time, I want you to envision the simple stroke as only being half of your leaf.

Step 2.

To clarify, I want you to make two simple strokes, one beside the other, running parallel with the page. Two simple strokes = one compound stroke. Once you've made the first simple stroke, return to the base of your leaf and complete your second stroke to finish the compound stroke. Be sure to leave a thin white line between the strokes, so that they aren't touching in the middle of the leaf.

This technique can serve as either the vein of the leaf or the illusion of a light source. This is an effect called negative space and is an integral part of watercolor.

We will explore this technique further when we move on to painting flowers, and you will see just how important it is to understand how white, or negative, space between strokes is absolutely essential for clarity in watercolor.

Step 3.

While the media is still wet, you can shape the tip of your leaf by applying gentle pressure where the leaf ends and using the toe of your brush to make the tip round or pointy.

Step 4.

I suggest filling a page or two with compound strokes before moving on.

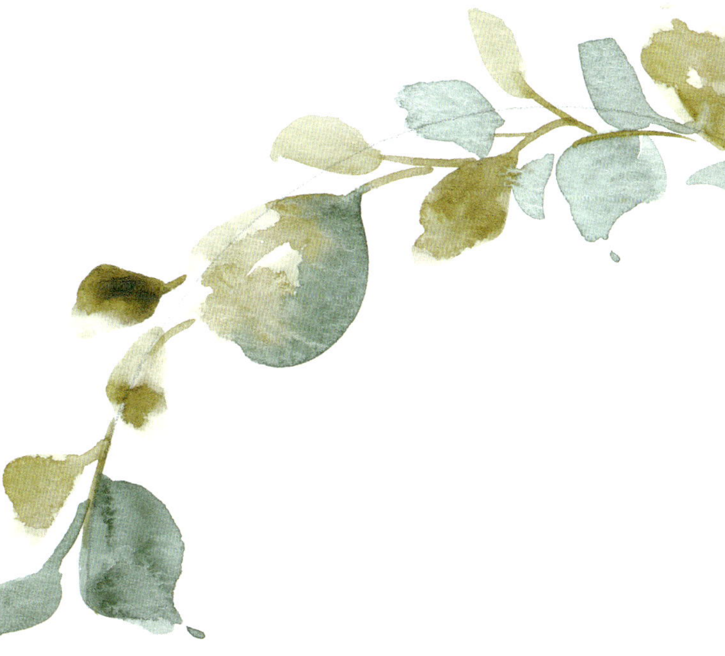

Movement and Variety

Once you feel good about your leaves, try injecting movement and variety of shape into the leaf by curving it to the left or the right so that it's slightly sideways. This will help when we put our wreaths together, lending an authentic appearance to the leaves. Think of the bottom portion of the leaf as the bottom lip of a mouth. Moving horizontally, return to the base and complete the top or upper lip, taking care to leave negative space (the thin white line) between strokes.

The final step is to make sure there are a variety of shapes and sizes of leaves. Allow some to be thick and others thin, using simple and compound strokes. Some leaves should be large, while others are medium and small. Variety, in conjunction with movement, are the foundation of compositions that feel both natural and peaceful. Consider now taking a scrap piece of paper and making as many different sizes, shapes and positioning of leaves as you can think of. Practice single leaves along with branches.

Gestural Stroke

We will use this kind of stroke often in our lessons, and it is my favorite! To gesture with our strokes simply means to loosely indicate the subject matter we're attempting to convey. It means we don't put a lot of focus or energy into making a leaf look like a leaf, but rather capture its essence.

To do this, you'll first want to loosen both your wrist and your hold on the brush. Begin by executing a few wrist rotations, forward and back to relieve any tension you might be carrying in your hand. Beginners have a tendency to grip the brush very tightly, whether in nervousness or wanting to have optimum control; however, for this technique, it is best to loosen your fingers so that the brush is resting in your hand rather than being choked.

Second, rather than thinking about an exact likeness, consider what a leaf or a flower might look like if you were to see it through a foggy window. We are not aiming to paint exactly what is in nature, but instead a loose interpretation of it. For example, at times even a small insignificant stroke with the brush can serve as a beautiful way to gesture a leaf or flower. To give you a few comparisons, to paint a gestural sailboat would be to paint a triangular shape on top (to act as a sail) and a half-circle on the bottom (to act as the base of the boat). It would *not* include the stern, bow, ropes, people and so on. Details are omitted and only the barest structure is left to identify the subject. To paint a gestural leaf, we are seeing it in its simpler, basic form, stripping away all the details.

The most alarming aspect of this technique is the "unfinishedness" of the object, which can lead to the artist wanting to continue adding details to make it look *more* like a leaf. This tendency and instinct to keep working can be challenging to overcome in the moment. The reward of restraint isn't revealed until the end of the painting when all the gestural strokes unite to create a beautiful effect.

The number one thing to keep in mind is instead of slow, steady strokes and controlled strokes, think: quick and flick. You're moving the brush somewhat rapidly around the page, the way a conductor flourishes his baton, relying on intuition to guide you.

Movement

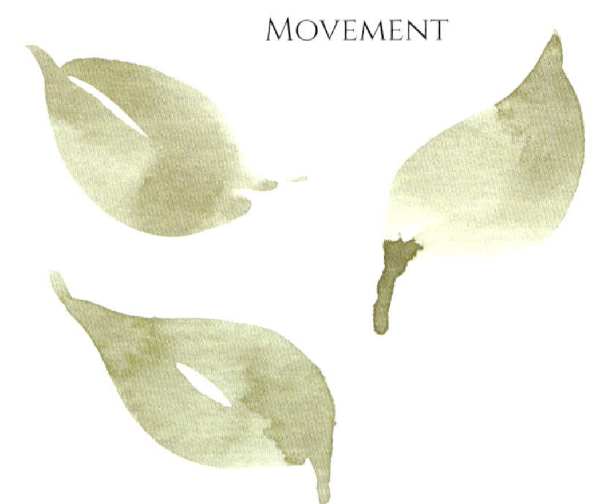

Example 1

Let's take a look at a leaf formed with a compound stroke versus a gestural stroke, so we can explore the differences. You'll notice that my compound leaf very noticeably has a beginning, middle and end. It's a complete story and "makes sense." A gestural leaf, by comparison, is much rougher in formation, left for interpretation; we can make guesses about where it begins and ends, but it is not fully clear. This is *okay*, and even beautiful. Standing alone, the leaf feels a bit odd and out of place, but when surrounded by other leaves and a flower, it all comes together.

Technique-wise, instead of two side-by-side simple strokes, I used one stroke, full belly, medium-to-firm pressure, and wiggled the brush downward.

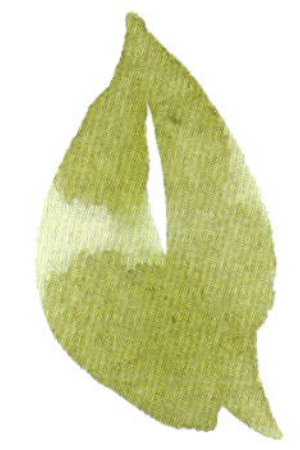

Compound

Gestural

Example 2

In this example, you can see that the first branch consisting of compound strokes is much tighter and controlled, versus the gestural branch, which has a much looser, watery feel.

Shortly, we'll cover what flowers look like using gestural strokes. For now, spend a little time working between the two styles, creating leaves. Strengthening these muscles will feel challenging at first, but this is crucial for mastering the gamut of loose watercolor.

Compound Branch

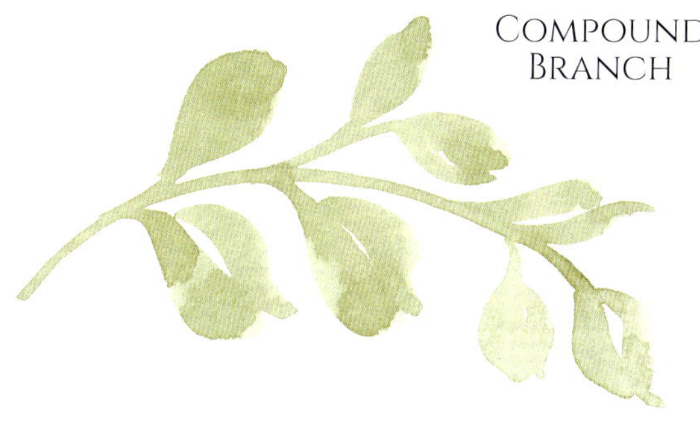

Gestural Branch

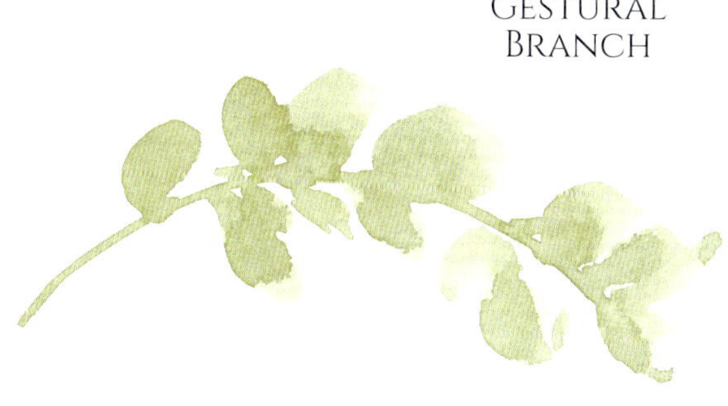

Eucalyptus Leaf Stroke

Supplies

One size 8 round brush

Canson 140-lb (300-gsm) cold-press paper

Palette

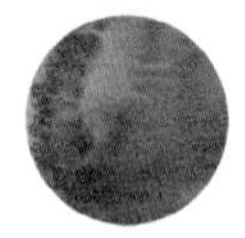

Greenish Umber

Payne's Gray

Practicing

Observe the examples provided and note the shape and positioning of the leaf. You might notice it is quite coinlike in shape, with some of the leaves having a point at the end, and others curved. Movement is key to executing this leaf, so we'll practice several angles so you'll be ready when we apply this to a later project.

Upward Leaf

Step 1.

Mix together Greenish Umber and Payne's Gray to BC (page 16). Using your size 8 brush, begin by painting a stem the length of a blade of grass. Angle it so it's facing toward the right.

Step 2.

Next, come back to the top of the stem and perform the first stroke. This is nothing more than the compound stroke reinvented. Rather than coming straight up, curve your brush out to the side, bristles belly down, before returning to the toe of the brush as you finish the stroke.

Step 3.

Finally, come back to the base of the stem and repeat on the right side. Practice this several times until the rhythm begins to feel natural and you produce a leaf with which you're satisfied.

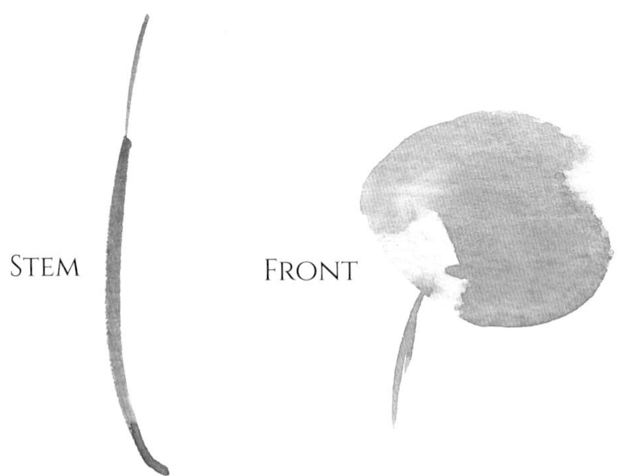

Sideways Leaf

Using the same mixture and brush, begin with a stem; however, this time, angle toward the left and make it slightly longer than the first stem we made. Return to the top of the stem and perform a compound stroke sideways that resembles lips. You'll start on the toe of your brush and quickly increase pressure until the bristles are flat (full belly) at the middle of the stroke before completing the stroke back on the toe.

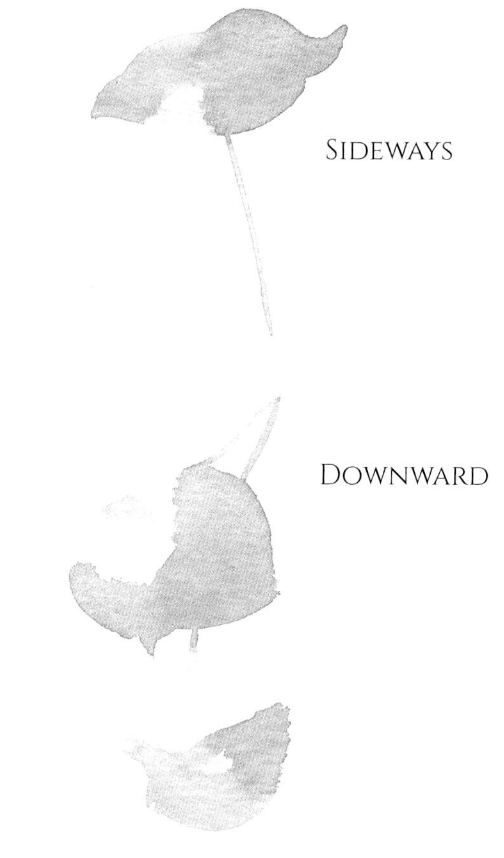

Sideways

Downward

Downward Leaf

Now, you will begin with a stem that starts at the top and is pulled downward and slightly right. With your size 8 brush, use the toe of the brush to create a stem. Continue by making the first half of a compound stroke, curving the brush slightly left, finishing on the toe with a point at the tip of the leaf. Next, return to the end of the stem and paint your second leaf. This time, paint the leaf sideways, starting on the toe, before coming belly down. End the stroke on the belly so there is no point.

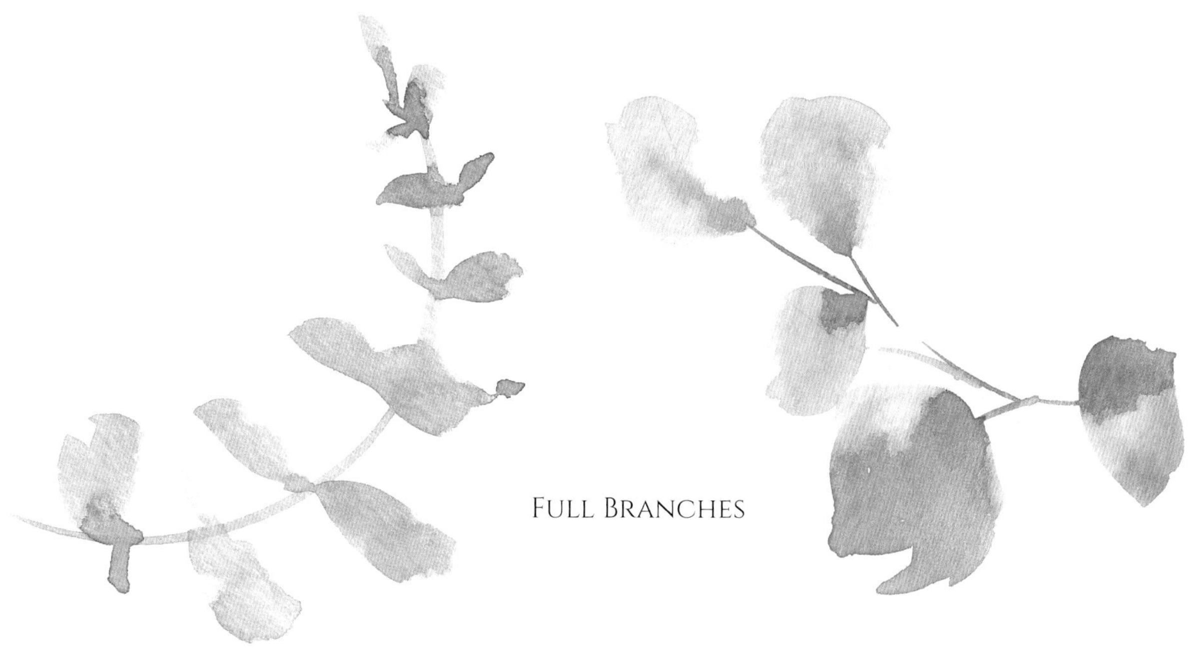

Full Branches

Eucalyptus Branch

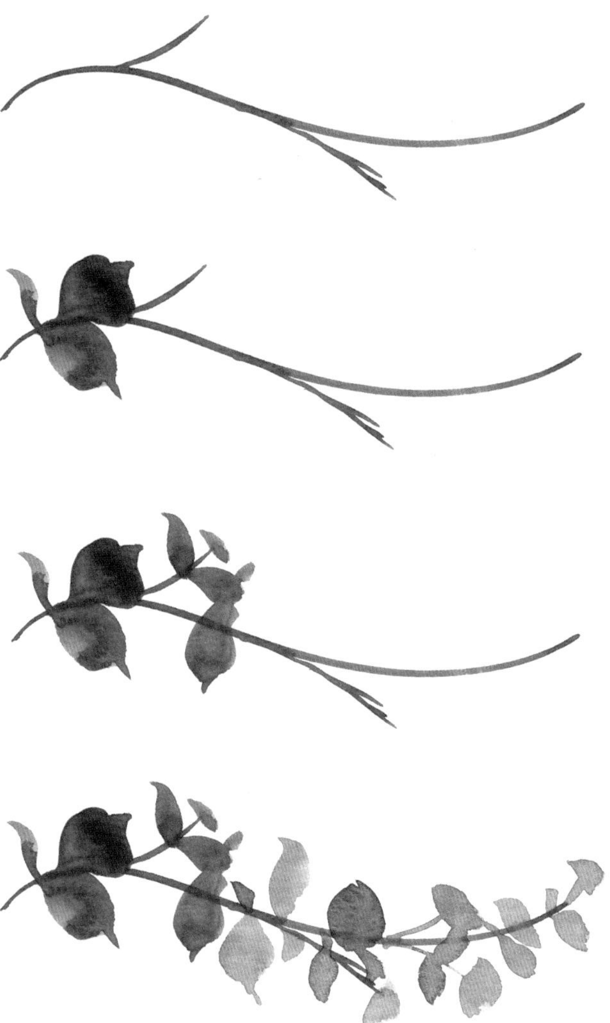

STEP 1.

Using your size 8 brush and Greenish Umber and Payne's Gray in CSC (page 16), begin with a branch. Stay on the toe of the brush and move in an up-down-up rhythm, so you have a line that looks like a smirk. Paint two smaller stems curving off the main branch.

STEP 2.

Next, paint your first two leaves. Starting at the top, to the left of the stem, use the toe of your brush to create a sideways simple stroke moving toward the branch. When you get to the branch, come down full belly and curve the leaf down and to the right of the branch, lifting up on the brush at the end of the stroke to end at the tip of the leaf.

Begin the next leaf by painting the first simple stroke curving to the left of the branch. Return to the base of the leaf and repeat this step on the right side so that it slightly overlaps the branch.

STEP 3.

Paint the next three leaves, using the same techniques. Begin the first leaf with two small sideways simple strokes. Just above that, paint a smaller simple stroke. On the main branch, paint a leaf that crosses the branch and ends at a point.

STEP 4.

Begin filling in the remainder of the branch, using the techniques found on page 32 of Movement and Variety. As you work, gradually decrease the size of the leaves as you make your way to the end of the branch.

The Pinwheel Flower

The pinwheel flower, named by yours truly due to its pinwheel-like appearance, is one of my absolute favorite flowers to paint because its structure can be used again and again with slight variations to make it feel like a new flower. A pinwheel flower can consist of three, four or five petals. It can include more, but once we reach seven or eight petals, it bears more of a fanlike appearance.

Supplies

One size 6 round brush

Canson 140-lb (300-gsm) cold-press paper

Palette

Permanent Rose

Step 1.

Using your size 6 brush, mix Permanent Rose to CSC and BC (page 16).

Step 2a.

Make a small circle, the size of a pea (about ¼ inch [6 mm] in diameter) with you HB pencil, or visualize the empty white space in the middle of the flower.

Step 2b.

Using the toe of your size 6 brush, make the first half of a compound stroke that is rounded at the top. I find it's easiest to begin at the base of the flower for formation, making one simple stroke, then coming back to the base to finish. This technique will need to stay loose, though, to ensure it doesn't appear too leaflike. I prefer to begin in the upper left-hand corner, working my way to the right; however, if you're left-handed, you may find it best to work in the opposite direction. No white space is needed between strokes; however, there should be a small amount of space between the full petals to keep the paint from merging.

Step 3.

Make your next petal, this one slightly larger than the first. Please note this petal might be much lighter than your first, not because it is a different consistency but because I have not reloaded the brush with more paint. You are welcome to do the same or you can reload the brush if you prefer your petals to closely resemble one another.

Step 4.

Make your third petal, angling it slightly downward.

Step 5.

Remember to leave a bit of space between your petals and in the middle. Make your final two petals.

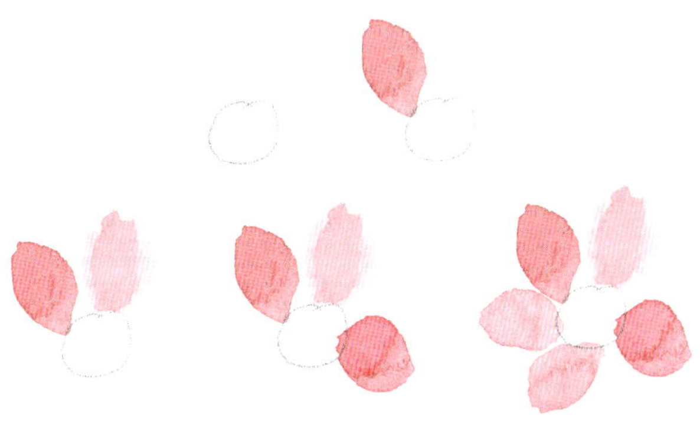

Pinwheel with Different Color Values

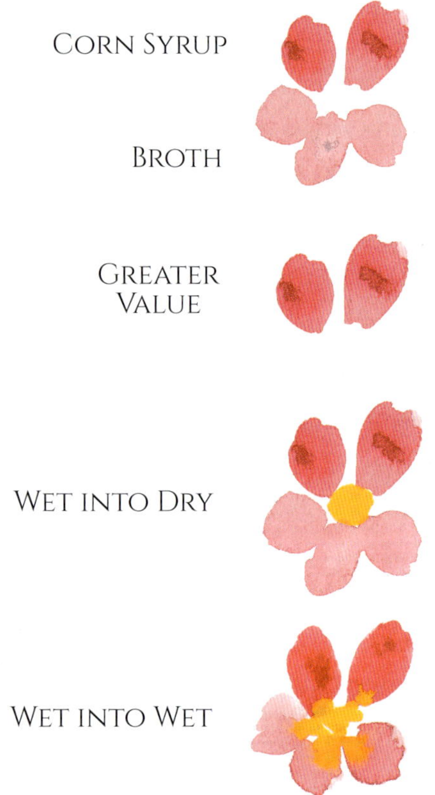

Supplies

Two size 6 round brushes

One size 4 round brush

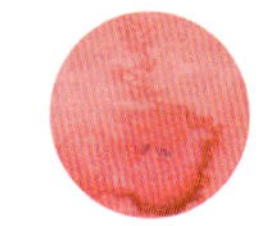

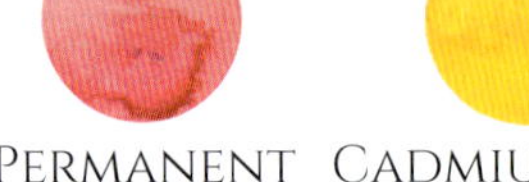

Permanent Rose

Cadmium-Free Yellow

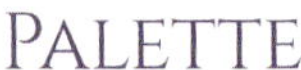

Palette

Make sure you have two piles of Permanent Rose, one at CSC and one at BC (page 16). By adding petals in different values (refer to page 21 for a refresh), the flower begins to take on a more natural appearance as we create a light source—the dark petals being shaded, and the lighter petals reflecting the light.

Step 1.

Begin by making two petals directly across from each other with a size 6 brush in CSC, leaving a pea-sized (about ¼-inch [6-mm]-diameter) circle in the middle. These two petals should be slightly darker than the others that you add in the next step.

Step 2.

Finish the flower, using your other size 6 brush by making three petals in BC. These three petals will be lighter. Be sure to leave a bit of space between the petals.

Step 3.

Next, mix up a pile of Cadmium-Free Yellow to CSC. Once the petals are dry, use your size 4 brush to add a small dab of paint to the middle of the flower. This is a wet-into-dry technique.

To do this using the wet-into-wet technique (page 29), you will paint all five petals in one fluid motion, using both size 6 brushes—one for CSC and one for BC. This time, paint the first two petals in CSC beside each other and the three bottom petals in BC. Have your size 4 brush preloaded with Cadmium-Free Yellow, so you can drop it into the center of your flower while the petals are wet. Gently poke at the edge of the center and allow the colors to merge.

Pinwheel in Different Positions

Next, let's have a look at a few different positions we'll use in a future lesson to create a forget-me-not stem.

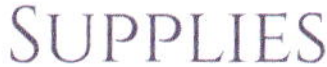

Supplies

One size 6 brush

Sideways: For this position, you will use your size 6 brush to create a simple stroke the same way you would a leaf, starting at the top and using the toe of your brush, pulling downward and gradually increasing pressure at the middle of the stroke. Next, you'll complete the petals the same way as you did for the open-faced pinwheel flower (page 37), starting at the middle with the largest petal and filling the area around with smaller petals.

Upward: Using the same technique as for sideways, you will slightly change the direction of that first petal by painting it horizontally instead of vertically. Then, fill in the accompanying petals.

Downward: Same as for upward, only this time you'll turn your paper upside down, and starting at the left and working your way right, complete one-half of the compound stroke and fill in the surrounding petals.

Closed: This petal begins with one fluid stroke, starting at the left on the toe of the brush and working right, applying more pressure to come down on the belly of the brush. Next, you will fill in the area above the petal with very small gestural strokes (page 32) to give the impression of petals peeking out from the other side.

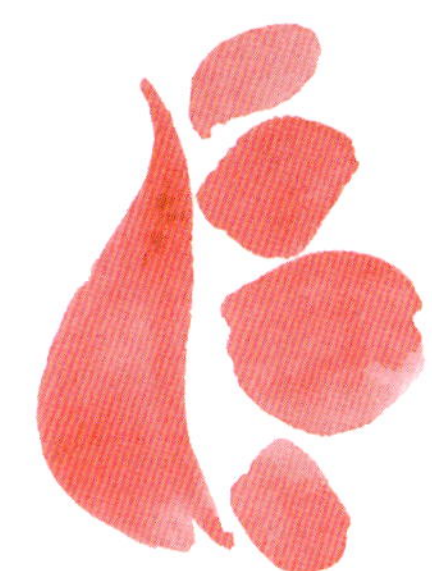

Sideways

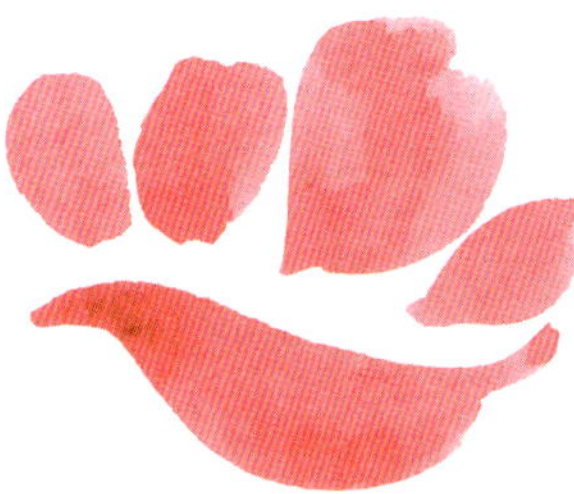

Upward

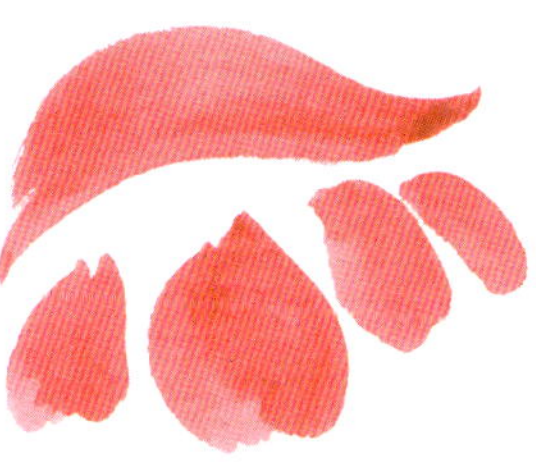

Downward

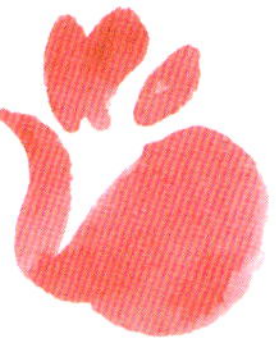

Closed

Gestural Pinwheel

As with our gestural leaves, there is a way to use strokes to form flowers that merely indicate toward the subject matter. Let's look at a few pinwheel flowers in loose controlled form beside their gestural sibling.

Note the differences. Observe that the gestural flowers have a "thoughtless" feel to them, but aren't any less beautiful. You'll likely need to spend ten to fifteen minutes practicing drills before you see any notable difference between controlled and gestural.

The size of brush you use to create a pinwheel flower will depend on how large the flower is itself. For a small pinwheel, for example a forget-me-not, we would use a size 2 or 4 round brush and create a stroke that is less formed than the simple stroke. For a larger flower—say, a wild rose—we would use a size 8 or 10 round brush.

Tips:

Consider using just a small marking to act as a petal rather than a stroke (as shown in closed form [page 39]).

Come up on the toe of your brush for thinner lines (as shown in sideways form [page 39]).

Put a bit more negative space in the middle of the flower and allow the petals to take on a more detached structure.

OPEN FACE CONTROLLED

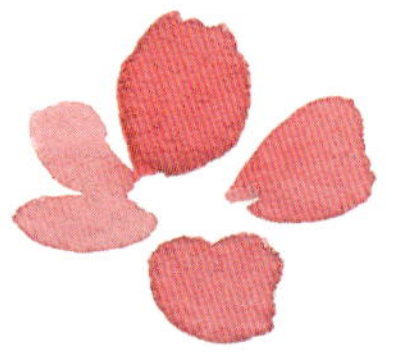

OPEN FACE GESTURAL

SIDEWAYS CONTROLLED

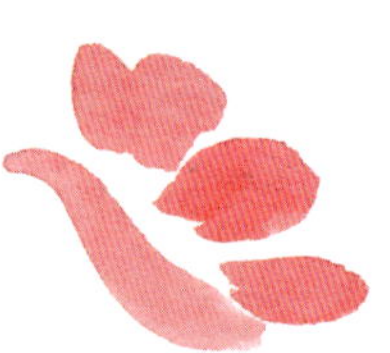

SIDEWAYS GESTURAL

CLOSED CONTROLLED

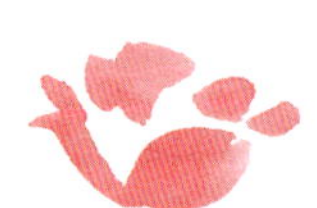

CLOSED GESTURAL

OPEN FACE CONTROLLED

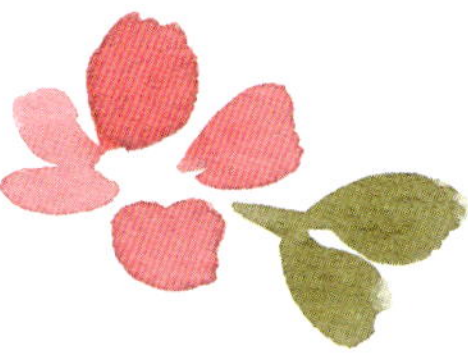

OPEN FACE GESTURAL

SIDEWAYS CONTROLLED

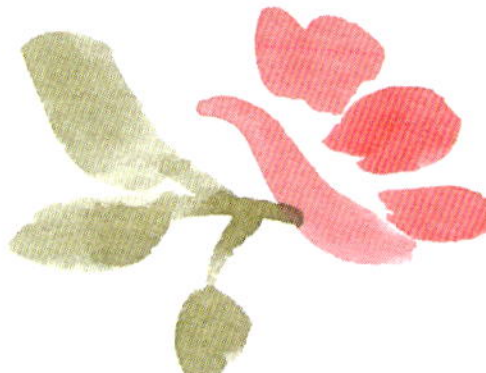

SIDEWAYS GESTURAL

CLOSED CONTROLLED

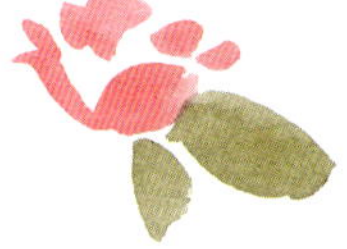

CLOSED GESTURAL

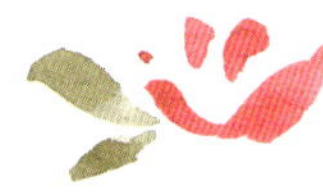

Now, let's add a few leaves in both controlled loose and gestural form. Again, note the differences in the overall feel of the structure. Controlled have fatter fluid strokes, whereas gestural are made with quick flicks of the brush.

GESTURAL OUTLINING

This is a technique we will be using often throughout the lessons to add an extra layer of interest to our flowers. Have a look at the images and note the differences. The controlled outlines around the pinwheel flower are very uniform and closely envelop the petals. The gestural outlines are more carefree and spirited, created using the tippy toe of the brush for fine lines. There is more room for variation, in thickness and also allowing the shape to be broken up so that it doesn't outline the entirety of the petal.

Take a few moments now to explore this technique by first painting a pinwheel, allowing it to dry and then, using a pointy brush (I recommend a size 6), create a loose outline around the petals.

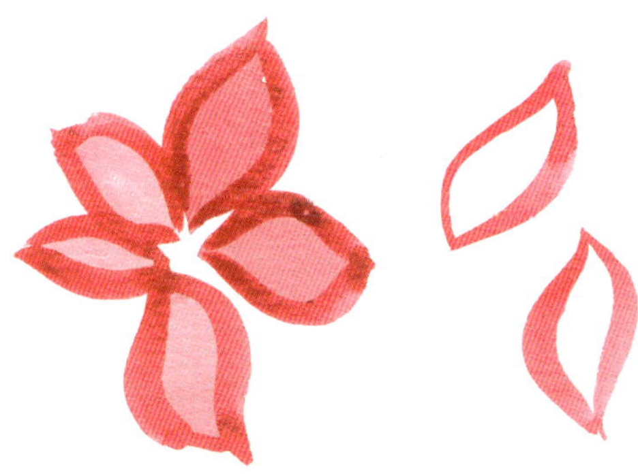

CONTROLLED OUTLINING

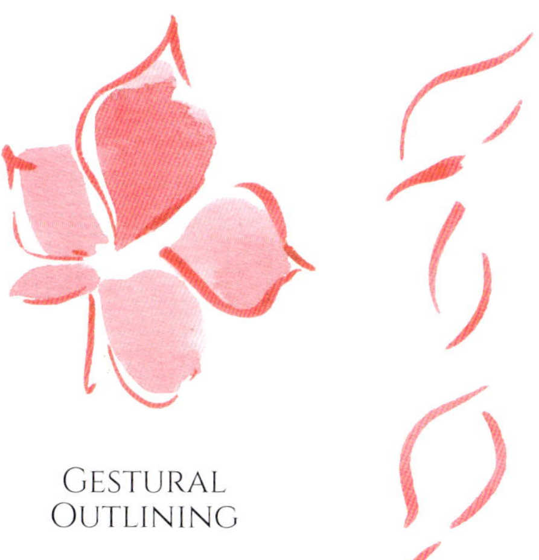

GESTURAL OUTLINING

Lavender Flower

Lavender is such a lovely, airy accent flower to add to compositions, and best of all, it's fairly simple to construct.

Supplies

Three size 4 round brushes

Canson 140-lb (300-gsm) cold-press paper

Palette

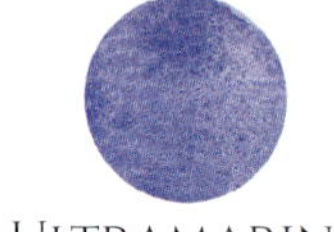

Ultramarine Violet

Rose of Ultramarine

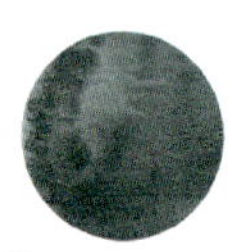

Greenish Umber

Step 1.

Mix Ultramarine Violet to CSC (page 16).

Step 2.

Mix Rose of Ultramarine to BC (page 16).

Step 3.

With a size 4 brush and the Ultramarine Violet in CSC, create the first flower at the bottom of the sprig. You'll be using the toe of the brush. Think about the shape of a hair bow as you're making your strokes.

Step 4.

Add the second and third flowers, using the toe of the brush to create small paddle-shaped strokes. Think of these as half of a hair bow, or if that bow was to be turned at an angle.

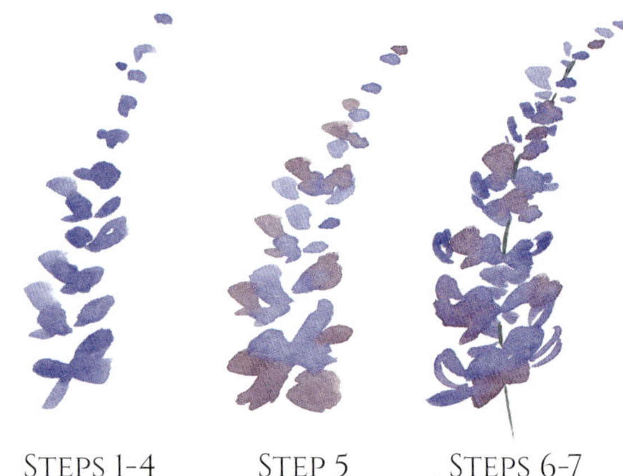

Steps 1–4 Step 5 Steps 6–7

Step 5.

Continue to the top of the stem, curving the direction slightly right, until you are making tiny gestural dots to indicate flower buds. The petals should be largest at the bottom of the sprig and gradually become smaller at the top.

Step 6.

Using a second size 4 brush, load it with Rose of Ultramarine in BC and add the same shape petals to the stem. These should be playing peek-a-boo from behind the original flowers. Your media may still be wet, which will allow for a gentle merging of colors. If not, the effect is still lovely. You can choose this technique by referring to page 29 for wet-into-wet technique.

Step 7.

Using a third size 4 brush, mix Greenish Umber to CSC and add a stem running through the middle of the flowers.

Step 8.

Lastly, add gestural outlining (page 41) in Ultramarine Violet in CSC along the outer edges of some of the flowers. Make a few more small dots at the top of the stem so that it's clearly leaning right.

African Daisy

In the final chapter of this book, we will have a look at using white tones to paint an African daisy. To better prepare you for this lesson, we're going to practice a bit beforehand. Also, to get you familiar with other brushes, I've included a few projects where we will use a filbert, one of my favorite brushes. As partial as I am to my round brushes, the shape of this brush will naturally give your flowers a whole different feel, making them more versatile.

Supplies

One size 6 round brush

One size 4 filbert brush

Canson 140-lb (300-gsm) cold-press paper

Palette

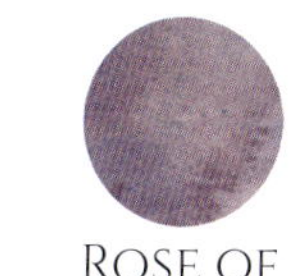

Rose of Ultramarine

Sepia

Green Gold

Lamp Black

Lamp Black + Green Gold

Rose of Ultramarine + Sepia

Step 1.

Using the size 6 round brush, mix together Rose of Ultramarine and Sepia to BC (page 16).

Step 2.

Using mid-pressure on the brush, paint a series of small strokes to complete a ring about the size of a quarter (1 inch [2.5 cm] in diameter), leaving a dime-sized (scant ¾-inch [1.9-cm]-diameter) white space in the middle. Refer to the image below to see how this looks.

Step 3.

Using your size 4 filbert brush, mix together Lamp Black and Green Gold to BC. Using the sample strokes as a reference, practice making simple strokes with the brush. If you have never used a filbert before, this will take some getting used to, as the brush does not have the pointed tip. You will still paint the same way as you would with a round brush, but the effect will be different. The ends of the petals will have a round shape instead of a pointy tip.

Mimic the bottom petal by using the side of the brush.

Mimic the second petal by using the entire brush, belly down.

Some of the paint will naturally come off the brush, so your last two petals will be a lighter color, which is wonderful for adding even more interest to paintings. Typically, we would need to decrease the value to do this, but simply using the paint on the brush will achieve the same result as long as there is enough water in the bristles.

Center

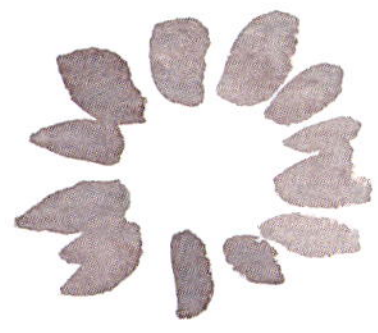

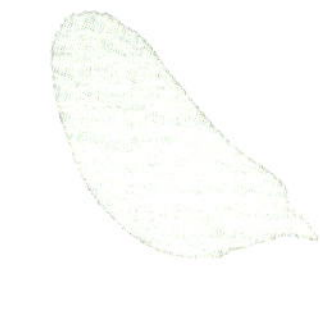

Practice Strokes

Step 4.

This time, I'd like you to practice wet-into-wet by painting the ring again the same way as you did in Step 2, but this time have your filbert brush preloaded with the Lamp Black and Green Gold mixture in BC to immediately touch the edge of the brush to the purple and make a few petals extending from the ring.

Refer to the image to see how this works.

Ideally, you should have a nice transition of color, starting with purple and gradually lightening to the white mixture at the tip of the petal.

We will revisit this concept in the near future when we paint the entire flower!

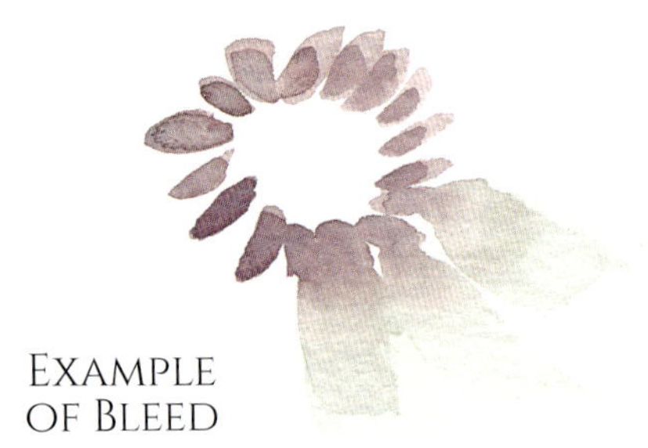

Example of Bleed

Rose

Oftentimes, roses can feel like complicated flowers; however, we're going to simplify the structure to make painting them both fun and beautiful.

In a future lesson, we will be painting a white rose, so we'll double up on practice now by using the same color, which will help prepare you for the project.

Supplies

One size 6 round brush

One size 10 round brush

Canson 140-lb (300-gsm) cold-press paper

Palette

Lamp Black

Raw Umber

Raw Umber + Lamp Black (Lesser Value)

Raw Umber + Lamp Black (Greater Value)

Step 1a.

Using your size 6 brush, mix Raw Umber and Lamp Black together to BC (page 16). This mixture will serve as the darkest and inner part of the rose, which I call the vortex.

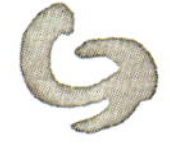

STEP 1B.

Create the vortex by painting two interlocking C shapes. One will be facing the right way, the other will be backward.

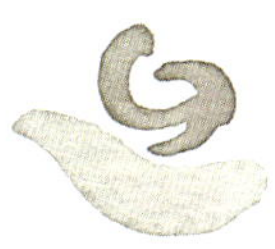

STEP 2.

Next, where the C shapes overlap at the bottom, create the third petal, which is done by sweeping the toe of the brush from the left to the right, gradually increasing pressure toward the middle and lifting up as you reach the other side. Don't reload the brush with paint, to ensure that this petal is lighter than the middle petals.

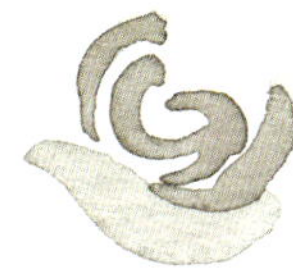

Tip: Be sure to leave negative space between your petals to act as a light source. It's okay if the petals run into one another other in certain places; you just want to make sure there is distinguishable white space between the petals as you move outward.

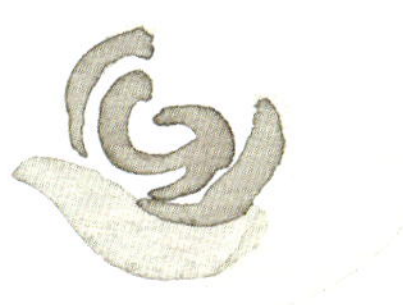

STEP 3.

Reload the brush with the Raw Umber and Lamp Black mixture. Use the toe of the brush to create two fine lines on either side of the rose.

Please note: There are some slight color differences between the inner and the outer petals even though we are still only using two colors blended together at different values. This is where my ratio of Lamp Black was slightly higher than the Raw Umber, resulting in a petal that is grayer than the previous petals. This is not something you need to attempt to do, but something that could occur as colors run together on your palette and are loaded on your brush.

STEP 4.

Switching to your size 10 brush, swirl it into your Raw Umber and Lamp Black mixture and begin a new pile. Add water to decrease the value so it is clearly lighter than the first mixture. This will give the impression that light is hitting the outer petals. On the bottom right side of the rose, paint the next petal the same way as you painted the third petal. Increase pressure on the belly so that this stroke is wider.

Step 5.

Reload the brush with the decreased mixture. On the left side, repeat Step 4, coming down almost full belly on the size 10 brush to create a slightly larger petal.

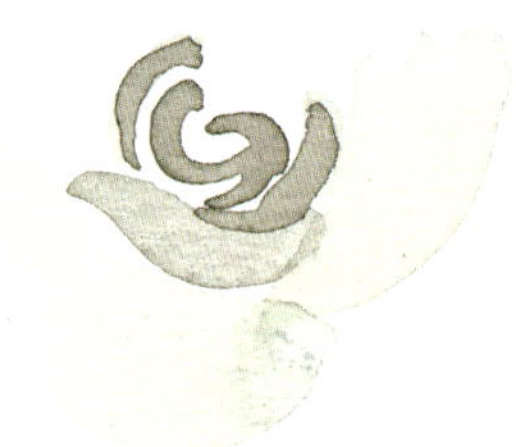

Step 6.

Reload the brush with the decreased mixture. For your next two strokes, arc the brush to almost mirror the petal below it, just slightly longer and wider. Above that, paint a thumb-sized rainbow-shaped petal.

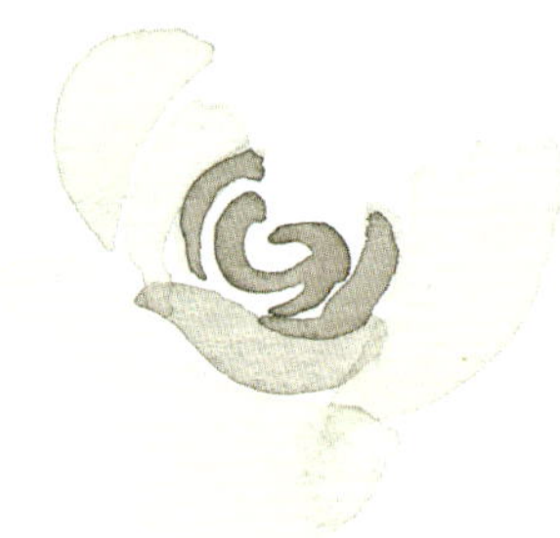

Step 7.

For this petal, you'll use both brushes. Load your size 6 brush with the Raw Umber and Lamp Black mixture (darker) we used for the vortex. Where the two bottom petals connect, paint a thin line that runs parallel to the edges of the petals. With a preloaded size 10 brush containing the decreased (lighter) Raw Umber and Lamp Black mixture, fill in the petal by painting a thick simple stroke on the left and a sideways leaf shape on the right, using the compound stroke technique, making the top side of the petal thinner and bottom wider.

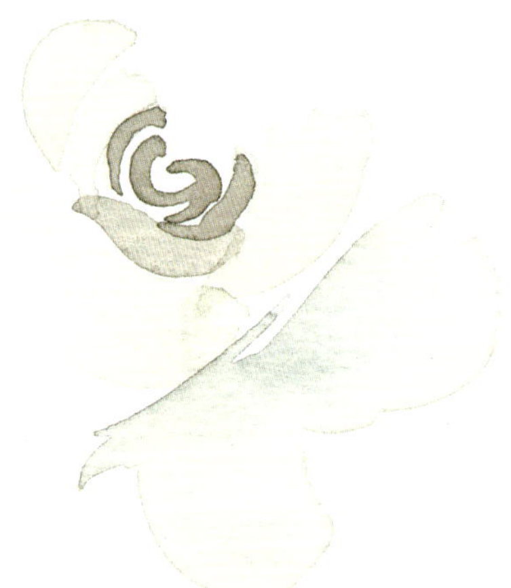

Step 8.

Next, you'll create the largest petal directly to the left, the same way you painted the previous petal. With your size 6 brush and using the lesser value Raw Umber and Lamp Black mixture, start with a thin line that runs parallel to the petal below it. Immediately use your size 10 brush, preloaded with the same mixture, to fill in the petal. This time, you will drag the brush in an up-and-down motion, almost as if you are painting a wall. Leave a small space between the next part of the petal and shape it the same way with minor differences. Add a little tail on the end to serve as a petal folded backward.

Refer to the demo petals I've included. Obviously, they need to be shaped a bit, but that is the general shape and will serve as a solid foundation for you to build on.

Step 9.

Using your size 10 brush, load it with the lesser value Raw Umber and Lamp Black mixture. Starting at the top, use the toe of the brush, gradually increasing pressure toward the middle of the petal and coming back to toe at the end to complete the simple stroke. Add one final stroke, using the toe of the brush to create a fine line just beneath the simple stroke.

Consider going through this lesson at least one or two more times before we get to the project on page 174; each time your muscle memory will get stronger and you will become more confident in your strokes, which will make painting the main lesson so much more enjoyable! If your rose didn't turn out all that roselike, no big deal! It's often a difficult flower to master on the first or even the tenth try! Give yourself grace and begin again.

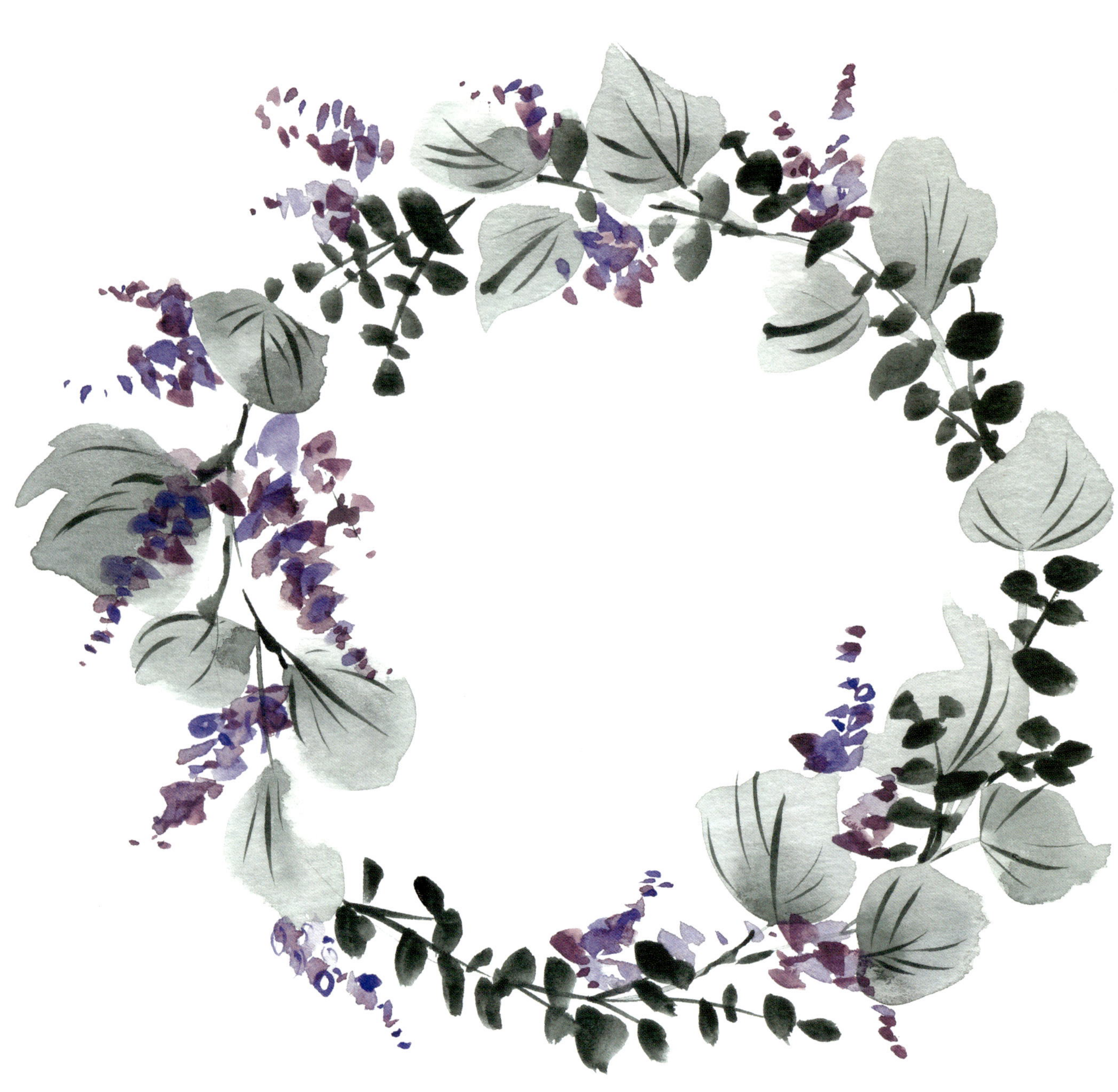

Beautiful, Well-Balanced Wreaths

When one hears the word *wreath*, the first thing that might come to mind is a Christmas wreath, brimming with poinsettia and pinecones; however, there are wreaths for all occasions, some quite complex in arrangement and others that fall under minimal decor. Beyond providing door candy, they are a wonderful subject for watercolor painters to study!

I chose to begin the project portion of this book with wreaths because not only are they beautiful and straightforward, but they also teach us a lot about composition, about how to balance the elements on the page in a way that makes the viewer feel at peace. They also help to alleviate anxiety in the new artist by providing a structure, thus relieving the artist of having to shape a painting. Whenever I feel unsure about what to paint or perhaps have only a small block of time, wreaths are my go-to project. With a bit of practice, painting them becomes the most lovely, relaxing and therapeutic activity.

Leaf Wreath

To get your feet wet, we will begin with an introductory wreath, consisting only of simple stroke leaves and gradually move on to more advanced techniques in the wreaths to follow. Simple though it may be, we will be using an arrangement of colors that is anything but plain, providing beautiful drama to our leaves and plenty of variety. Let's head in now!

Supplies

Two size 6 round brushes

Canson 140-lb (300-gsm) cold-press paper

HB pencil

Dust-free eraser

Palette

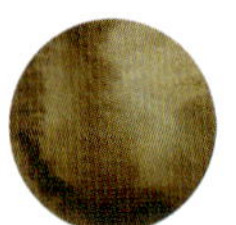

Sepia

Sap Green

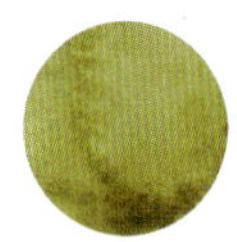

Sepia + Sap Green

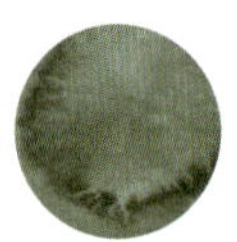

Greenish Umber

Preparing the Palette

Prior to beginning the lesson, use a size 6 brush to mix Sepia and Sap Green together to CSC. (Refer to page 16 for a refresh on consistencies and the abbreviations we'll be using to indicate color value.) Next, use the other size 6 brush to mix Greenish Umber to BC. Set these brushes off to the side for now.

A Note on Shaping Wreaths

To set ourselves up for success and prevent our wreath from going cockeyed or crooked, we will be tracing a circle to serve as the foundation. Having a few firm boundaries will allow us to work intuitively later on.

If you've ever painted a wreath that ended up looking square or ovalish, the reason could be you neglected to stay on track, so to speak. Although I encourage play and "winging it" in many cases, for wreaths I highly suggest finding a circular object you can trace. I like to use small dishes or the lids of large candles.

Lastly, at times, I'd like you to attempt to detach yourself from the intimacy of the painting and observe with a gracious eye. Look at your work as though you are seeing it for the first time. Realize that you're creating an experience as much as painting and that not every tiny detail needs to be perfect to be beautiful. Above all, this is supposed to be *fun*! You are meant to be soothed, invigorated and romanced through the act of painting. So, please don't forget to enjoy yourself along the way!

STEP 1.

Lightly trace a circular object at least 8 inches (20 cm) in diameter on your paper with a pencil. If the idea of free-handing the remainder of the wreath sounds overwhelming, you are more than welcome to lightly pencil a few guide points (the places you intend to place leaves) and erase them at the end.

Next, using your size 6 brush loaded with the Sepia and Sap Green mixture in CSC, make your first leaf branch and a few guides points—the smaller stems protruding from the main branch. Note: You may need to swirl the brush through the paint before this step if the paint has dried.

STEP 2.

Begin attaching leaves to your guide points, with a combination of simple and compound strokes, using CSC. I began with two simple stroke leaves on the left and a compound stroke on the right. For a refresher on strokes, see page 30.

STEP 3.

Using your other size 6 brush with the Greenish Umber in BC, fill in the remainder of the guide points with leaves. You can follow along with my stroke choices or take liberties here (which I always encourage!). Remember to think of movement and variety (page 32) by playing with positioning and different sizes of leaves to make the wreath feel natural, the way it appears in nature.

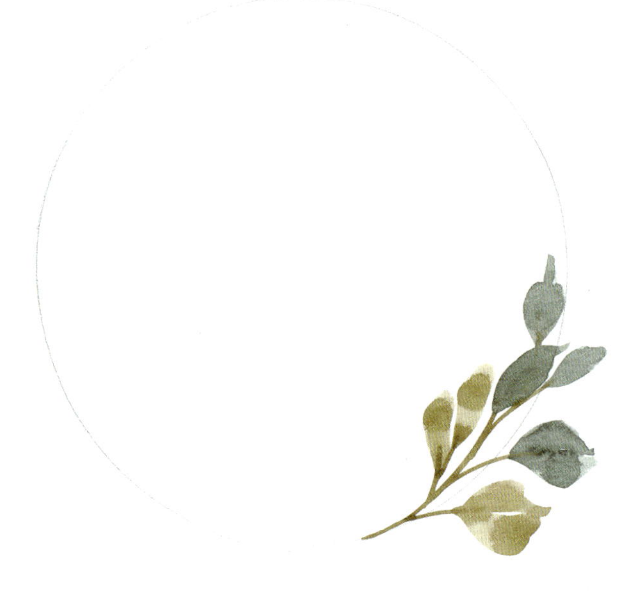

STEP 4.

With your size 6 brush loaded with Sepia and Sap Green in CSC, connect your branch, using the toe of the brush by beginning a new one at a natural beginning point from behind a leaf. Refer to the image to the right to see where that was on my wreath. Also, remain mindful of staying on track, so to speak, not venturing too far inward or outward from the pencil line.

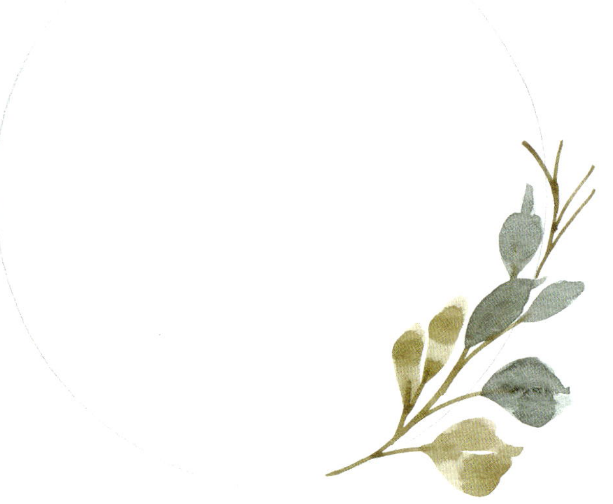

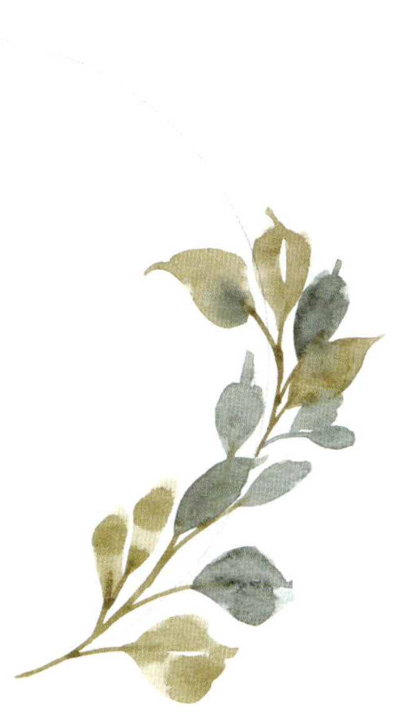

STEP 5.

Continue to fill in the leaves, using both colors and consistencies, painting some of the leaves using wet-into-wet technique. Detailed instructions for this can be found on page 29. As I did, you can paint a leaf, using the Sepia and Sap Green mixture in BC, and then while it's wet, drop in Greenish Umber in CSC. Allow two leaves in different colors to touch to create a bleed. More about bleeds can be found on page 26.

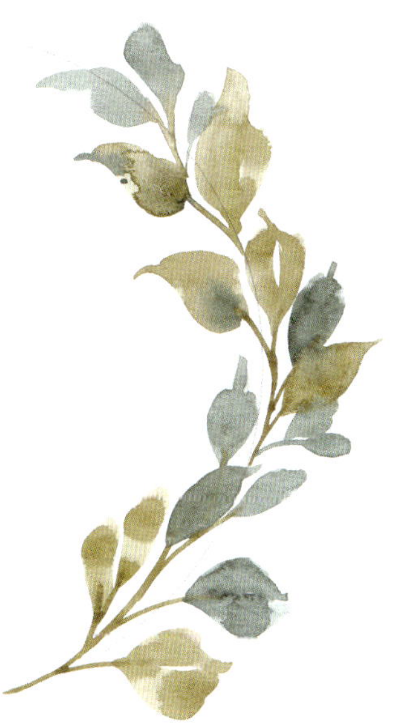

STEP 6.

There's no need to wait until your leaves are dry in one area before moving on to the next; however, you'll need to be aware of timing if you're working on a wet-into-wet leaf. Be careful of hand placement as well, so as not to smear the palm of your hand through the leaves. Add the next portion of the wreath in a similar manner as the previous steps.

STEP 7.

Go slowly. I can't emphasize this enough. Do NOT feel the need to complete your wreath in one fluid session. Continue to fill in the wreath, using the same strokes, utilizing movement and variety. You can take liberties here with the consistency, making some leaves extra interesting by invoking wet-into-wet and allowing other leaves to remain a single color. Let the colors run together and resist the temptation to "fix" every little thing you deem a mistake or flaw.

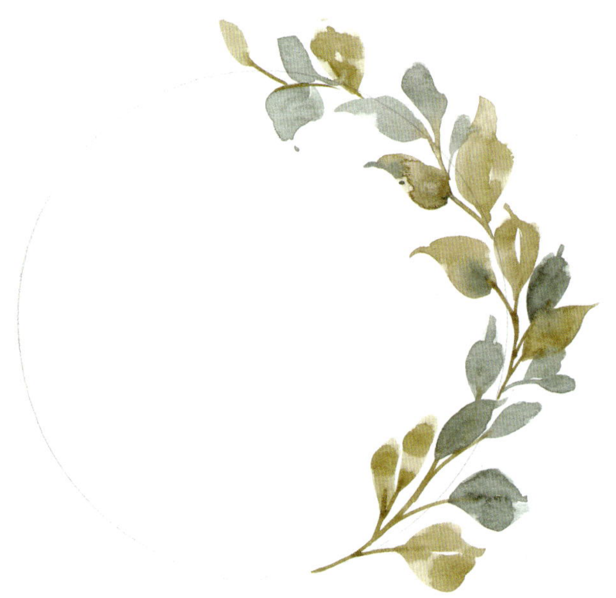

STEP 8.

Take care to make sure your leaf at both the top middle and bottom middle are the highest and lowest parts of the wreath. If you do not do this, your wreath will begin to take on a square shape.

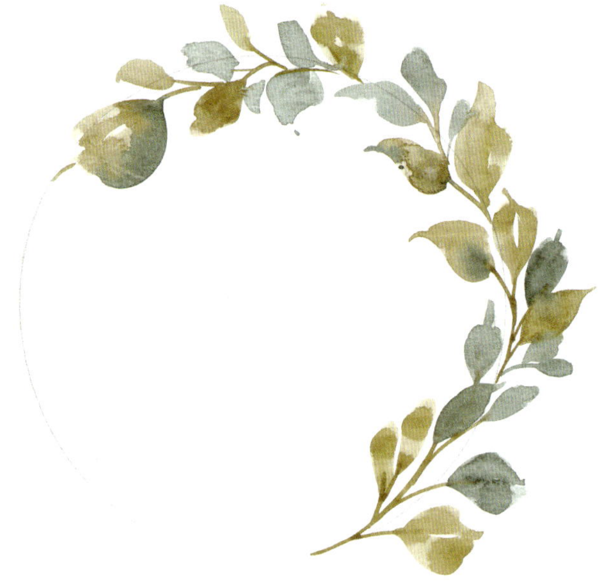

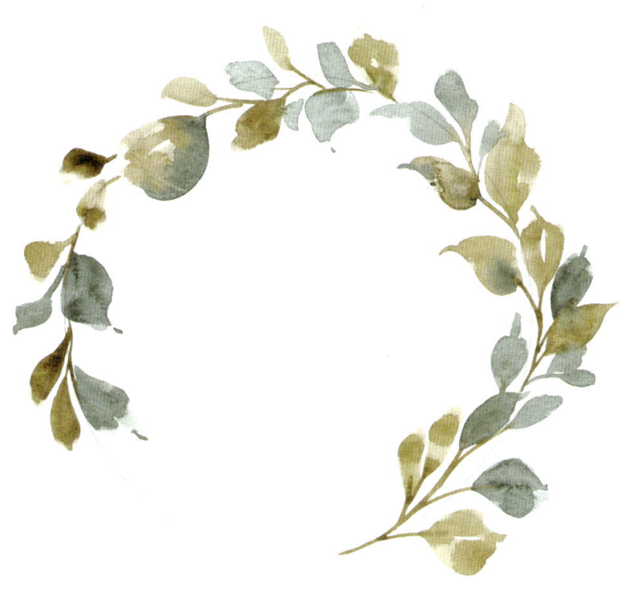

Step 9.

Continue to make your way around the circle slowly, pausing to reflect on what areas need to be thickened up and where others might benefit from being left sparse. Don't feel the need to overwhelm your wreath with a leaf in every nook and cranny. As I've said already, there is great beauty in the parts of the painting you leave open.

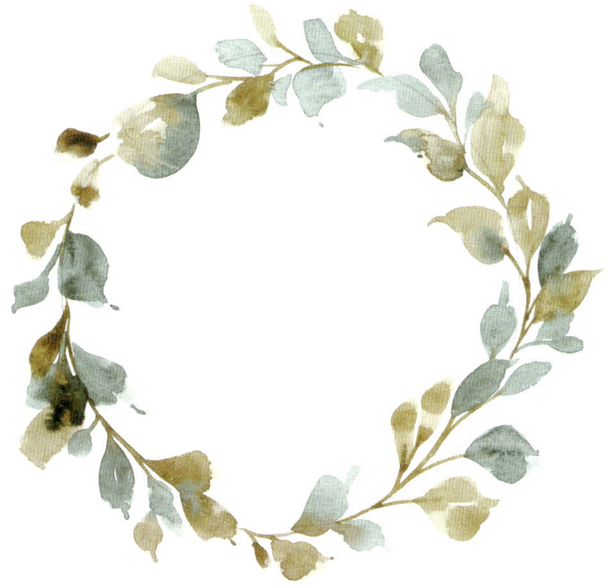

Step 10a.

Finish the last portion of the wreath, ensuring the bottom middle leaf is at the lowest point of the wreath.

Step 10b.

Take a moment to observe your wreath as a whole. Does it feel balanced? Or does it feel too sparse? If so, see what you can do about remedying this. You may need to put in a few more leaves. Sometimes all that's missing is erasing the pencil line, so you may want to do that first (once everything is completely dry) and then decide whether your wreath could benefit from extra touches.

Step 10c.

Erase the pencil lines once the wreath is completely dry.

Lavender and Eucalyptus Wreath

This wreath combines two of my favorite things: lavender and eucalyptus. Now that you have a better understanding of how to balance the shape of a wreath, you're ready to tackle an extra element. For this lesson, you'll be referring back to pages 42 and 34, where we practiced this flower and these leaves in our stroke guide.

Supplies

Two size 4 round brushes

One size 8 round brush

Canson 140-lb (300-gsm) cold-press paper

HB pencil

Dust-free eraser

Palette

Rose of Ultramarine (Flowers)

Ultramarine Violet (Flowers)

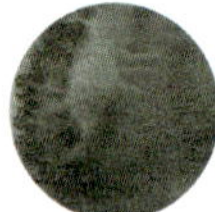

Greenish Umber (Leaves)

Payne's Gray (Leaves)

Payne's Gray + Greenish Umber

Preparing the Palette

Using a size 4 brush, mix Rose of Ultramarine to BC (page 16). Load it and set the brush off to the side.

Using the other size 4 brush, mix Ultramarine Violet to CSC (page 16). Load it and set the brush off to the side.

Lastly, using the size 8 brush, mix together Payne's Gray and Greenish Umber to two separate piles, one BC and one CSC.

Step 1A.

Trace an 8 inch (20 cm) circle shape very lightly in pencil.

Step 1B.

Retrieve your size 8 brush and swirl it through the Payne's Gray and Greenish Umber Gray BC mixture until the brush is completely saturated. Following the line, paint the first five leaves, using the downward technique demonstrated on page 35.

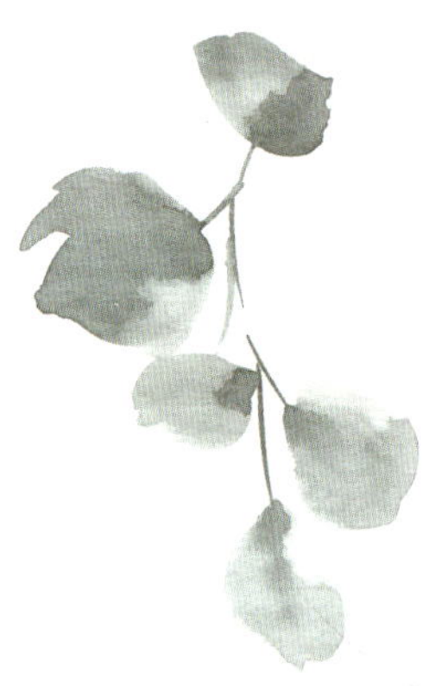

Step 1c.

While the leaves are still wet, use the same mixture in CSC to drop in a tiny bit of color at the base of the leaves. Refer to the wet-into-wet technique on page 29 if you need a reminder.

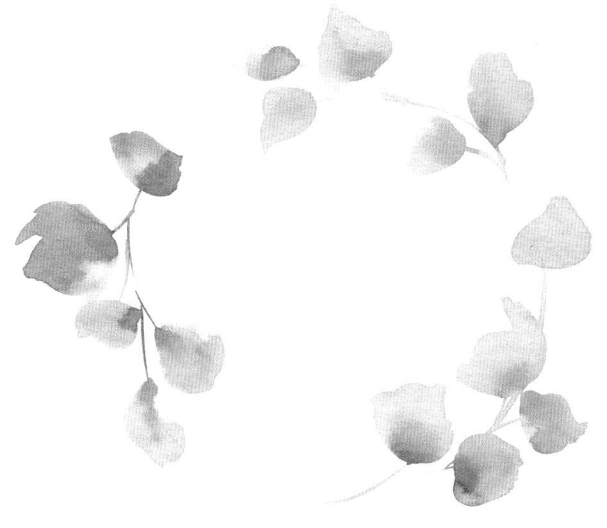

Step 2.

Follow through with the next two groupings of leaves, using the upward and sideways techniques demonstrated on page 34 and 35. Be mindful to leave gaps for the smaller eucalyptus and lavender.

Step 3.

With your size 8 brush, begin adding the smaller eucalyptus stems in the gaps between your large branches, using the Payne's Gray and Greenish Umber mixture in CSC. Be mindful to maintain the shape of the wreath and pause between strokes to see which areas need to be filled and what areas are best left with room to breathe.

Step 4.

Repeat Steps 2 and 3, adding a few more small branches where there is natural space for them.

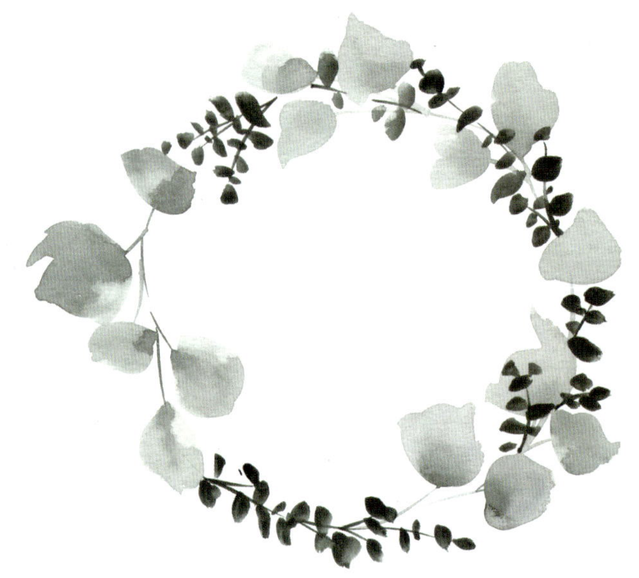

Step 5.

Next, using your size 4 brushes, add the lavender between gaps and poking out from behind larger leaves. Using the toe of the brush, begin with Ultramarine Violet in CSC and then, while wet, add in the Rose of Ultramarine in BC. The colors will softly merge the way they did in our exercise on page 42.

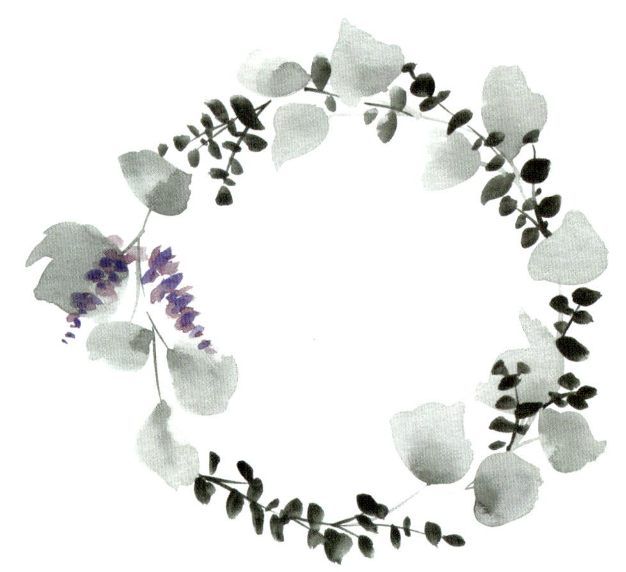

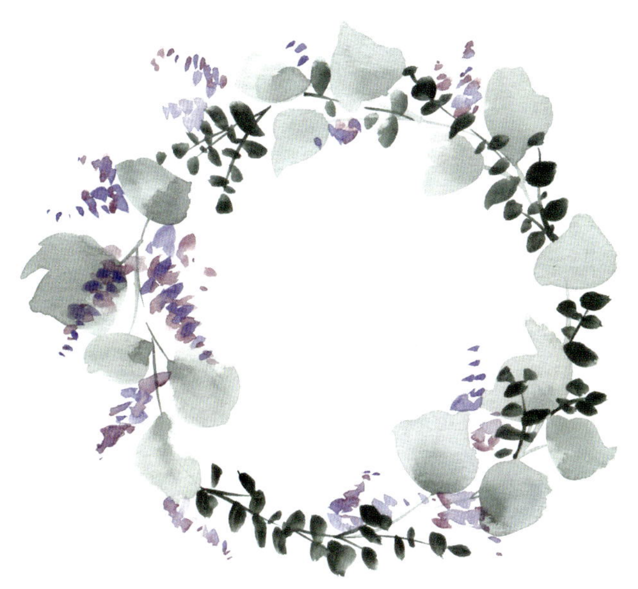

Step 6a.

Repeat Steps 2 and 3 and fill in the gaps.

Step 6b.

Lastly, using your size 4 brush, mix Rose of Ultramarine to CSC and add darker gestural markings, using the toe of the brush to indicate smaller buds. See page 40 for more info on gestural petals. I opted not to include the stems in the lavender branches, for a looser look. You can also decide to leave them as is, or refer to the examples in our practice lesson for how to add a stem.

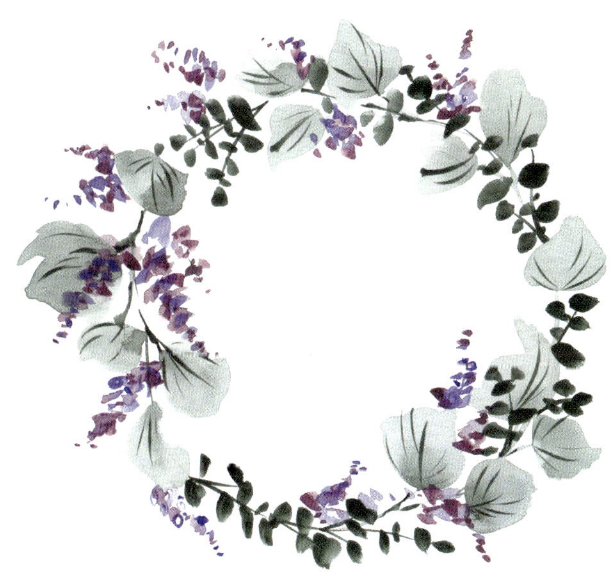

Step 7a.

Optional: If you would like to, be sure your leaves are dry and then, using your size 8 brush and Payne's Gray and Greenish Umber in CSC, add gestural lines in your leaves to indicate veins. Refer to page 32 for a refresher on how we create fine strokes.

Step 7b.

Once everything is completely dry, erase any pencil lines.

Autumn Wreath

One of my most favorite things to paint during fall are the autumn leaves. The colors are achingly beautiful, and I can never resist putting them on a wreath with a few berries. To make this lesson a bit different, we'll be creating a three-quarter wreath with some lovely branch work. We'll still be using the simple stroke method (page 30); however, we'll aim to employ variety by making some of the leaves pointy and others more paddlelike.

Supplies

Three size 6 round brushes
Canson 140-lb (300-gsm) cold-press paper
HB pencil
Dust-free eraser

Preparing the Palette

Use a size 6 brush to mix together Scarlet Lake and Cadmium-Free Yellow to CSC and BC (page 16) in two separate piles.

Using a second size 6 brush, mix together Cadmium-Free Yellow and Raw Umber to CSC and BC.

Lastly, using your third size 6 brush, mix together Scarlet Lake and Raw Umber to CSC and BC.

Step 1.

Trace a circle shape with an 8-inch (20-cm) diameter, but instead of leaving it whole, erase a small portion of the top left-hand side so there is a small gap about 3 inches (7.5 cm) wide.

Palette

Scarlet Lake (berries)

Cadmium-Free Yellow (leaves)

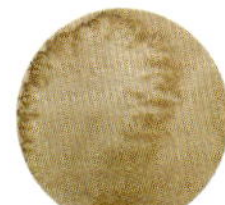
Raw Umber (leaves & branches)

Cadmium-Free Yellow + Raw Umber

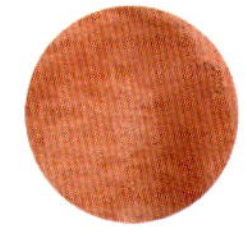
Scarlet Lake + Raw Umber

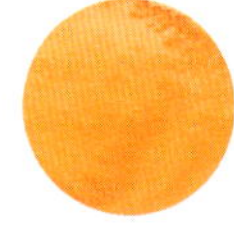
Scarlet Lake + Cadmium-Free Yellow

STEP 2A.

With a size 6 brush loaded with Raw Umber in BC, begin to make slightly curved lines, following the pencil line, using the toe of the brush. If you need a refresh, refer back to page 32 where we covered how to paint a gestural branch. The only difference here is that some will overlap.

STEP 2B.

One at a time, take the remaining two size 6 brushes and swirl each one through the Scarlet Lake and Raw Umber, Scarlet Lake and Cadmium-Free Yellow and Cadmium-Free Yellow and Raw Umber, so that all three size 6 brushes are loaded with a different color of paint. Your first brush will need to be refreshed with Raw Umber in BC.

Important: You don't have to stay exactly on the circle, but you also don't want to stray too far inward or outward. Utilize the toe of the brush, alternating between light to mid-pressure to get a variation of thick and thin lines. Refer to the diagram for branch examples.

STEP 3.

Repeat Step 2 until your wreath is thick with branches and smaller guide points (the same way we did in the Lavender and Eucalyptus Wreath lesson on page 56). You may notice some of the branches are darker than others. This is not due to a different color but because at times the brush will have more or less paint on the bristles, which will result in a variety of shades within a single color.

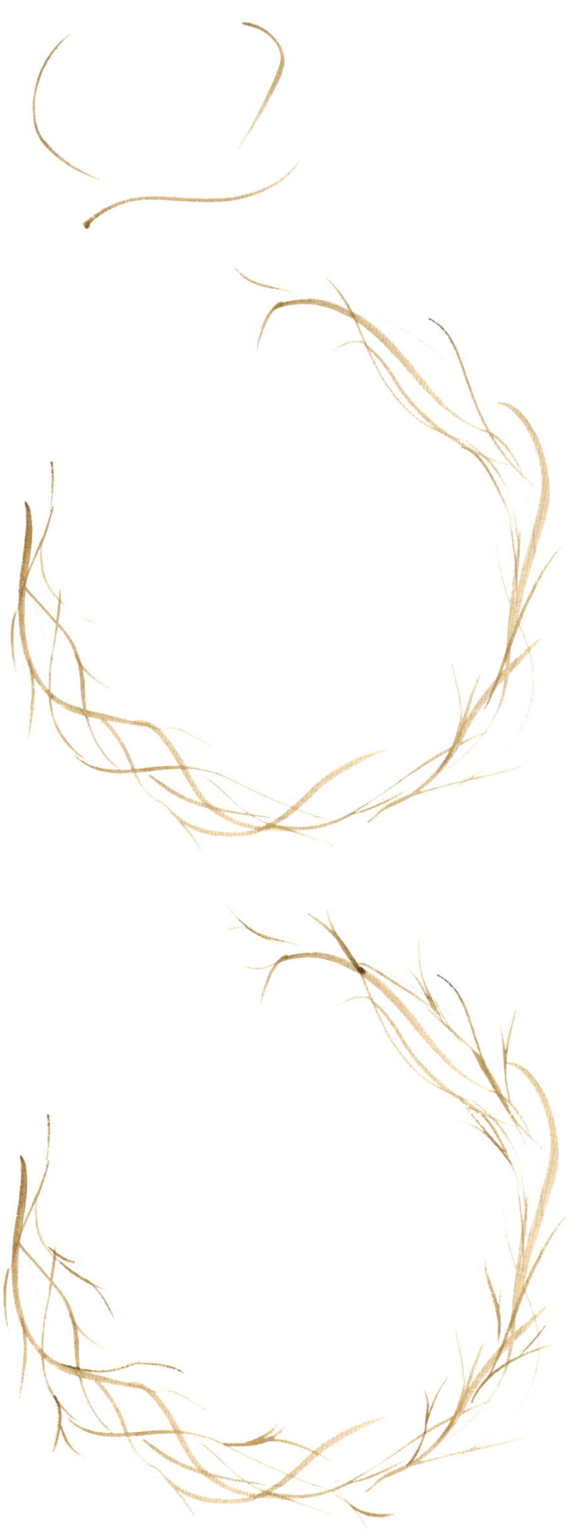

Step 4a.

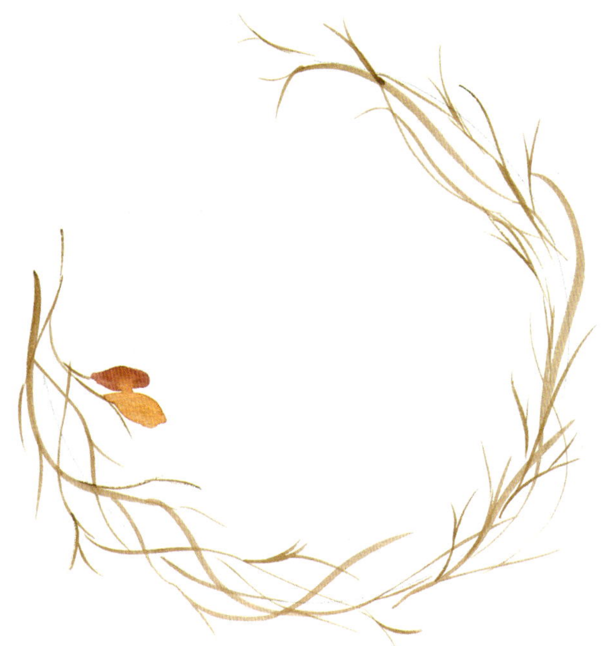

Once your branches are fully dry, you can begin with any color or follow along with me. I'll start with the size 6 brush loaded with the Scarlet Lake and Raw Umber in BC and create my first simple stroke extending from the guide point. Because your branches will not look exactly like mine, there is no need to be concerned with a different beginning location. Rather than walk you through each leaf painted, I want you, the artist, to think of how you would like to compose the piece. Think of it as a playground and its main desire is to be played with. There are no wrong leaves. You can only create beauty, so have FUN. Work from the left to the right side of the paper so as to avoid smudging any wet paint. Refer to page 32 for a refresh on shape variety and leaf posture.

Step 4b.

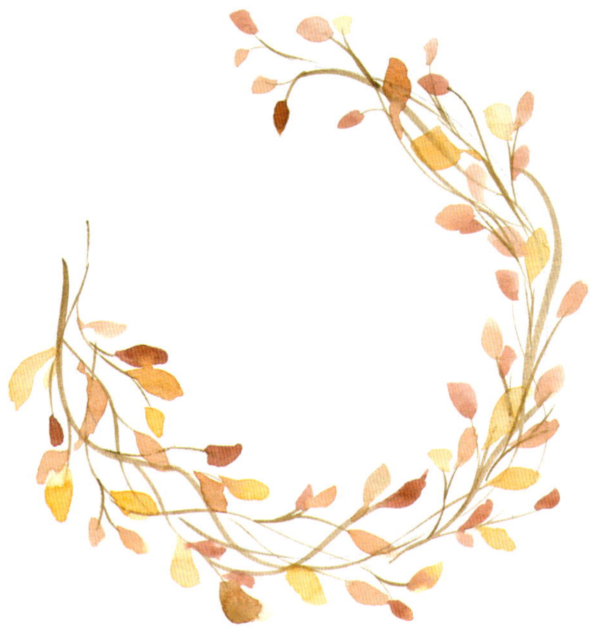

Using your size 6 brush loaded with the Scarlet Lake and Cadmium-Free Yellow mixture in BC, put another simple stroke leaf beside it so the colors are touching.

Step 5.

Now that we are very familiar with the simple stroke technique and have painted a wreath together, I'd like to encourage you to take liberties here, alternating different consistencies and colors as you build the wreath.

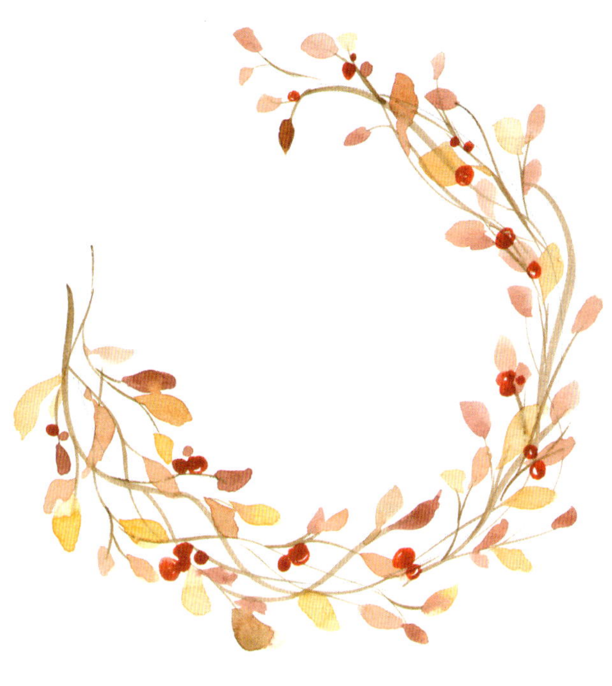

Step 6.

With your size 6 brush loaded with the Scarlet Lake and Raw Umber CSC mixture, begin adding small berries, ranging from lentil- to pea-sized (about ⅛ to ¼ inch [3 to 6 mm] in diameter), using the toe of the brush. Pick a few places to cluster the berries along the branch or nestled against a leaf. If you prefer to follow along with my exact placement, that's completely fine, but again, I'd love for you to take liberties here.

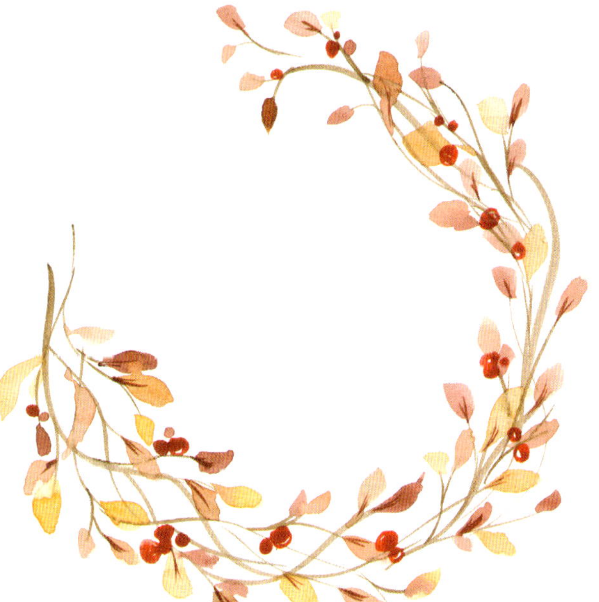

Step 7a.

With a size 6 brush and the Scarlet Lake and Raw Umber mixture in CSC, you can choose to do as I did and add a few veins, using quick, thin strokes utilizing the toe of the brush. For a refresh how to do this, refer to "Pressure" on page 24.

Step 7b.

When the art is dry, erase the pencil lines.

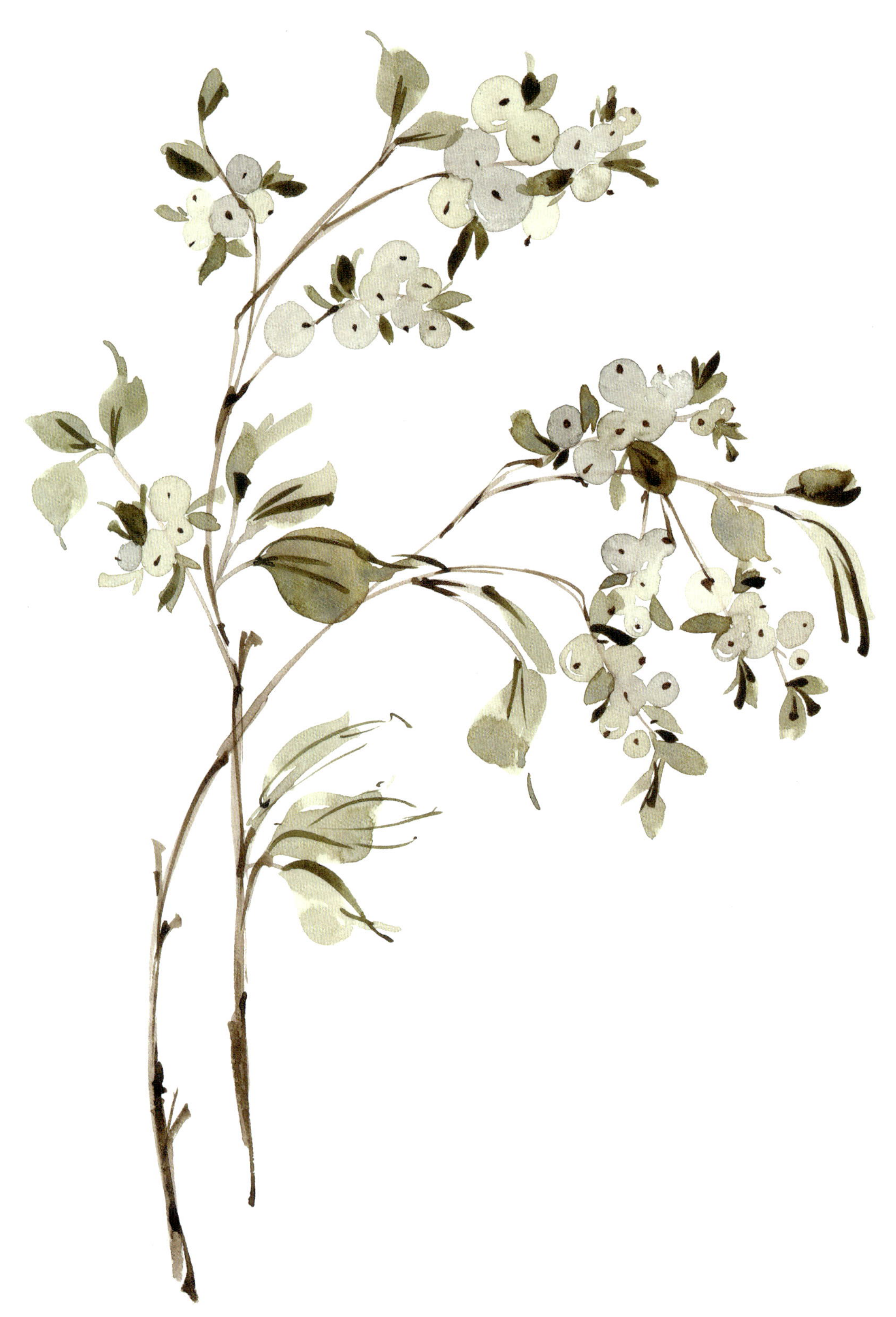

Dainty, Charismatic Blooms

Often referred to as filler flowers, the blooms that surround and accompany the larger, more prominent focal flowers are equally as important as the more glamorous ones. Strong backup vocals can make or break a song. The same goes for florals. We do our compositions a disservice by not recognizing the importance of filler flowers when we underestimate their value.

Some of my most *favorite* flowers are filler flowers. As we move through the projects in this chapter, together we will explore the expressive nature of the flowers that, done well, can stand alone or serve as the perfect addition to a floral composition. I can't wait to show you all that's in store—let's head in now!

Forget-Me-Nots

Forget-me-nots, in my humble opinion, are the perfect flowers with which to begin our filler flower portion of the book. They have a sweet, dainty nature and are chock-full of personality, leaning on the gestural technique (page 32) to come alive. Rather than focusing on each individual flower, we're going to think of the cluster as a whole, building up density as we go by playing with movement and variety (see page 32).

We will have four working piles to draw from as we paint these flowers, two consistencies for each mixture. I'd like you to have different versions of these colors for versatility. In real life, every little detail is gloriously shown through the petals, center and stamen. On paper, however, we have to take care to insert the details—as well as omit them. Because we are always aiming for loose representation, we will focus on not overwhelming these tiny blooms with petal nuances, but rather playing with color in a way that allows these flowers to be distinguishable from one another. We do that with color value (see page 21). By having a range of blueish purples in different consistencies, we can alter the petals' color in each flower to create a cluster that is definable, if only loosely.

Take a look now back at the discussion on page 38, where we covered the technique used for pinwheel flowers in great detail. We will be using that structure here to make our cluster of flowers.

Yellow Added Wet

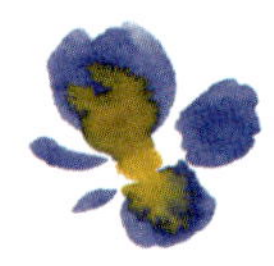

Yellow Added Dry

Open Face

Side

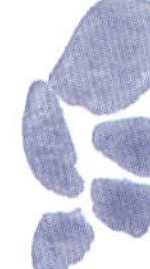

Upward

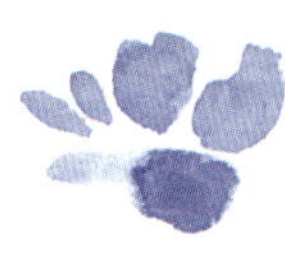

Downward

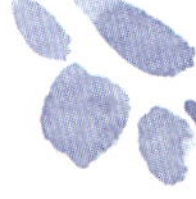

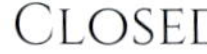

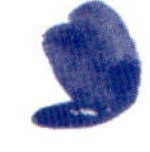

Using Both Colors

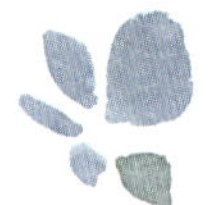

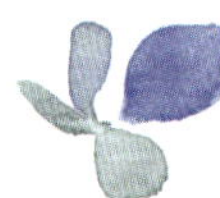

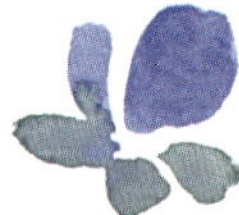

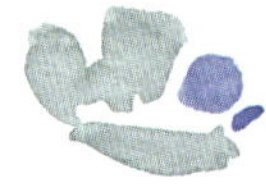

Cluster

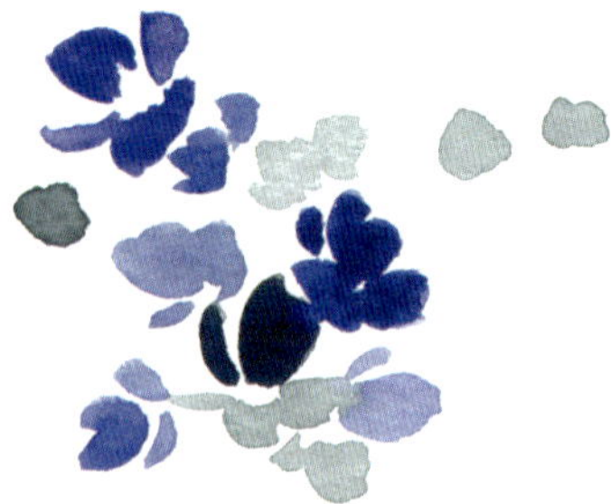

Supplies

Two size 2 round brushes

Canson 140-lb (300-gsm) cold-press paper

Palette

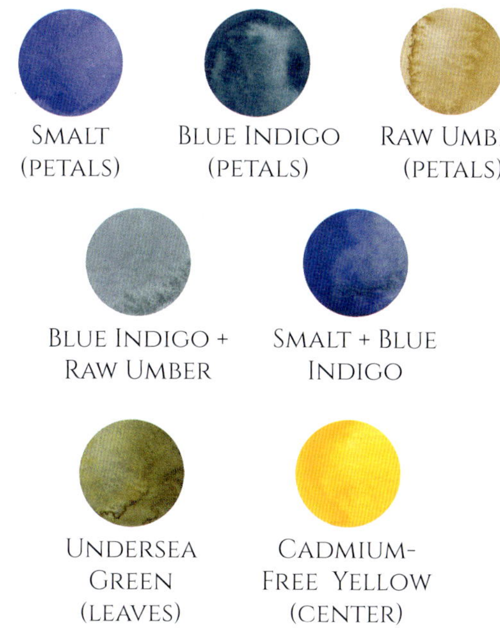

Preparing the Palette

Mix together the Blue Indigo and Raw Umber to both BC and CSC (page 16).

Mix together Smalt and Blue Indigo to both BC and CSC.

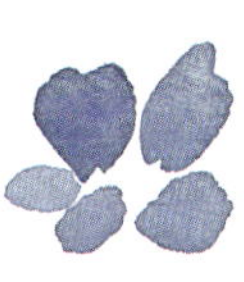

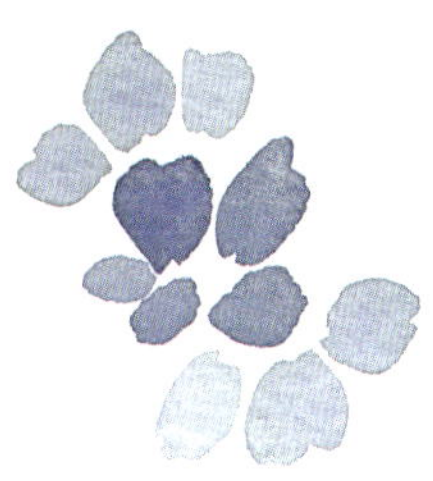

Step 1.

Using a size 2 brush, load it with the Smalt and Blue Indigo mixture in CSC and make an open-faced pinwheel flower. Remember to leave a small circle in the middle and white space between the petals to act as negative space. Vary the size of the petals the same way we did in our pinwheel exercise (page 37), beginning with the top left petal and working right, making the first three petals largest and the bottom two smaller.

Stay mindful that not every stroke needs to look like a petal. As we've worked through our material, you now know a small dot of color can gesture a petal and go a long way in providing clarity to the flower as a whole. For a refresh of gestural pinwheels, see page 40.

Step 2.

Using the same brush, create the next two flowers by creating an upward flower to the upper left of the open-faced flower, and a downward flower toward the bottom right of the open-faced flower. This time, use the mixture in BC. Start with the middle petal, making it the longest, and then add the two shorter petals.

STEP 3.

Using your other size 2 brush, load it with Blue Indigo and Raw Umber in CSC. Create the next clustering of flowers to the lower left of the first cluster. Use CSC for the middle flower and BC for the two additional flowers.

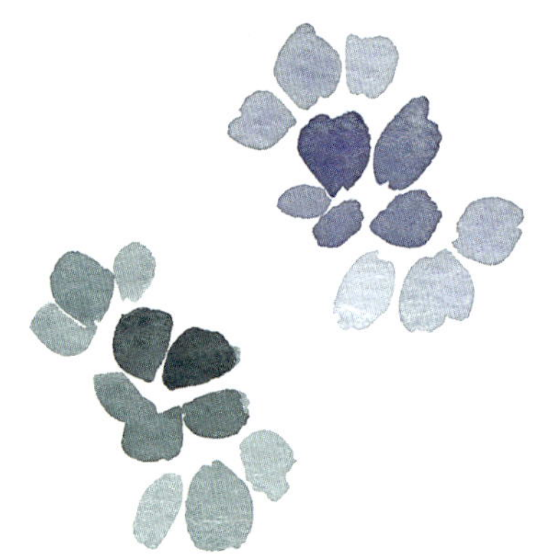

STEP 4A.

We'll make the highest point of our stem now by forming a tight clustering of flowers at the top of the page, slightly deviated to the left. They should be smaller than the flowers in the middle of the page. This time, I'd like you to use both mixtures in CSC, executing a variety of positions. Using both your size 2 brushes, make three open-faced pinwheels tightly together. These appear as the royal blue flowers angling toward the left side of the paper.

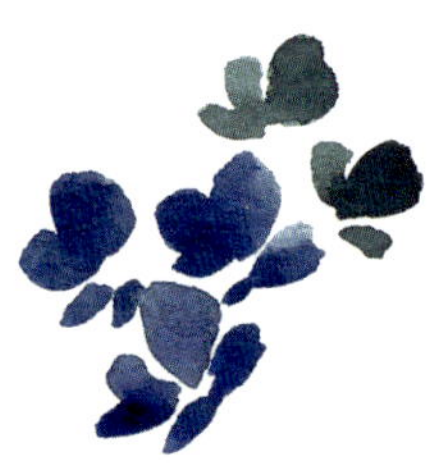

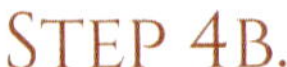

STEP 4B.

Next, using your size 2 brush with the Blue Indigo and Raw Umber CSC mixture, make two sideways pinwheels to the right.

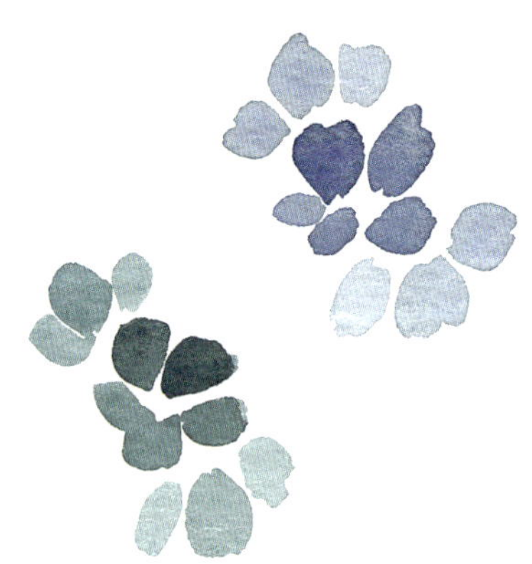

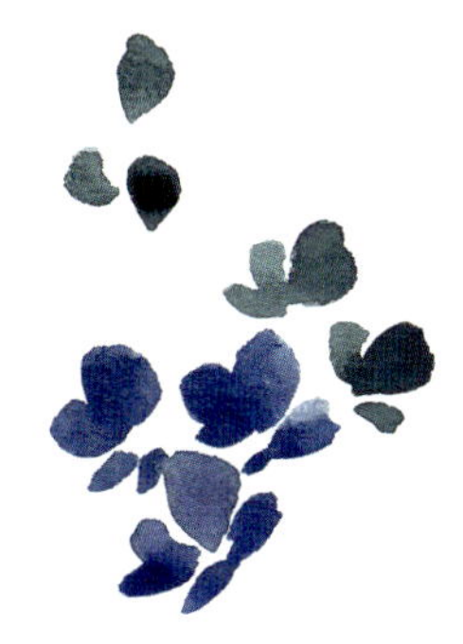

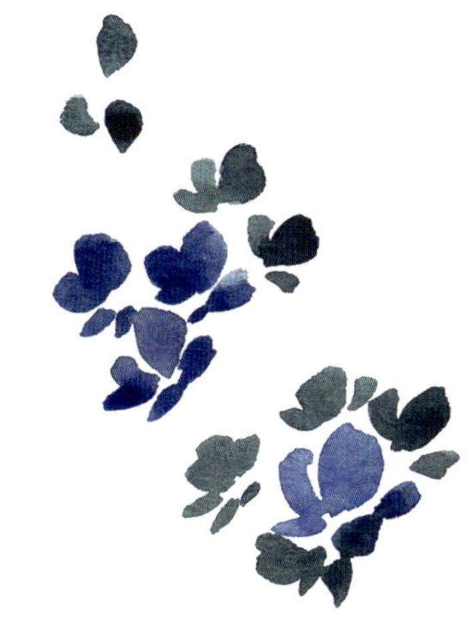

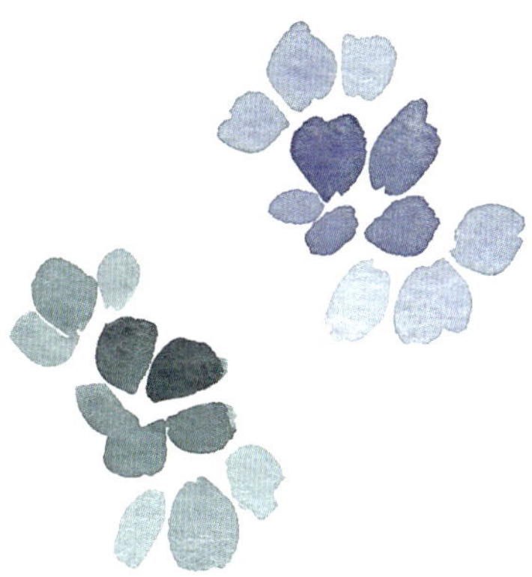

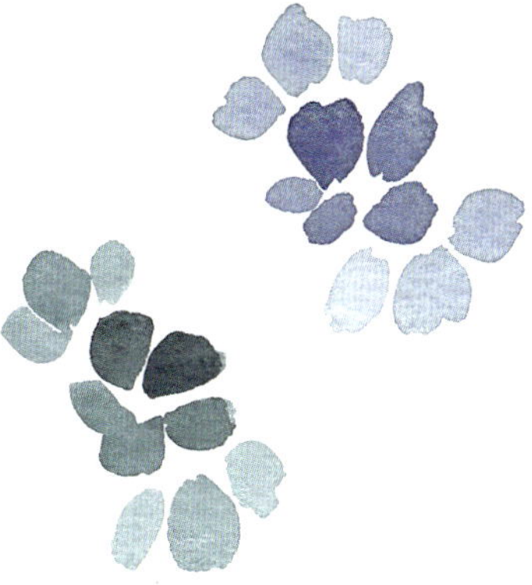

STEP 5.

At the very top, make a few gestural, kernel-sized marks using the same brush to indicate the buds of the flower.

STEP 6.

Continue to make small gatherings of clusters, moving back and forth between colors. For the next batch, paint the open-faced pinwheels in BC, using the Blue Indigo and Raw Umber mixture, and the sideways flowers in Smalt and Blue Indigo, using CSC.

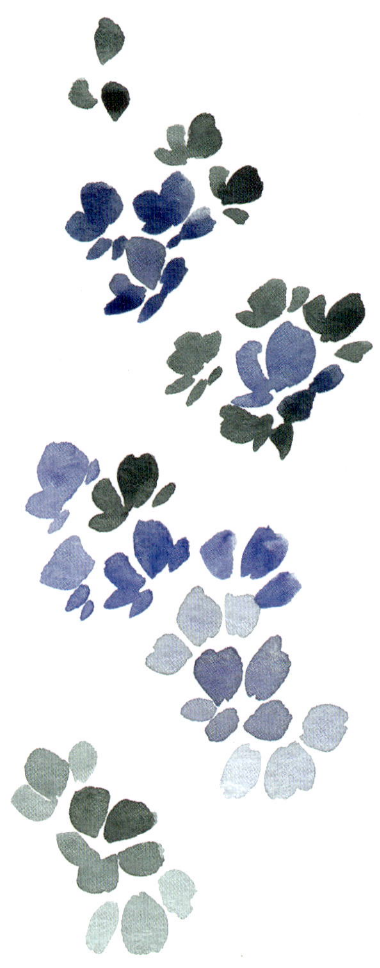

STEP 7.

Fill in the next area, just above our middle cluster, with more pinwheels.

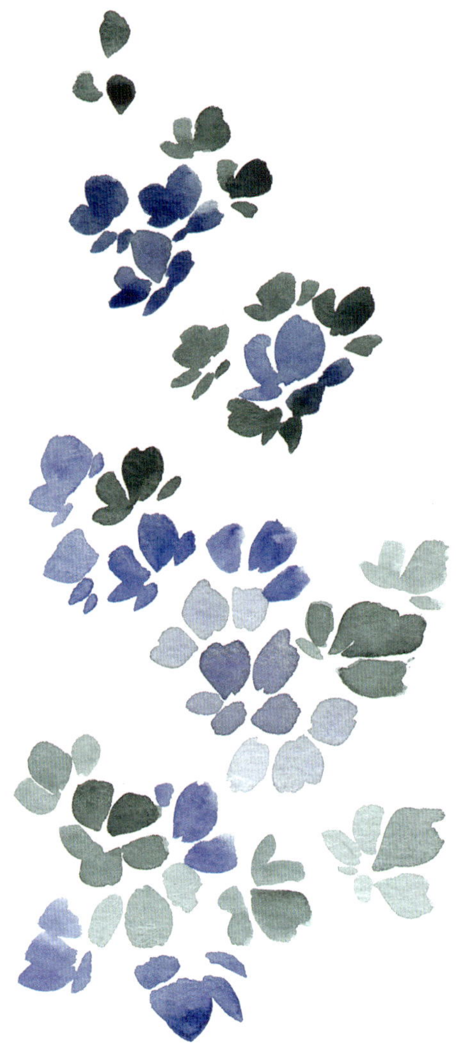

STEP 8.

We will finish the pinwheel portion of this project by adding to our original clusters plus a few additional flowers to help shape the overall structure. As always, alternate consistencies for best variety.

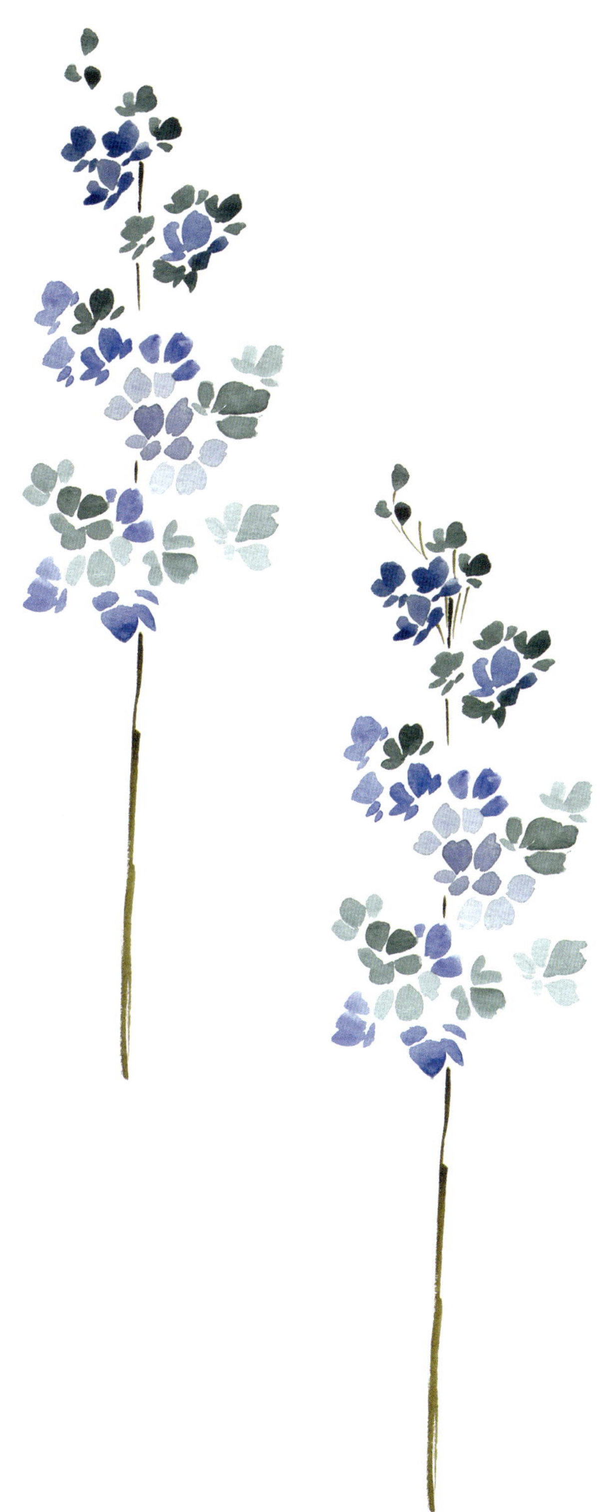

Step 9a.

Using a clean size 2 brush, mix Undersea Green to CSC and BC.

Step 9b.

Paint a main stem running through the middle of the clusters in CSC. This is just to give you an idea of how it will stand. We'll pull it all together soon by attaching the flowers to smaller stems. It would be easiest to create this with a downward stroke. Begin at the top and using the toe of the brush, make a continuous fine line. At the very end, apply a bit more pressure to thicken it up at the bottom.

Step 10.

This is where you will begin to make connections between the flowers and the main stem. Using the same mixture in CSC and your size 2 brush, come up on the toe for very fine lines. Leave a few stems unattached for a more gestural feel.

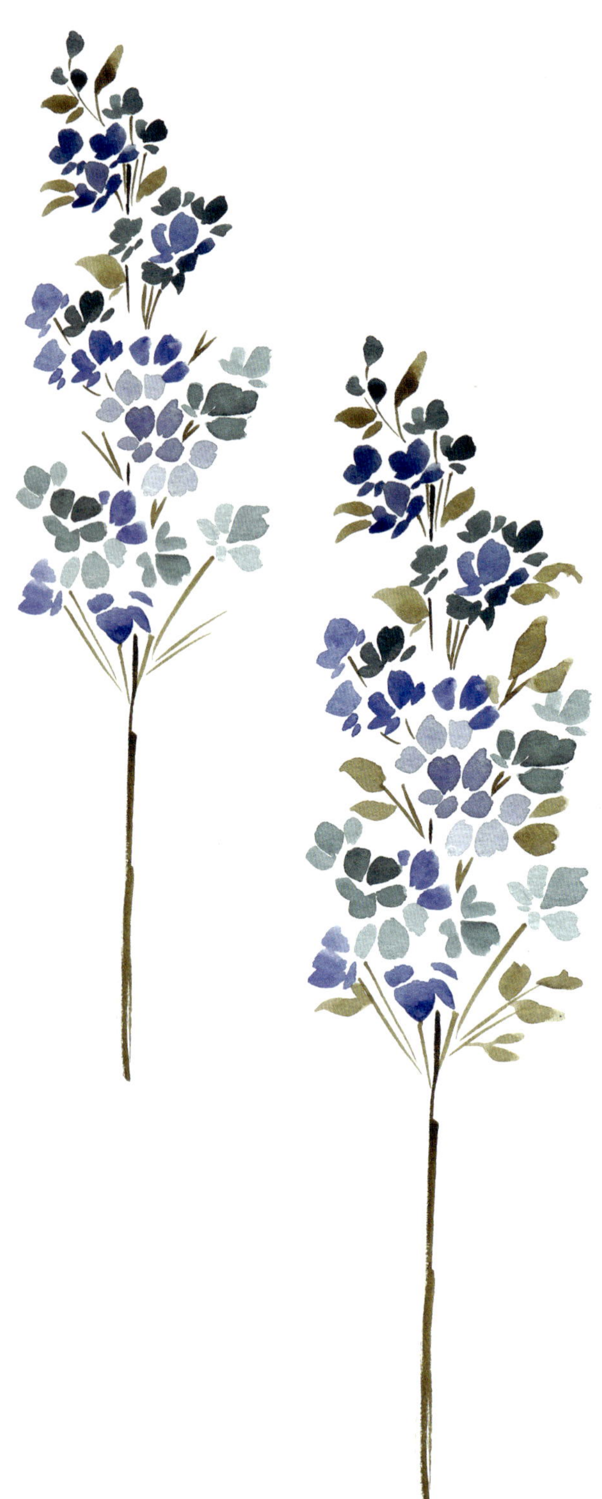

Step 11A.

Finish making connections between the main stem and flowers, and create a few stems where we will later attach leaves.

Step 11B.

Using your size 2 brush and the Undersea Green mixture in BC, begin adding leaves using simple stroke formation (see page 30 for a refresh). These should be smaller versions, tack-sized, than those we practiced earlier in the book to match the size of the flower.

Step 12.

Fill in the remainder of the leaves using a variety of thick and thin simple stroke leaves in both BC and CSC, still using Undersea Green.

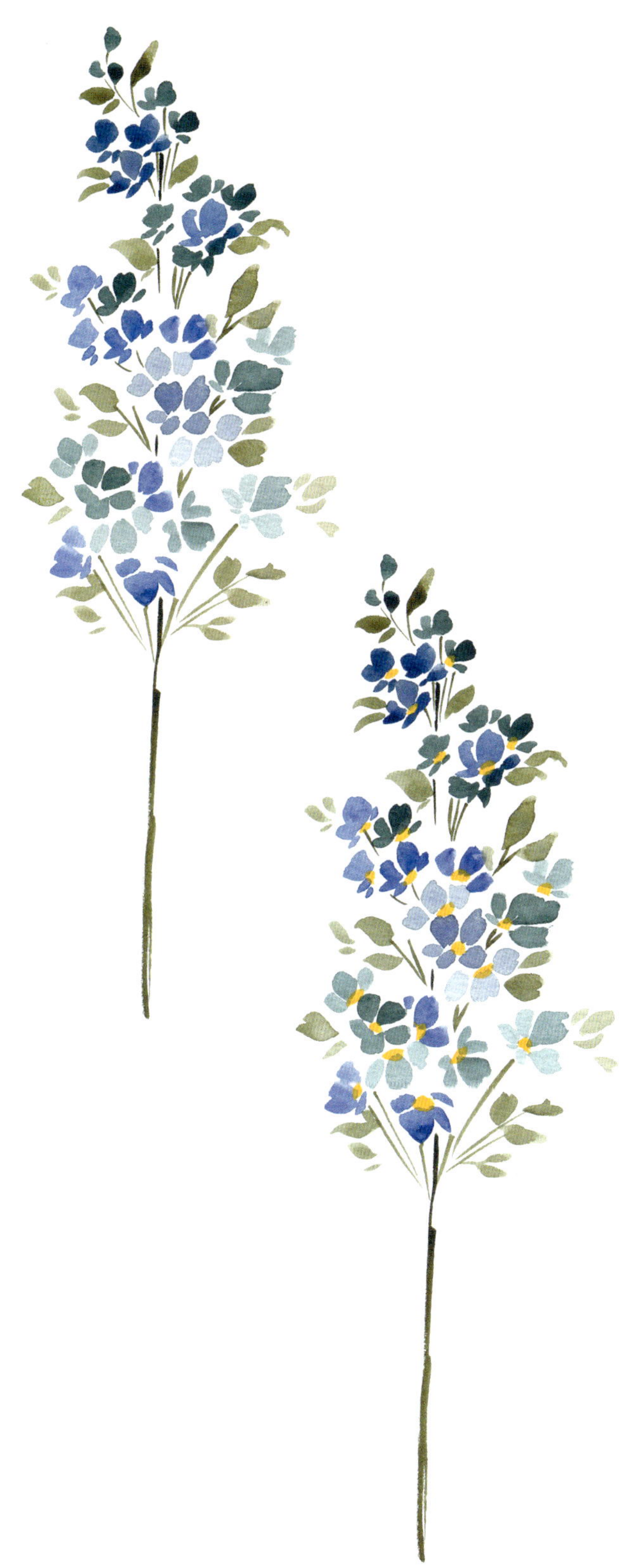

Step 13.

Add in a few gestural leaves in BC. Play with movement and variety (page 32) by altering the size and shape of the leaves.

Step 14.

Lastly, rinse the size 2 brush, then mix Cadmium-Free Yellow in CSC and begin filling in the center of the flowers. As with our leaves, there is a way to play with size and shape so that the centers don't look so "copy and paste." Although there is no special "technique" per se, you can continue to utilize movement and variety by using the very tippy toe of the brush for a small dot, as well as the side of the brush for more of a pronounced middle. I've indicated the difference in the final image.

Yarrow

As with many filler flowers, Yarrow has a tendency to cluster together, specifically in small, medium-sized and large bundles. Depending on the variety, sometimes it resembles the shape of a rainbow if you're looking at it straight on. It has a very erect, stiff posture with almost no curve to the main stem, yet retains the playful pinwheel structure, making it the perfect accent flower to add to a composition. Rather than a smooth petal formation, it has an almost forklike edge that gives it a personality all its own. Yarrow comes in many colors, but I've chosen pink for its lovely variation. Later on, you may want to research this flower and try out different colors for new results!

Supplies

One size 2 round brush
One size 6 round brush
Canson 140-lb (300-gsm) cold-press paper

Palette

Helios Purple (Petals)

Undersea Green (Leaves)

Preparing the Palette

Mix the Helios Purple to BC and CSC (page 16).

Prior to beginning this project, I'd like you to create a third version of Helios Purple by swirling the BC version on the palette and adding water to decrease the value, and thus creating LC (Lightest Consistency). We're really going to play with range with this flower, since we will only be using a single pigment. See more on color value on page 21.

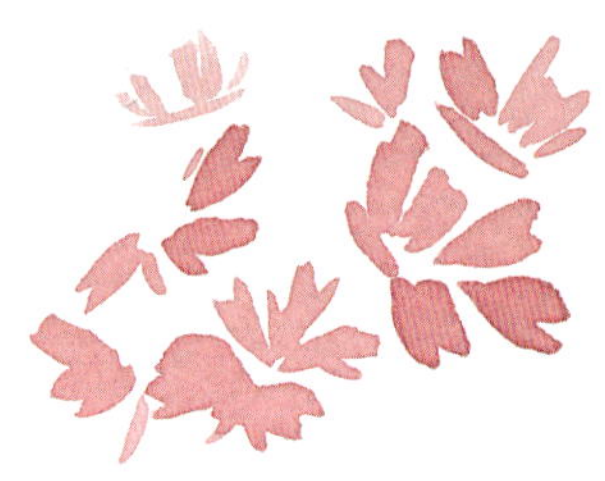

Step 1.

Using your size 2 brush in Helios Purple in BC, begin your first cluster of pinwheel flowers near the top of the page. This will indicate the highest point, and we won't paint beyond here. Take note that the majority of these pinwheels will be flat—as though we're looking at them on their side. To properly achieve the structure, rather than using the compound stroke method to bring the ends together, we will use small, short strokes that are disconnected to create the different parts of the petals. Think simple strokes with a fine tip, which are achieved by coming up high on the toe of the brush. Be sure to lean into positioning so that the flowers are facing different directions. See page 39 for a refresh on position possibilities.

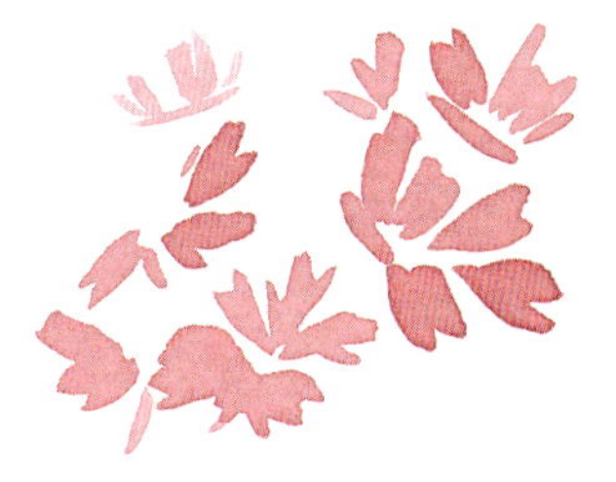

Step 2.

Still using your size 2 brush in BC, create your next bundle of pinwheels directly to the lower left side of your first bundle.

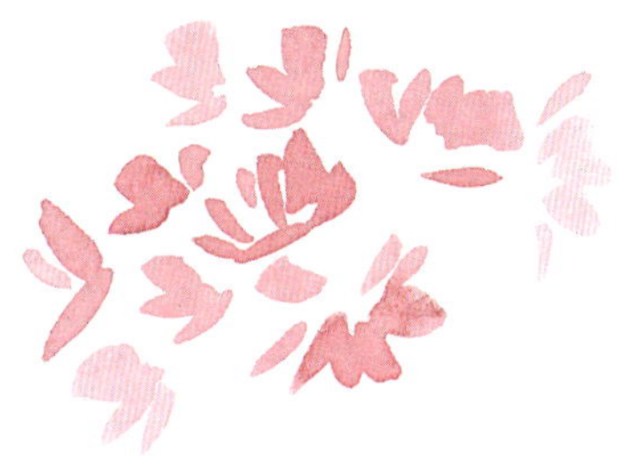

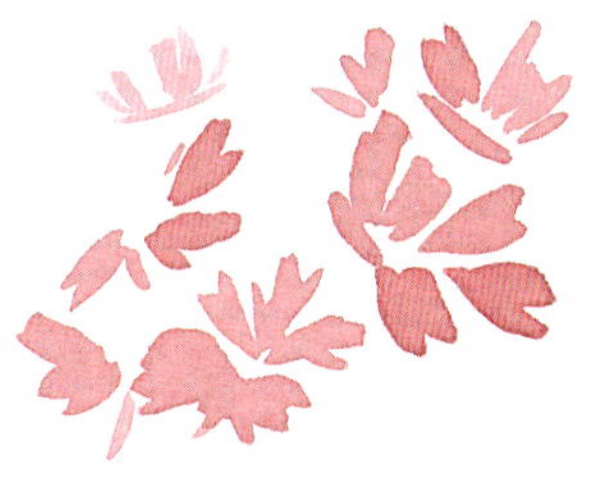

Step 3.

Repeat the previous steps, this time creating a cluster directly to the lower right side of your first bundle.

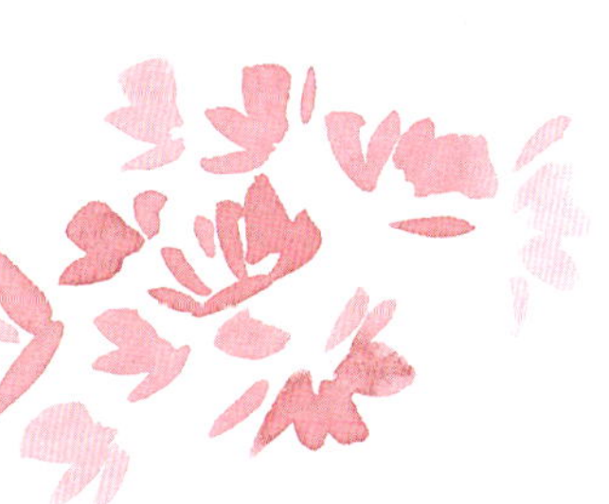

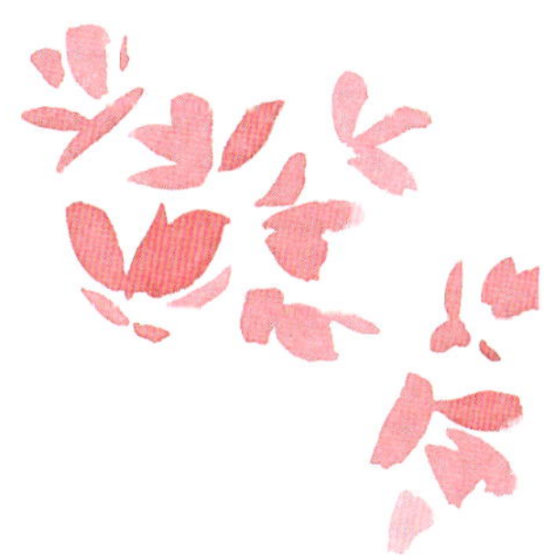

Step 4.

Using your size 2 brush in CSC, add another batch of pinwheels to all three clusters. Take advantage of our gestural stroke (page 32) by using just a tiny line or even a dot to serve as a petal. Not every flower needs to have structure. In fact, not giving every flower structure will allow those that have it to shine!

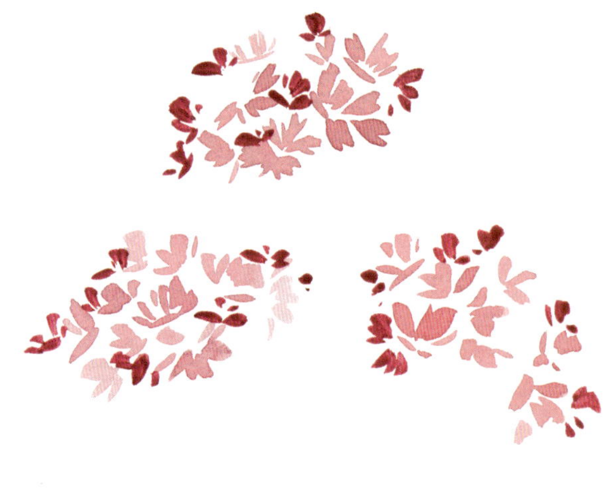

Step 5.

Lastly, rinse your size 2 brush thoroughly and load it with the third version of the Helios Purple in its lowest value (the lightest color). Finish off the clusters with pale petals, stacking them above and to the side of the existing flowers.

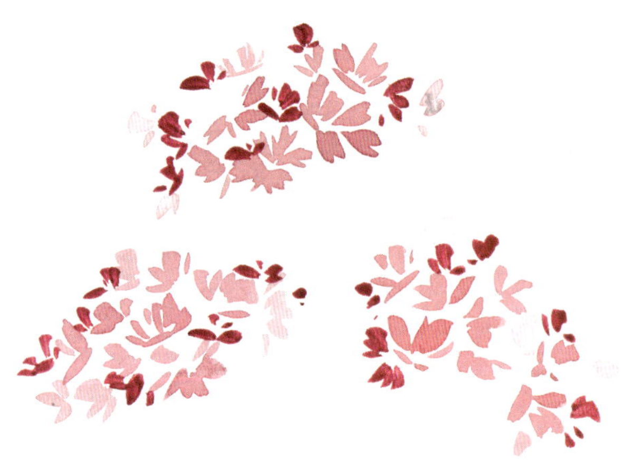

Note: *Because this is such a dainty flower, I am opting not to include centers with this lesson. If you were to look at yarrow in real life, you would see that the center is highly detailed, which works famously in nature; however, trying to capture all of this in watercolor could potentially take away from the playful structure of the petals. Leaving the middles open is actually one of my favorite techniques to give rest to the composition.*

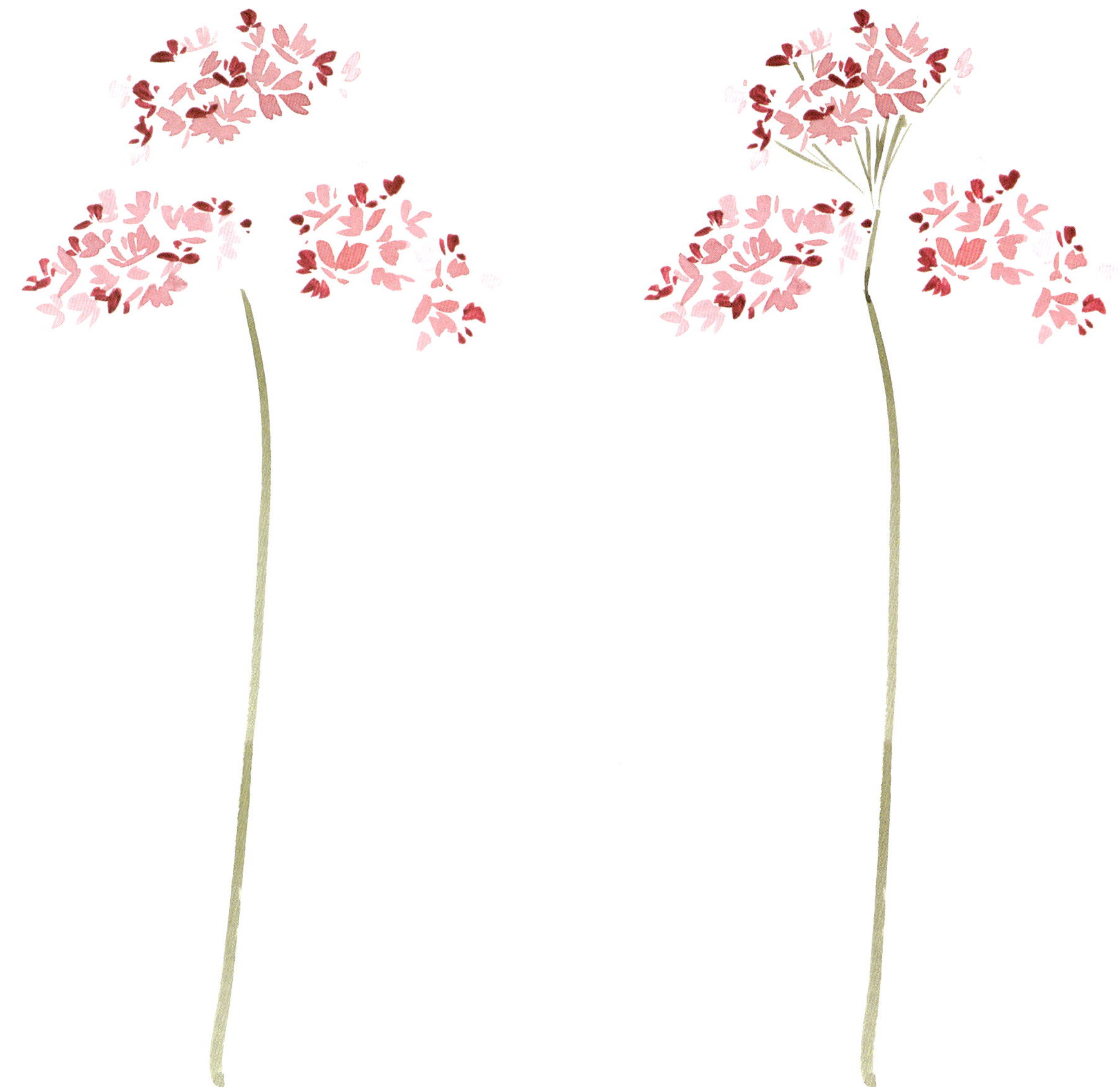

Step 6.

With your size 6 brush, mix Undersea Green to BC and CSC. Using mid-pressure, paint a long, straight main stem running through the middle of the clusters in BC. It should be about the thickness of a strand of spaghetti. Leave it disconnected from the clusters for now.

Step 7.

Next, still using your size 6 brush in BC, you'll attach the flowers to the main stem with finer stems. For this, come up on the tippy toe and use light pressure. Don't feel the need to connect every single flower. Some can remain detached to maintain that loose feel.

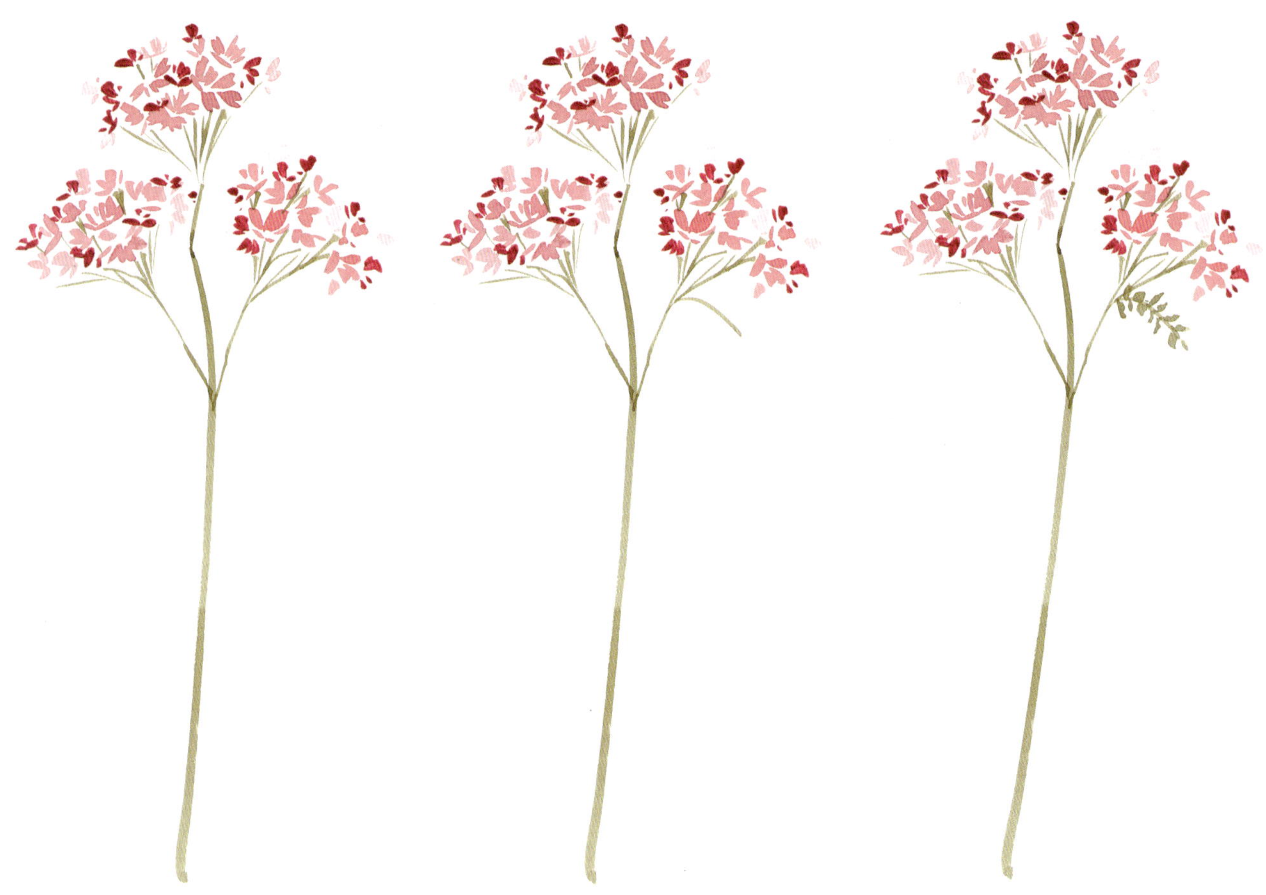

Step 8.

Finish connecting the small stems to the main stem.

Step 9.

Using your size 6 brush loaded with Undersea Green in BC, paint a branch extending just below the cluster on the right.

Step 10.

To create the leaves, use the same brush and mixture. Come up on the toe of the brush and paint gestural markings and squiggles to represent leaves.

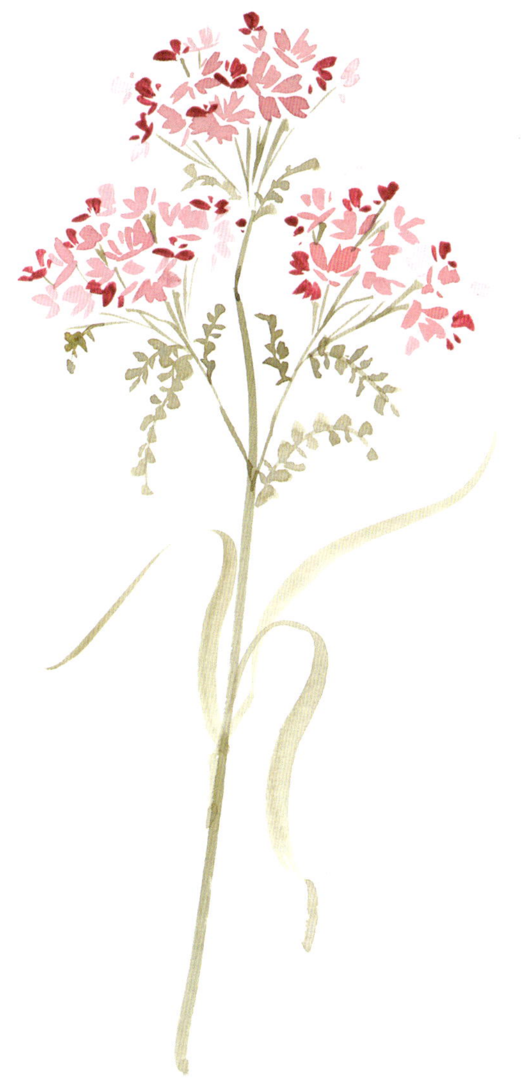

Step 11a.

Continue adding branches and leaves around the main stem where it feels natural. Remember to use variety in size, shape and positioning.

Step 11b.

Still using your size 6 brush loaded with Undersea Green in BC, paint three long leaves extending from the main stem using the simple stroke technique (page 30).

Step 12.

Using Undersea Green in CSC, layer the darker color on top of the tiny leaves, the main stem and the long leaves. For a refresh of gestural outlining, see page 41. These lines of contrast go far in creating depth and shadow in loose compositions.

Aubrieta

This flower is more of a bush or shrub, but it still makes for a lovely filler flower! We'll jazz things up a bit by using a filbert brush, which will give the petals a whole different feel. Although I have yet to paint this flower in my professional career, this project really warmed me to them. Let's get to it, then!

Supplies

Two size 4 filbert brushes

One size 6 round brush

Canson 140-lb (300-gsm) cold-press paper

Palette

Purple Lake (Petals)

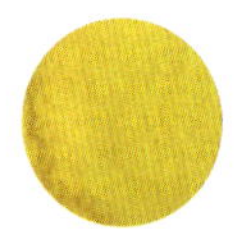

Green Gold (Center)

Greenish Umber (Leaves)

Preparing the Palette

Using a size 4 filbert brush, mix Purple Lake to BC and CSC (page 16) in separate piles. Load the brush with BC.

Before We Begin

If you need a refresh, see page 43, where we practiced using the filbert brush to paint an African daisy. Also note we will be using a four-petal pinwheel flower structure to create this flower (see page 37). We will also be using the layering effect referencing wet-into-wet technique (page 29). As for their size, your flowers should be roughly the size of a nickel (⅞ inch [2.2 cm] in diameter); however, varying the size slightly larger and smaller is suggested.

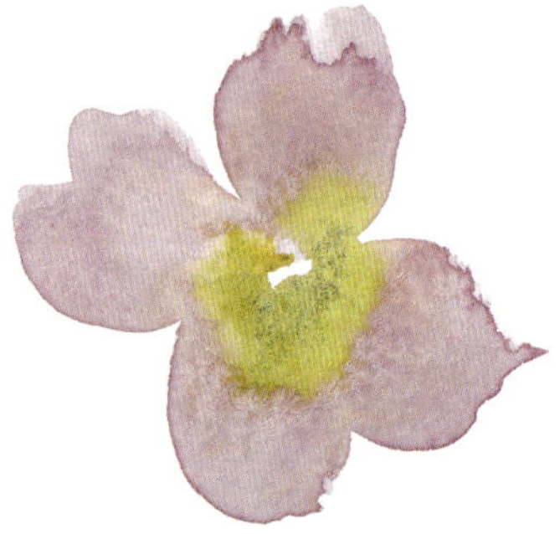

Step 1A.

With your size 4 filbert brush loaded with Purple Lake, paint four petals in BC, using the filbert-stroke technique (page 43). Be sure to leave a dot of open space (the size of a tack) in the center.

Step 1B.

While the media is wet, use your size 6 round brush to drop Green Gold in CSC into the middle of the flower. It should flow thoroughly through the petals. If not, you can glaze the petals (see page 28) and begin again.

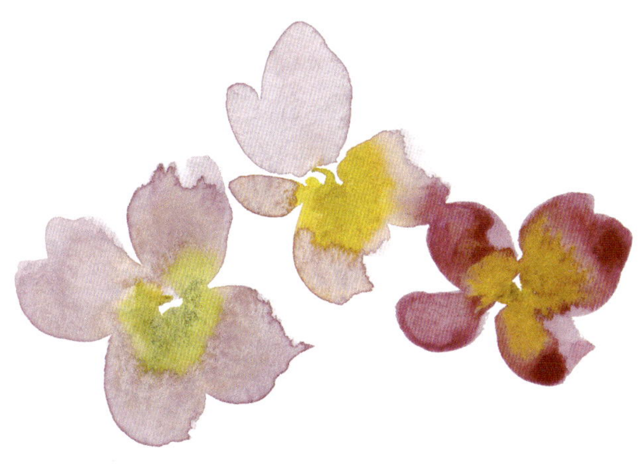

Step 2a.

Now, we will elevate the process by painting two flowers, one after the other, using the wet-into-wet technique. Paint the first flower in BC, and then while the flower is damp, use your other filbert brush to paint a flower that appears to be resting just off to the side of the first flower, allowing the different consistencies to merge and bleed.

Step 2b.

While the media is wet, use your size 6 round brush to drop Green Gold in CSC into the middle of the flower. It should flow thoroughly through the petals. If not, you can glaze the petals (see page 28) and begin again.

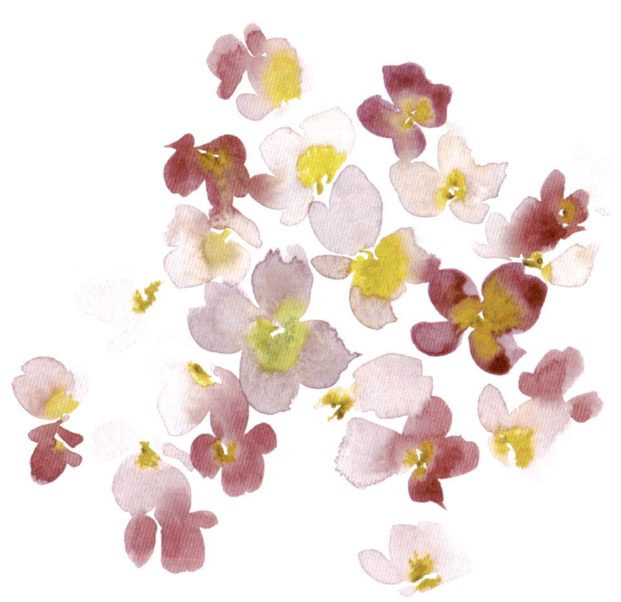

Step 3.

Continue to add flowers in both consistencies, allowing the outside petals of each individual flower to touch. Play with positioning and variety here, painting flowers in several but similar sizes and peeking out from behind others. These may show as three-petal or even two-petal flowers, since the other petals would be hidden by the flower blocking it. This means you'll need to use the side of the filbert for thinner lines, which will leave them appearing more gestural. This clustering effect gives the composition a more natural feel, rather than a bunch of disconnected flowers floating on the paper.

Step 4.

Be sure your flowers are dry, and then using your filbert brush loaded with CSC, paint a few very dark flowers on top of the lighter flowers, so they are layered.

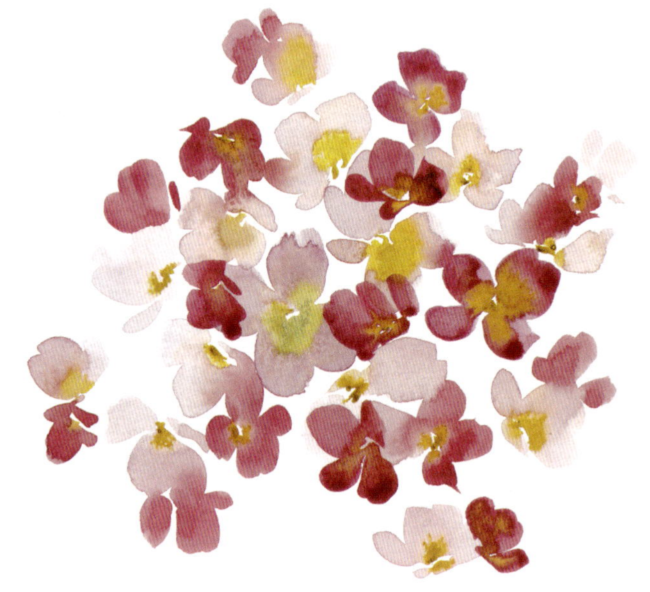

Step 5.

Rinse one of your filbert brushes, and mix together Greenish Umber in BC and CSC. Load the brush with BC and begin painting gestural leaves (page 34) between the flowers so the cluster begins to fill in and thicken. Utilize both the side and belly of the brush.

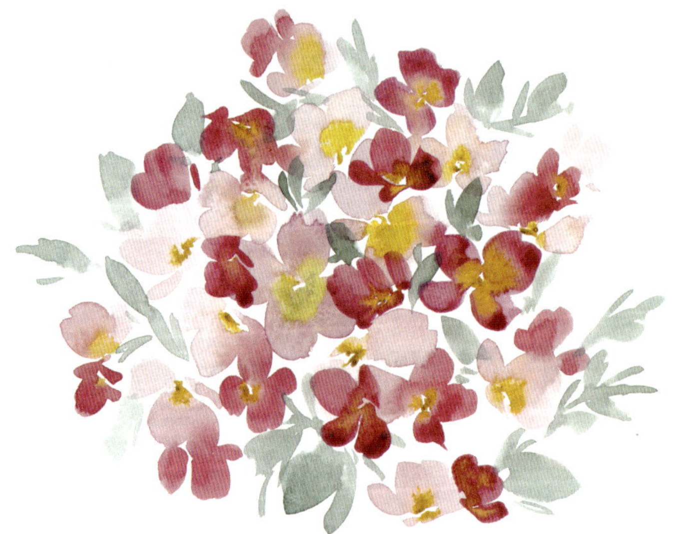

STEP 6.

Rinse your size 6 round brush and load it with CSC Greenish Umber to add darker leaves and gestural veins on top of the lighter leaves. Don't be afraid to keep things super loose. We have many detailed flowers in this book, but sometimes an uncomplicated, simple flower is the perfect addition to a composition, providing rest and balance.

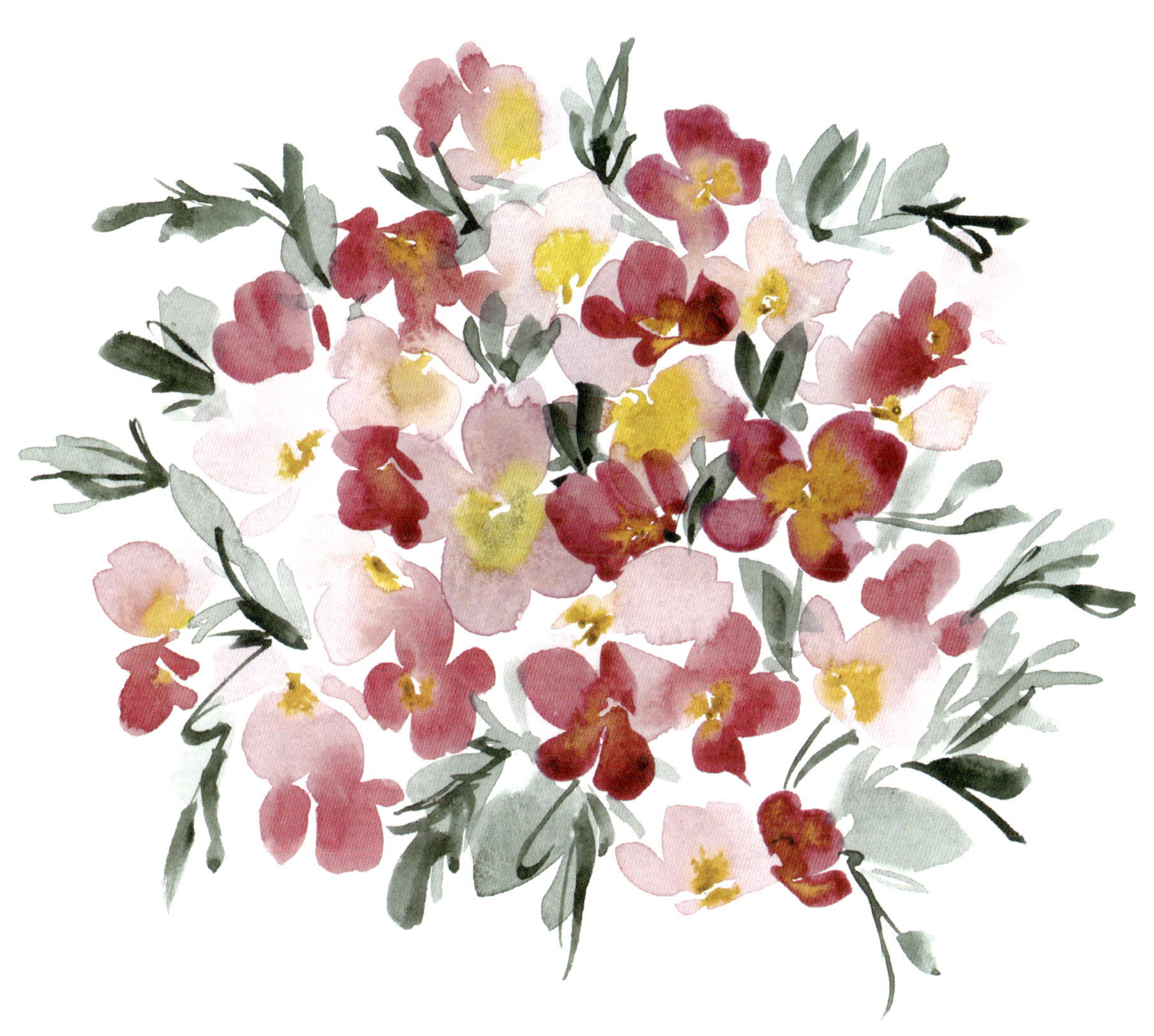

Snowberry

Doesn't the name snowberry *sound like something you might find perusing the lands of Narnia? I was rightly enchanted when I came upon these tiny, delicate globes, ranging from pale white through meringue to dusty pink. They* do *look good enough to eat, though I would advise against it—ha! Berries are one of the loveliest filler accents to add to compositions so we're going to have fun with this one. Also, as we conclude this book, we are going to make a thorough study of working with white tones. To give you a small taste of what's in store, we will opt to paint with white tones with this lesson, keeping things very simple by using just two colors to create white.*

Supplies

Two size 6 round brushes

One size 2 round brush

Canson 140-lb (300-gsm) cold-press paper

Palette

Sepia (Branch, Berries and Leaves)

Lamp Black (Berries)

Cadmium-Free Yellow (Berries)

Undersea Green (Leaves)

Lamp Black + Sepia (BC)

Lamp Black + Sepia (LC)

Lamp Black + Cadmium-Free Yellow (LC)

Sepia + Cadmium-Free Yellow (BC)

Sepia + Cadmium-Free Yellow (LC)

Undersea Green + Sepia (BC)

Preparing the Palette

Mix together Lamp Black and Sepia to BC (page 16) and then dilute it further by adding water to decrease the value. We'll call this lightest consistency (LC).

Mix Lamp Black and Cadmium-Free Yellow to LC.

Mix Sepia to BC.

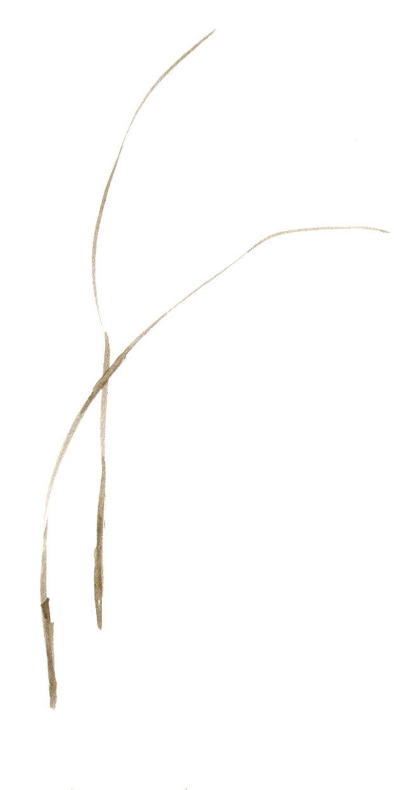

Step 1.

Using one of your size 6 brushes and Sepia in BC, start by painting the two main branches on which the berries will sit.

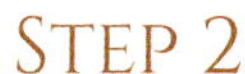

Step 2.

Paint a few more stems that will carry leaves and berries. Play with pressure here to get a variation of thin and a bit thicker branches that curve slightly to the right.

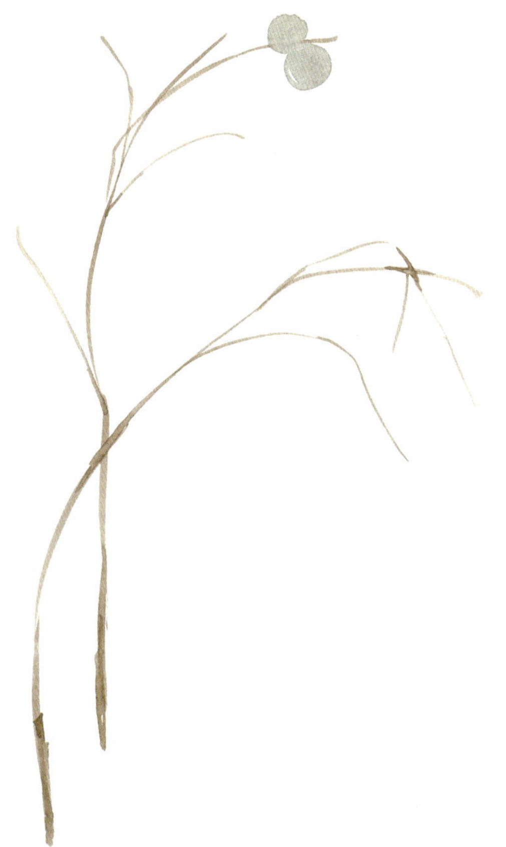

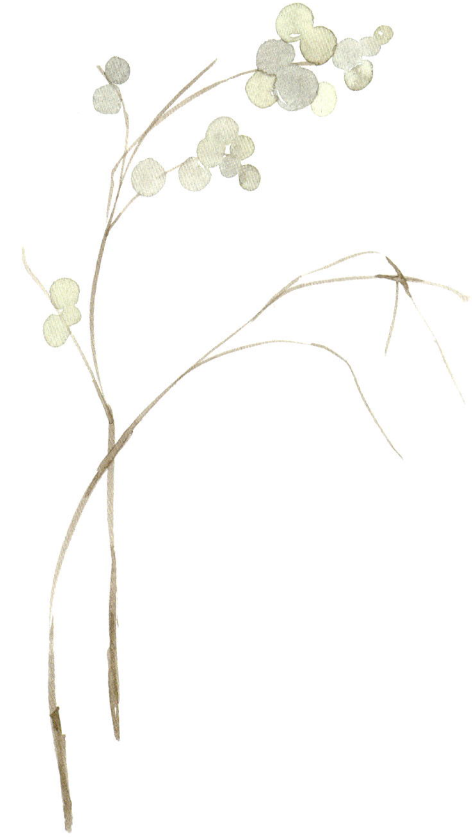

Step 3a.

Using your size 2 round brush, load it with the Lamp Black and Sepia mixture in BC and paint a circle roughly the size of a marble (about ½ inch [1.3 cm] in diameter) on the stem.

Tip: To remove the branch mark running through the berry, simply rub the brush lightly over the mark until it disappears.

Step 3b.

Without reloading your brush, immediately paint another marble-sized circle, using the first berry as a launching point. This berry should rest against it so that there is a clear distinction between the two except for the place where they are touching.

Step 4.

Alternating mixtures (your size 2 brush loaded with Lamp Black and Cadmium-Free Yellow in BC, and your size 6 brush loaded with Lamp Black and Sepia in BC) continue to add berries along the smaller stems in a clusterlike formation. You'll want to play with size, shape and position as you move along, for optimal variety. Some of the berries should be tucked behind others, so there appears to be depth in the cluster.

Tip: You can also opt to leave a small sliver of white space to act as a light source, as I did with the second berry.

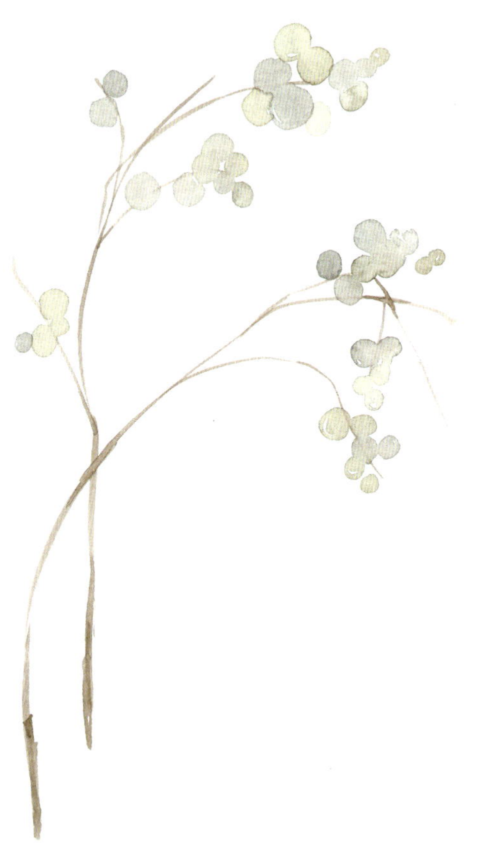

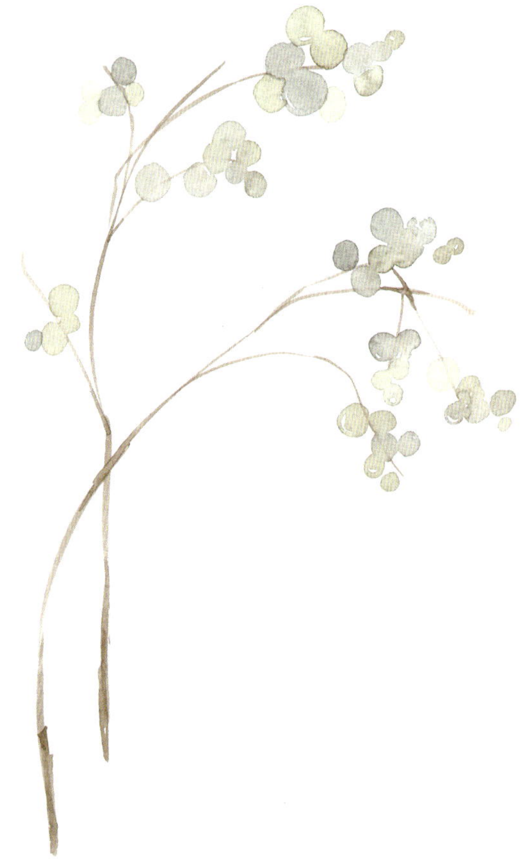

Step 5.

Repeat Step 4 on the other branch.

Something to keep in mind: It's fine and even favorable to allow some berries to merge together as one. As long as there is distinction between some of the berries, there will be enough definition to give the subject clarity. You'll notice there are areas of my painting where it's a bit of a conglomeration of sizes and color, where the berries have come together as one. Later, when we add details, the structure will return.

Step 6.

Using both mixtures (Lamp Black and Cadmium-Free Yellow, and Lamp Black and Sepia) in LC, add more berries to the existing clusters.

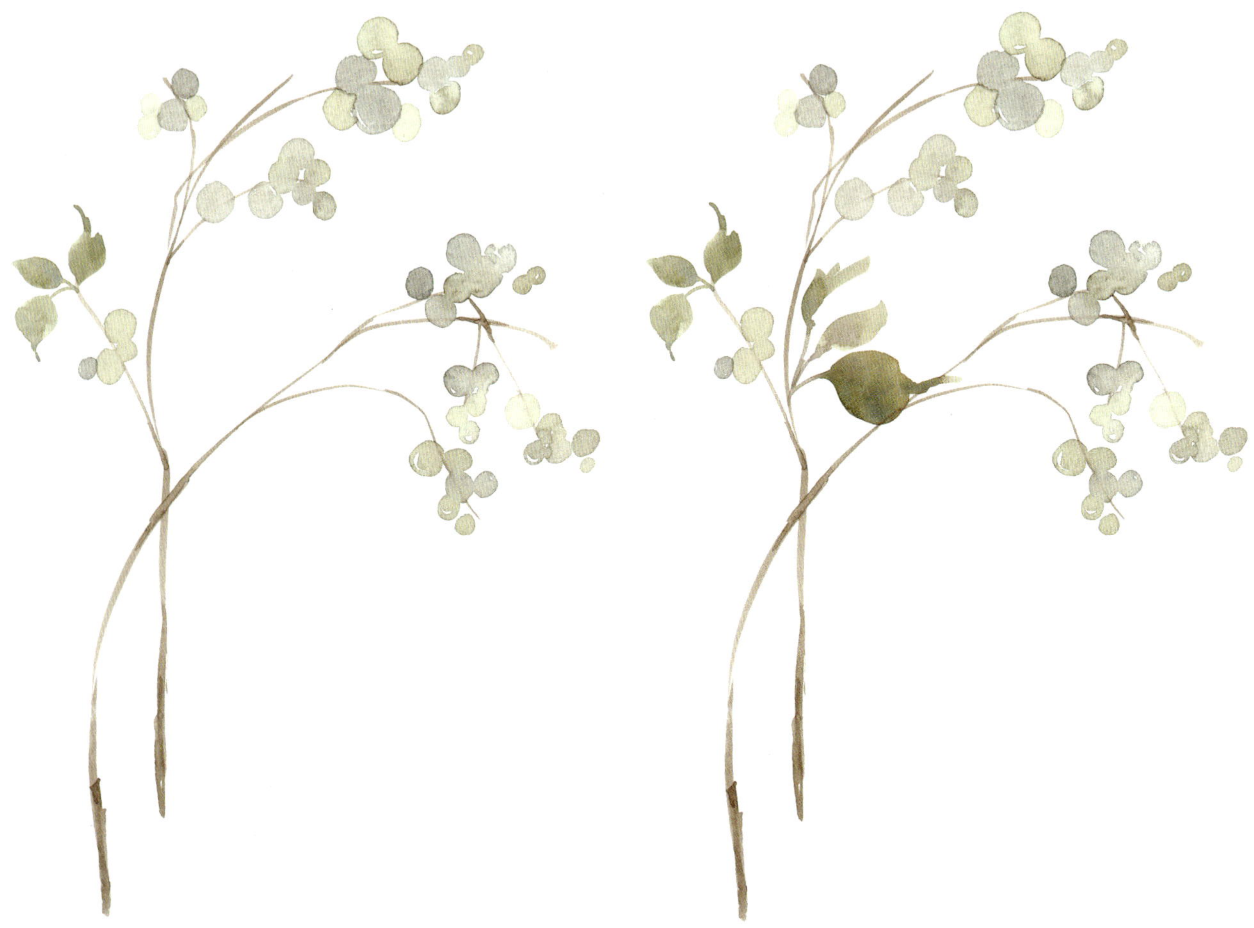

Step 7.

Load your second size 6 brush with Undersea Green in BC and paint the first three compound leaves (page 31) on the main branch. Be sure to play with positioning so that they are facing different directions and don't appear stagnant. Load your second size 6 brush with Sepia in BC.

Step 8.

Paint three more leaves on the main branch using Undersea Green in BC. While wet, drop in Sepia in BC for wet-into-wet (see page 29 for a refresh).

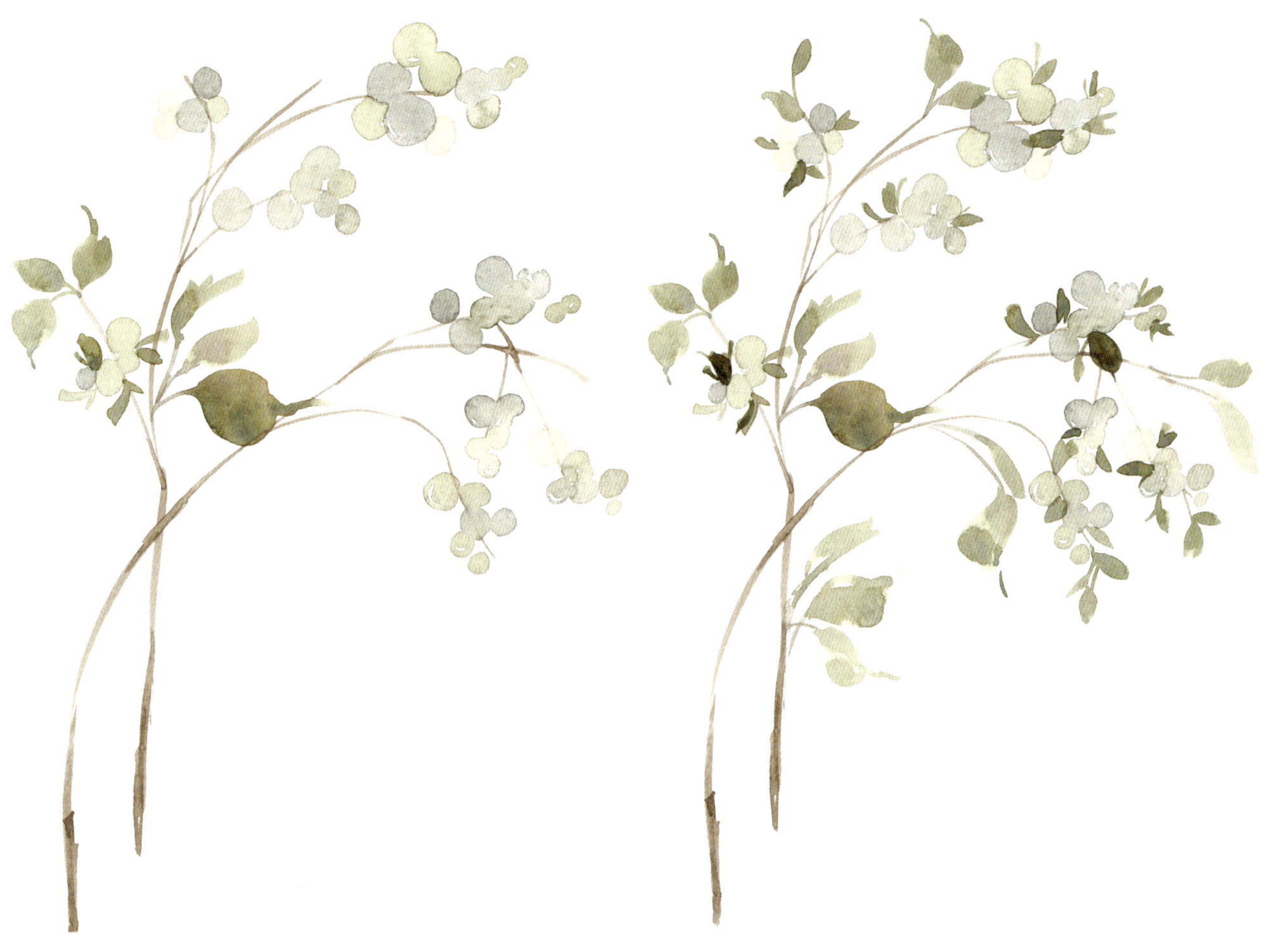

STEP 9.

Attach smaller leaves to the berry cluster, using your size 6 brush loaded with Undersea Green in BC. Employ the gestural leaf method (page 34).

STEP 10.

Continue adding leaves until the clusters and stems are filled in to your liking. As you near the end of the stems, consider adding a few gestural leaves to lend even more variety to your composition.

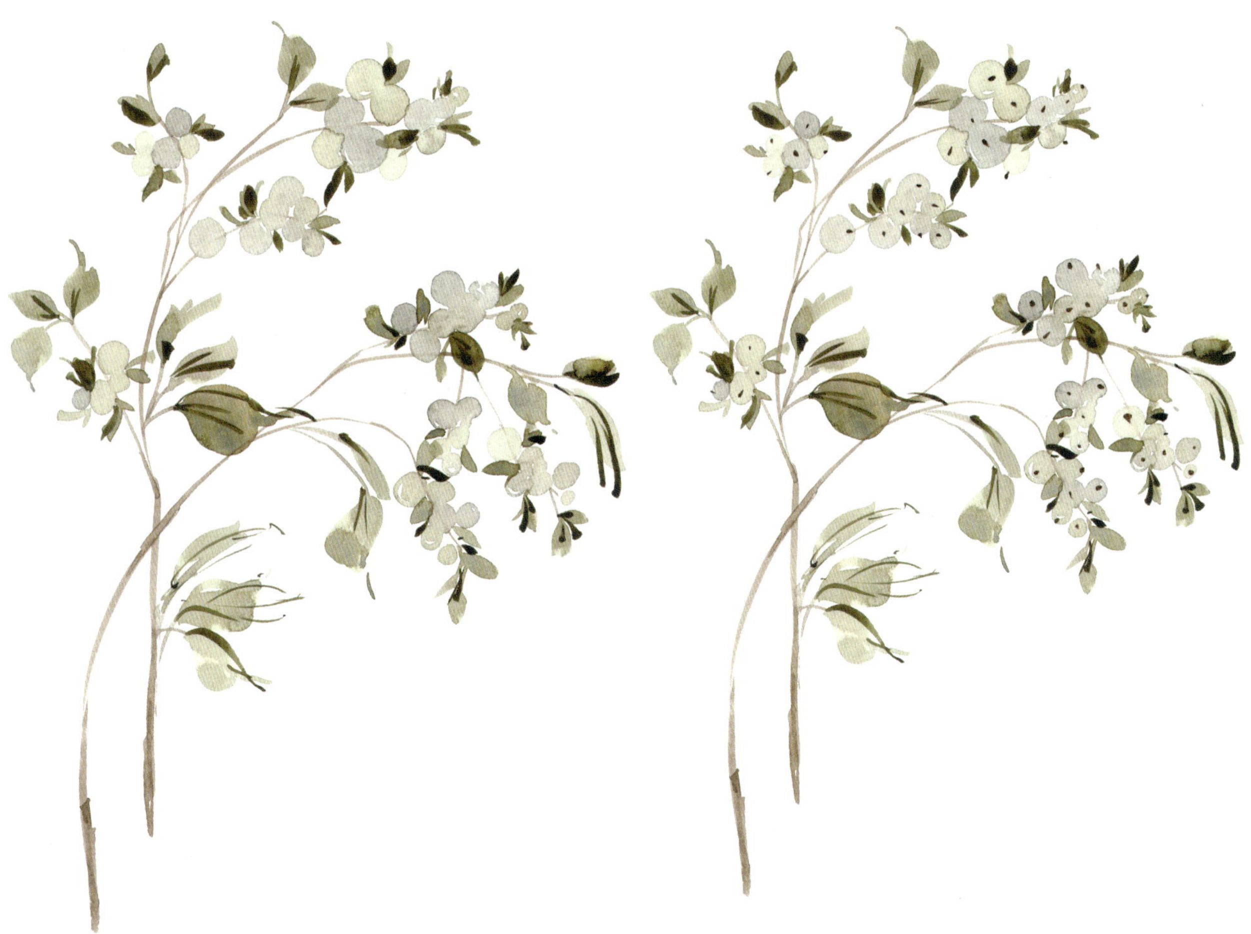

Step 11.

Load your size 6 brush with Undersea Green and Sepia in CSC, and add gestural outlines to your leaves.

Step 12.

Load your size 2 brush with Sepia in CSC, and add small dots to the edges and center of the berries to indicate which position they are pointing.

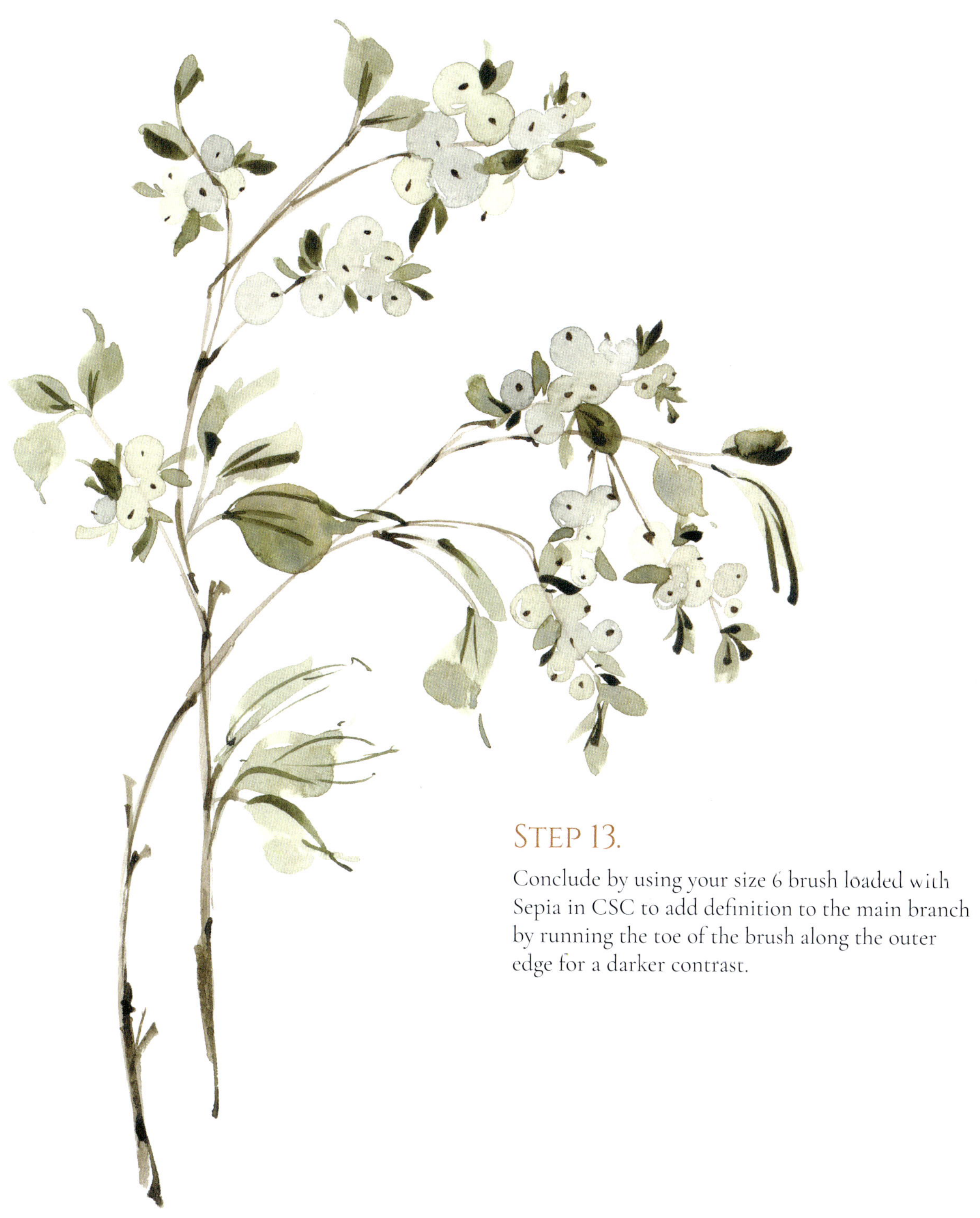

STEP 13.

Conclude by using your size 6 brush loaded with Sepia in CSC to add definition to the main branch by running the toe of the brush along the outer edge for a darker contrast.

Delphinium

Delphiniums, much like forget-me-nots (page 66), have a sweet, ruffly formation with a complex structure we are going to simplify by staying loose and gestural with our strokes. If you are familiar with the flower called stock, delphiniums are nearly a doppelgänger. They grow in many colors, from sky blue to eggplant purple. I've chosen a pink/purple combo that feels both carefree and romantic. We will rely once again on our pinwheel flower (page 37) for basic structure, elevating it by creating multiple layers.

SUPPLIES

Three size 6 round brushes

Canson 140-lb (300-gsm) cold-press paper

PALETTE

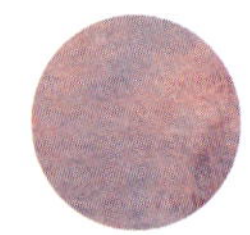
ROSE OF ULTRAMARINE (FLOWERS)

PERMANENT ROSE (FLOWERS)

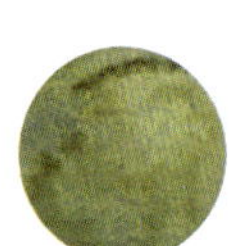
UNDERSEA GREEN (LEAVES)

SEPIA (LEAVES)

HOOKER'S GREEN (LEAVES)

PERMANENT ROSE + SEPIA

FULL FLOWER

BOTTOM LAYER

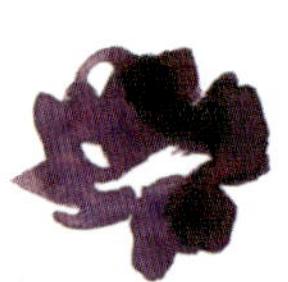
TOP LAYER

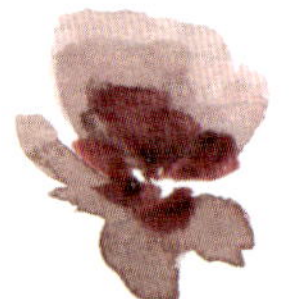
SIDE ANGLE

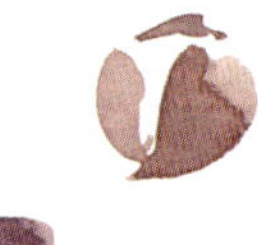

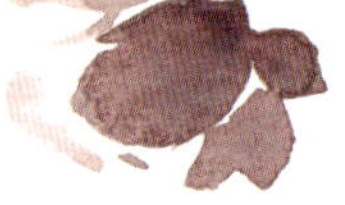
DOWNWARD ANGLE

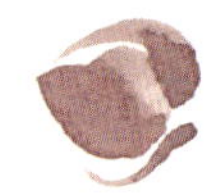
BUDS

PREPARING THE PALETTE

Mix Rose of Ultramarine to BC and CSC (page 16).

Mix Permanent Rose to BC and CSC.

Mix Permanent Rose and Sepia to BC.

Mix Undersea Green to BC.

Mix Hooker's Green to BC.

Using one size 6 brush, load it with Rose of Ultramarine in BC. Set it off to the side.

Next, load a second size 6 brush with Rose of Ultramarine in CSC. Set it off to the side.

Lastly, load the third size 6 brush with your Permanent Rose and Sepia in BC, and set it off to the side.

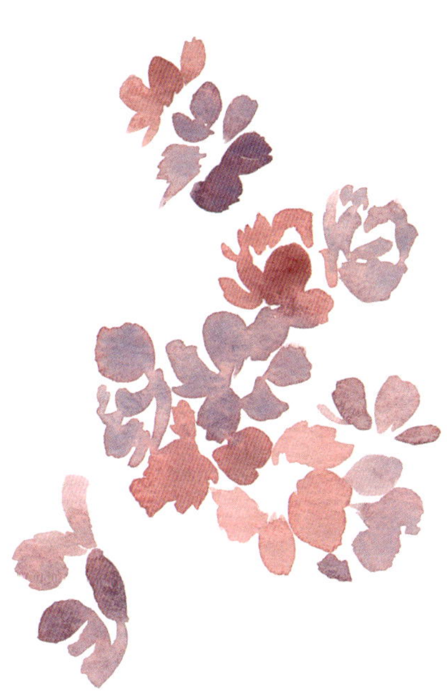

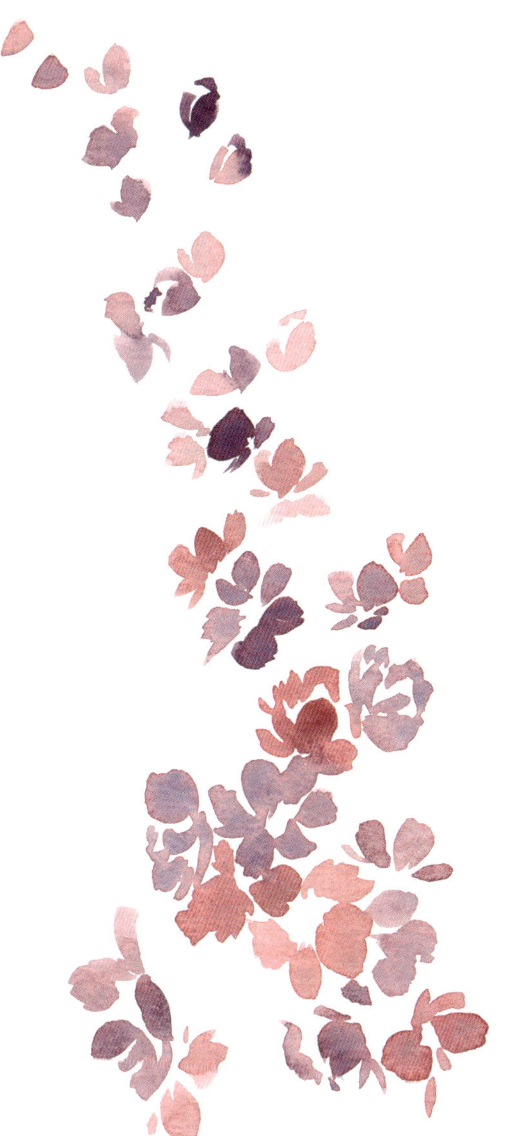

STEP 1.

We will begin our cluster in the middle of the page. Using your size 6 brush with Rose of Ultramarine in BC, and your other size 6 brush with Permanent Rose and Sepia mixture in BC, begin painting pinwheels in a variety of angles and sizes. (For pinwheel shape and structure review, see page 39.) This means you'll have open-faced, sideways, downward- and upward-facing flowers, as well as some that peek out from behind larger flowers.

STEP 2.

Repeat Step 1 again until your cluster begins to fill in, angling it slightly to the left. Make an effort to include buds as you near the top of the stem, using the closed structure formation on page 39. Remember these should be the smallest, kernel-shaped flowers.

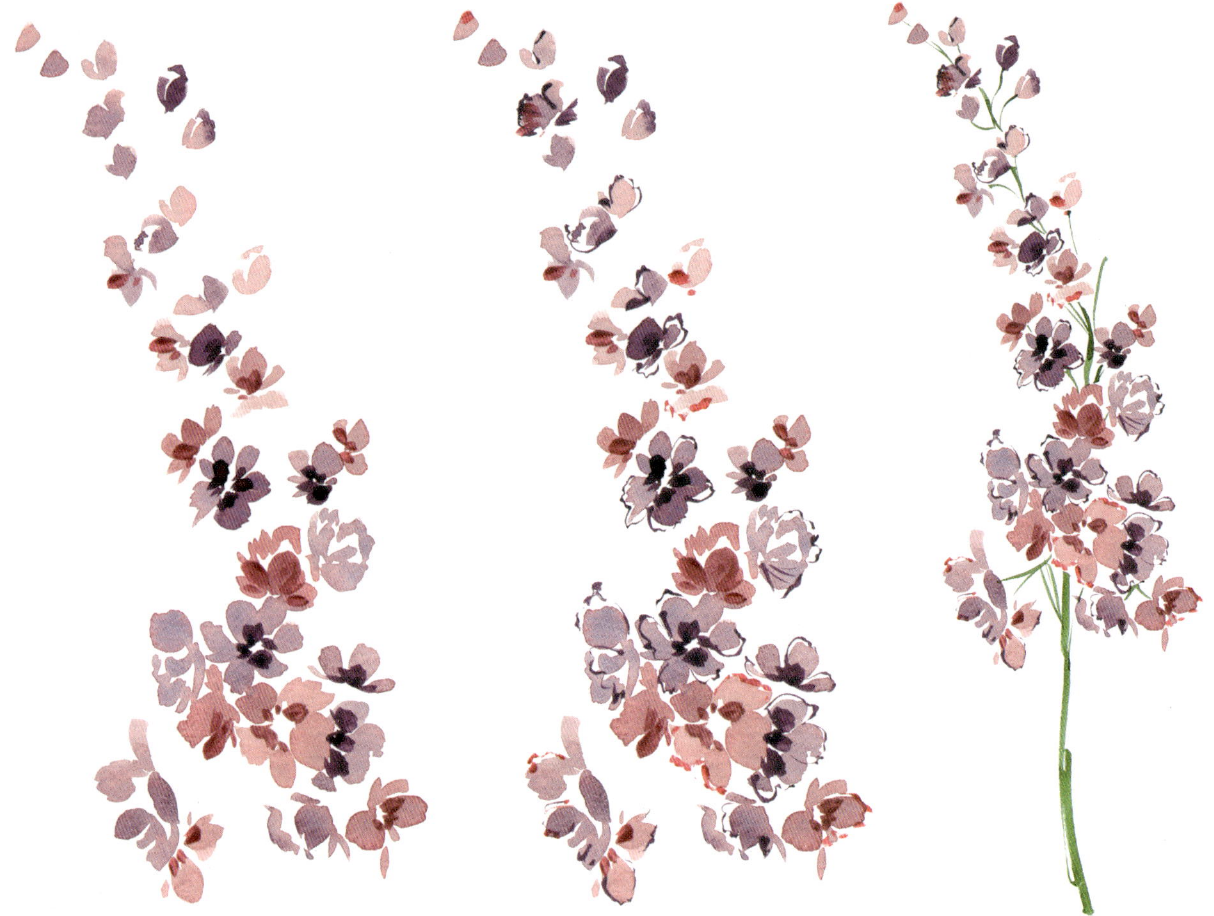

Step 3.

Load your size 6 brush with Rose of Ultramarine in CSC to create the top layer of the purple flowers. Refer to the diagram on page 92 for a closer look. Load your other size 6 brush with Permanent Rose and Sepia in BC to create the top layer of the pink flowers.

Step 4.

With both size 6 brushes again in CSC, add detail frilling to the edges of the bottom layer petals, using the gestural outlining technique on page 41. Be sure the brushes you're using are nice and pointy so as to create those very fine lines.

Tip: *Prior to moving on to Step 5, rinse your brushes thoroughly to remove all pink and purple hues. Check your water and change it out for a fresh cup if there's a strong pink tone.*

Step 5.

Using both size 6 brushes, mix Undersea Green to BC, and then Hooker's Green to BC, a separate pile for each color. Using the brush with Hooker's Green, paint a stem that runs through the middle of the flowers. Connect the smaller flowers and buds so that they all extend from the main stem.

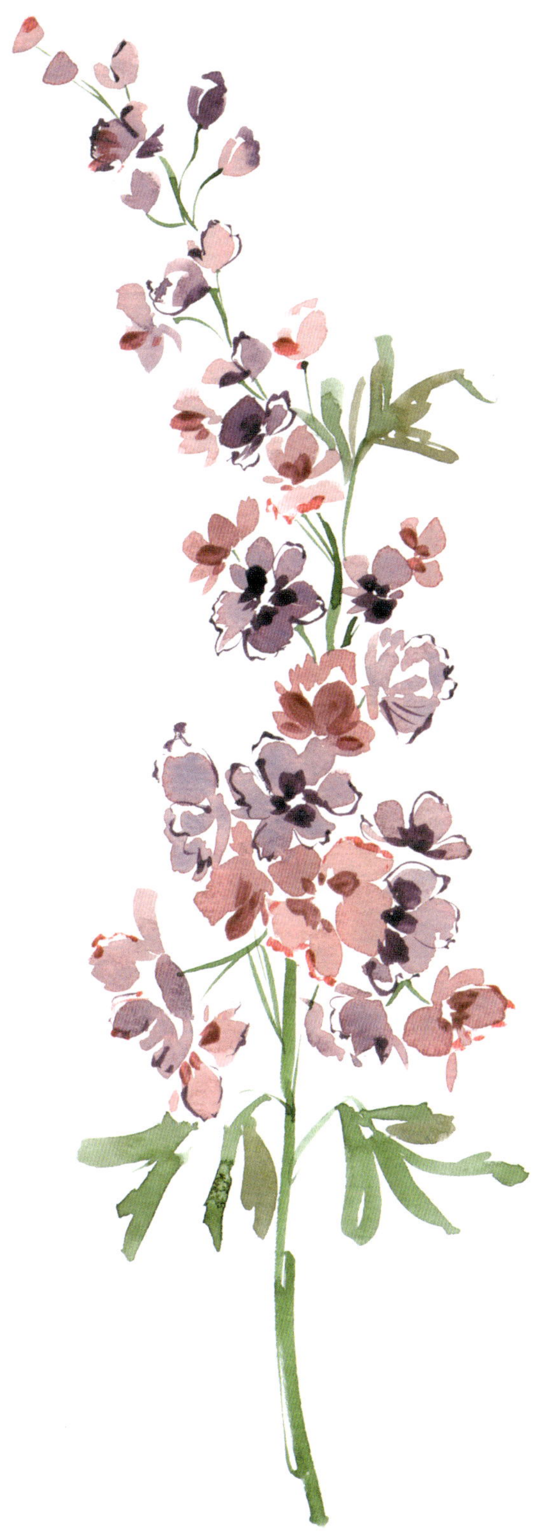

STEP 6.

Leaves are the most forgiving of subjects and so this is where I once more encourage you to take liberties and make this painting your *own*. If you need a refresh on gestural leaves, see page 34.

If you would like to follow along with me, I began with my size 6 brush loaded with Hooker's Green in BC to paint the top leaf. While it was wet (see the wet-into-wet technique on page 29 for a quick review), I added a few more gestural strokes on the end of the leaves, using Undersea Green in BC. Repeat these steps to create two more leaves extending from the main stem. Again, there is room to play and explore here, so feel free to create leaves that sing for *you*.

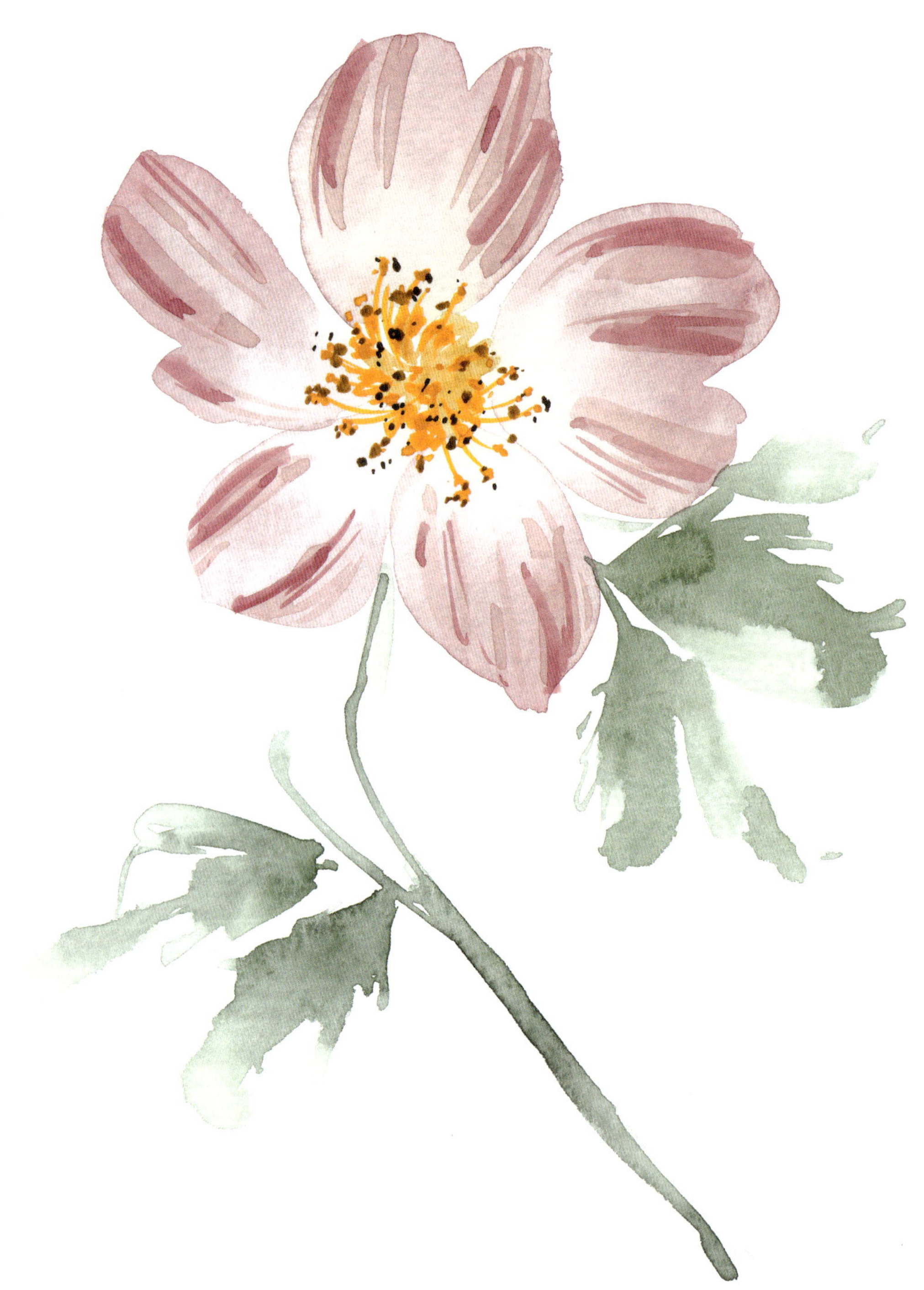

Center Stage Flowers for Every Occasion

We've come to the chapter of the book that features all my favorite showstopping flowers—I'm so excited! Narrowing down this list was certainly not the easiest task, as there are so many beautiful blooms from which to choose; however, I've selected what I feel to be the loveliest of the bunch; florals that bring joy to my botanical-loving heart. In the following projects, we will learn much about how to approach what seems like a complicated flower at first glance. And we'll discover how to notice the details without becoming overwhelmed by them, something that is absolutely crucial for success when painting with watercolor.

Iceland Poppy

Poppies come in many shapes, colors and sizes, so it was rather a challenge to pick just one for us to do together. I've chosen an Iceland poppy, which we will paint in a lovely shade of red-peach. You'll see the structure is almost cuplike, with petals resembling the shape of paper fans and a texture something akin to crinkly tissue paper. What's most important is what you see when you look at this flower and what it is you want to draw out, so be sure like always to spend a few minutes on the Web finding pictures for inspiration. Because we don't aim to overwhelm the flower with all the details, we'll focus on the areas we do want to draw the eye and will allow rest in other places.

Supplies

Two size 8 round brushes

One size 6 round brush

Canson 140-lb (300-gsm) cold-press paper

Preparing the Palette

Mix Red Deep and Cadmium-Free Yellow to BC (page 16).

Mix Red Deep to CSC (page 16).

Mix Sap Green and Raw Umber to CSC and BC.

Mix Cadmium-Free Yellow to BC

Palette

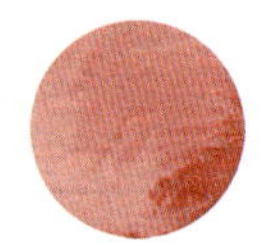

Winsor & Newton Red Deep (flower)

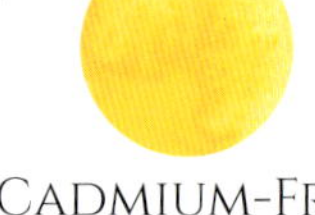

Cadmium-Free Yellow (flower)

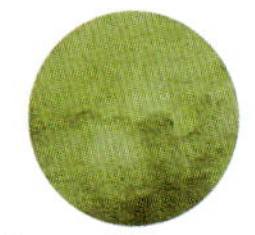

Sap Green (leaves)

Raw Umber (leaves)

Winsor & Newton Red Deep + Cadmium-Free Yellow

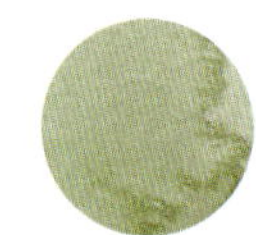

Sap Green + Raw Umber

Step 1A.

Using your size 8 brush and the Sap Green and Raw Umber mixture in CSC, paint the center of the flower just above the middle of the page. It should be about the size of a dime (scant ¾ inch [1.8 cm] in diameter).

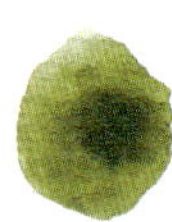

Step 1B.

Load your size 6 brush with Cadmium-Free Yellow in BC. Also load your size 8 brush with the Red Deep and Cadmium-Free Yellow in BC and set it off to the side. You'll be using it in a moment to create the bleed.

Step 2.

Using the size 6 brush in Cadmium-Free Yellow in BC, paint a ruffled ring around the center. This is done using a series of short, gestural strokes, which we covered on page 32. This doesn't need to be perfect at all because in a moment we'll be dissolving the shape.

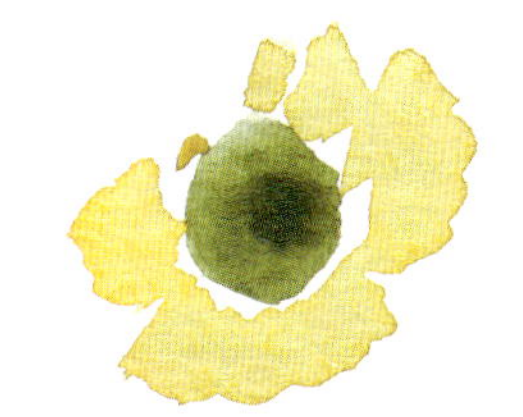

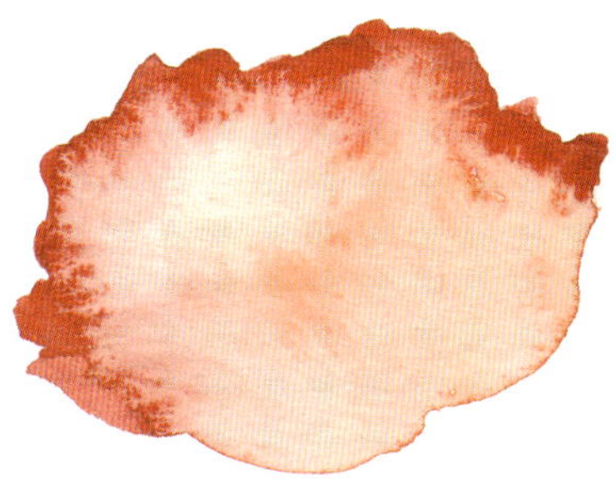

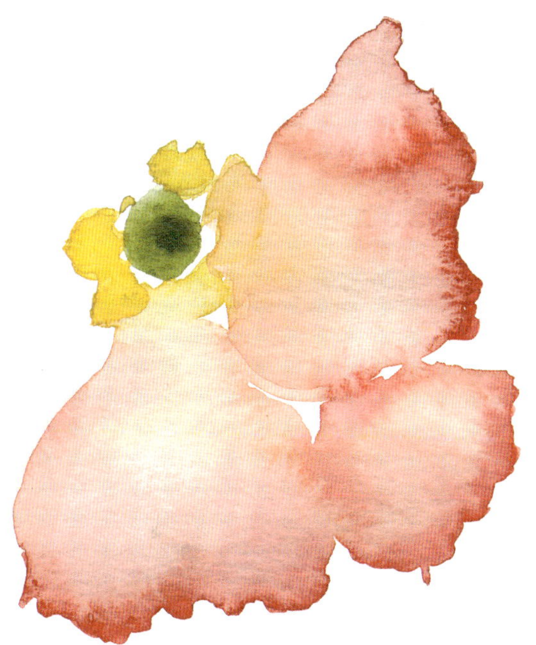

Step 3.

Quickly pick up your preloaded size 8 brush with the Red Deep and Cadmium-Free Yellow mixture in BC. To create a bleed, touch the toe of your brush against the yellow ring wet media and complete a wide, simple stroke. Be sure to lift up at the belly once you reach the edge of the petal, so it doesn't have a point at the edge as it would if we were painting a leaf. Return to the yellow ring and repeat this step so you have a compound stroke (see page 31 for a refresh). Repeat this step to complete the first three petals.

Quickly load your size 8 brush in the Red Deep CSC mixture, touch the toe of your brush to the edge of the petals and drag it the length of the petal to create a ruffled edge and cast a splash of red back through the petal. Repeat this step one more time before the media dries, for an even more striking effect. Ideally, you should have a very dark edge that transitions to peach, then to yellow.

Tip: *For a proportion gauge, your petals should be three to four times longer than your green center.*

Step 4.

Complete the other petals and actions in Step 3. You'll notice the colors dry two to three times lighter than how they appear when wet, so don't be afraid to drop in a lot of color in CSC along those edges. If they end up looking too faint after they've dried, simply glaze the petal in an even coating of water and start again. (For a glazing review, see page 28.)

STEP 5.

Using the size 8 brush in the Red Deep and Cadmium-Free Yellow BC mixture, add a few gestural lines (page 32) to the petals. Invite variation in the thickness of lines by using both the toe and the belly of the brush. Feel free to take liberties here and place them where they feel most natural and special for your flower.

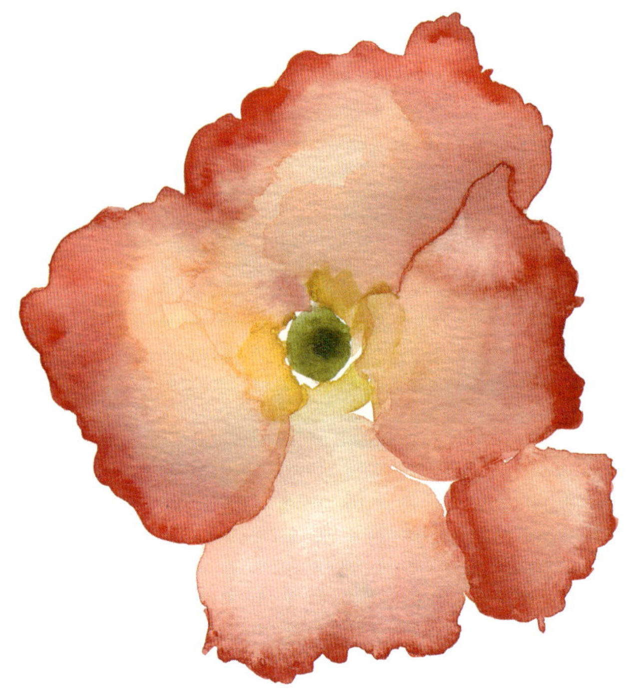

STEP 6.

Using Cadmium-Free Yellow in BC, complete the center by painting thin, fine lines that curve slightly as they extend outward. Refer to the "Pressure" discussion (page 24) for a quick refresh. Use your pointiest size 6 brush and come up high on the toe.

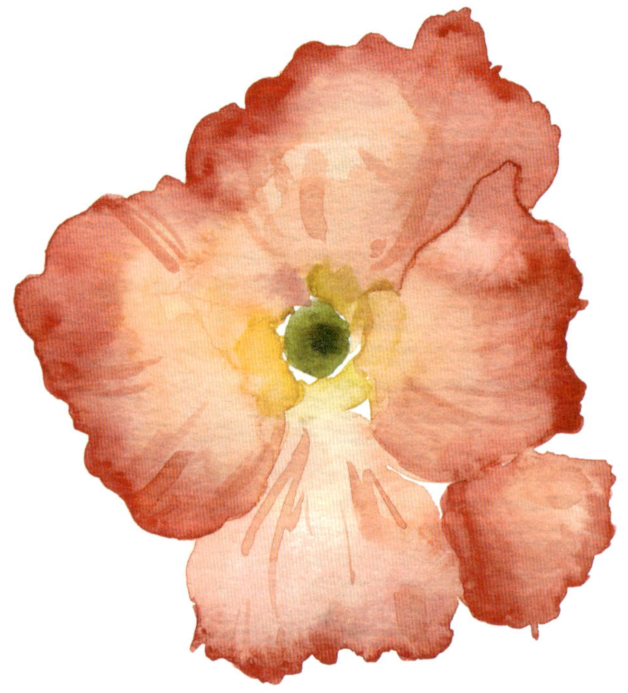

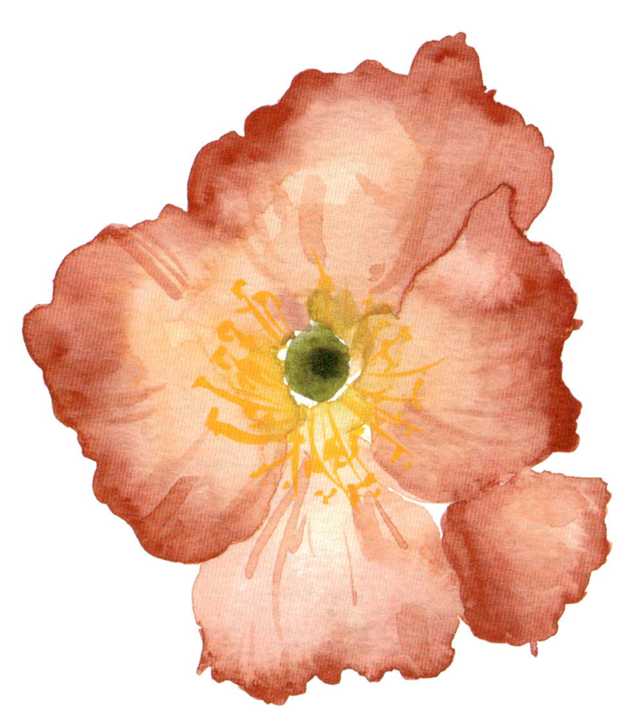

Step 7.

Finish off the center by adding in the Sap Green and Raw Umber mixture in CSC around the green center to darken the area and pull the eye toward the middle of the flower. Your size 6 brush is best for this step.

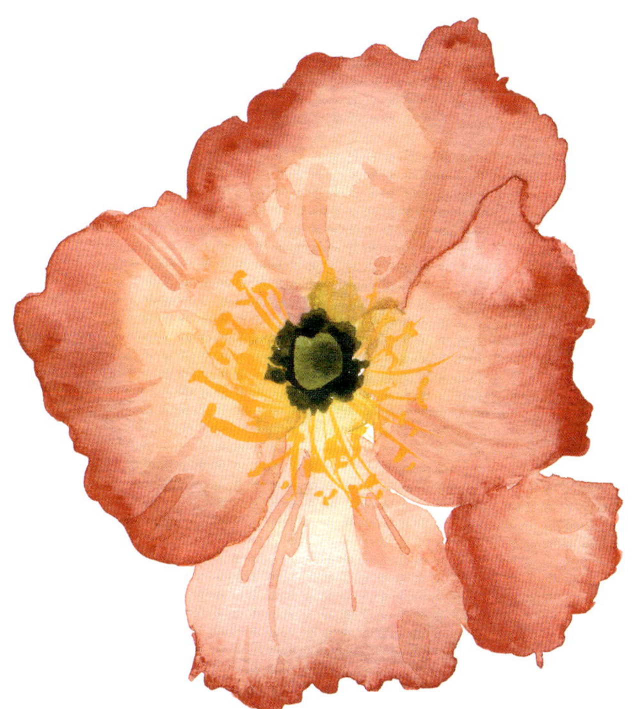

Step 8a.

Using your size 8 brush in the Sap Green and Raw Umber mixture in BC, paint a stem extending from the middle of your flower or where it looks most natural. I used the toe of my brush to curve it snakelike, left-right-left, and then used medium pressure to thicken it at the end of the stem.

STEP 8B.

As we did in our Delphinium lesson (page 92), create a few leaves using the gestural technique on page 34. Use your size 6 brush in the same mixture as used in Step 8a. Remember, there is no rhyme or reason to this style of leaves. Anything goes—embrace this! Try to get loose with your strokes by flicking the toe of your brush around somewhat wildly along the leaves. Start with the BC, and move to CSC to add more interest along the edges of the stem and leaves.

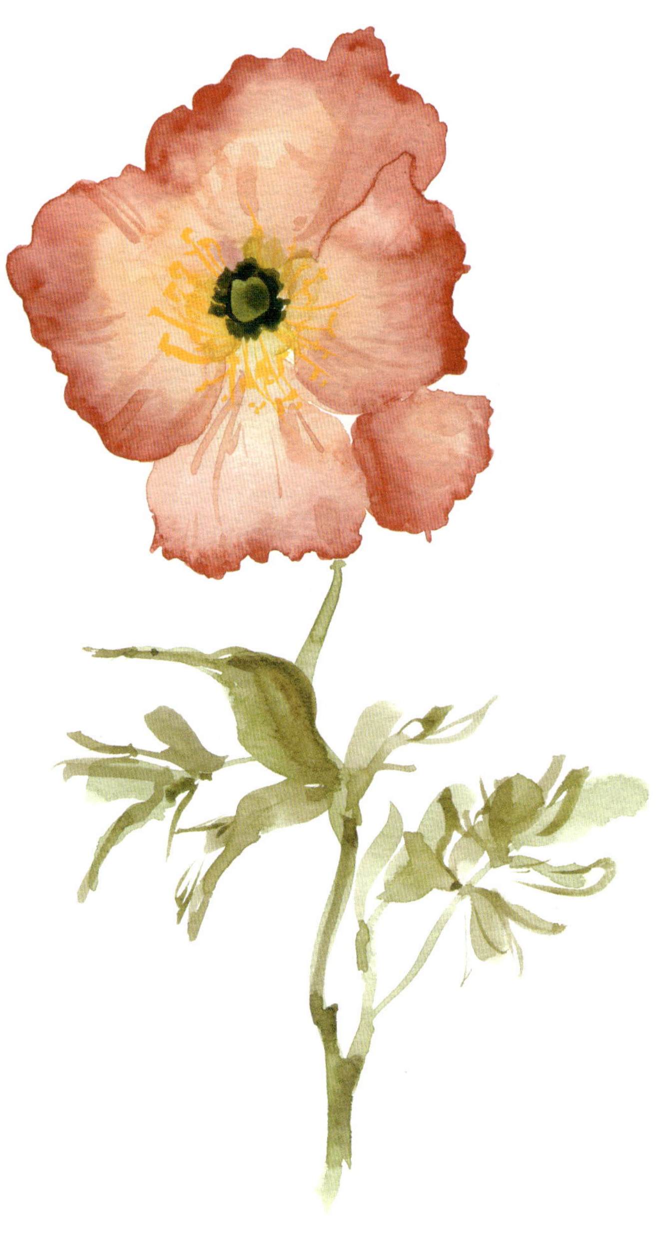

Cosmo

The cosmo is the Lady Gaga of pinwheel flowers. She's got sass, style and sophistication, and you just can't help but stop and stare when you pass her by. We're going to be using our filbert brush again for this lesson to give the petals a different shape and help draw out those darling ruffled edges. We'll be painting an eight-petal cosmo, mostly open-faced, at a slight angle.

Supplies

One size 4 filbert brush

One size 6 round brush

Canson 140-lb (300-gsm) cold-press paper

HB pencil

Palette

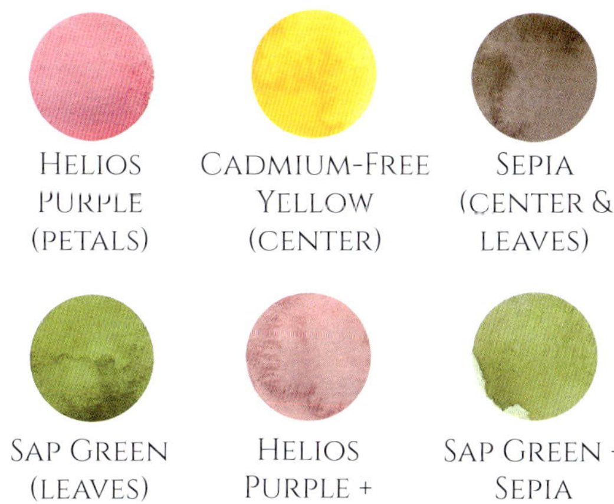

Preparing the Palette

Using your size 4 filbert brush, mix Helios Purple to BC and CSC (page 16).

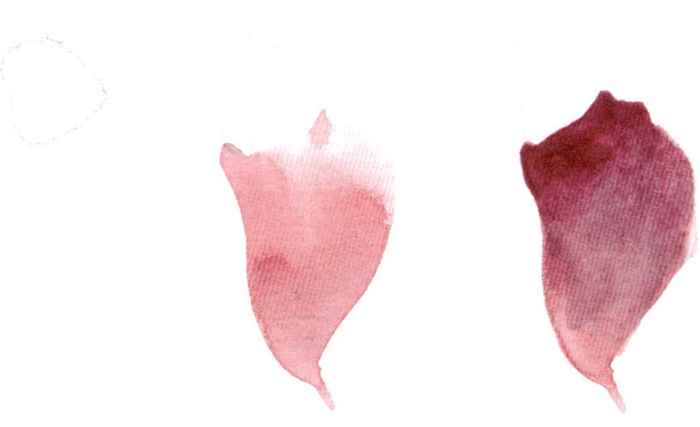

Step 1.

Lightly pencil in the center of the flower in the middle of the paper, roughly the size of a gumball (½ inch [1.3 cm] in diameter).

Step 2.

Load your size 4 filbert brush with Helios Purple in BC, and create your first and shortest petal extending from the bottom of the center, using the compound stroke formation (page 31). The second half of your petal should be slightly shorter than the left side.

Step 3.

While the petal is still wet, load your size 6 round brush and drop in Helios Purple in CSC at the base of the petal, closest to the center. This will create a beautiful gradation of color.

Step 4.

Allow the petal to dry for a moment and then, still using your size 6 round brush and the CSC mixture, come up on the toe to create very fine, dark lines running through the length of the petal.

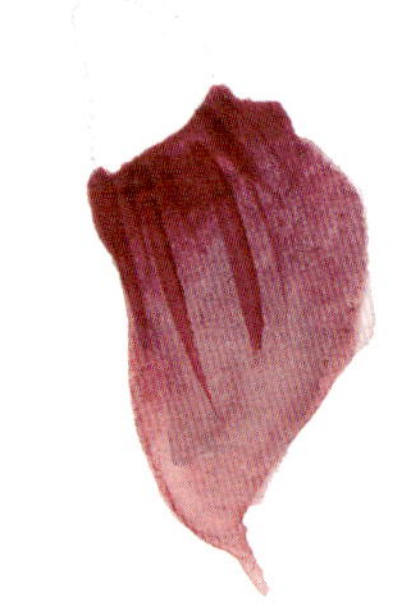

Step 5A.

Follow Steps 2 through 4 to create the next four petals: For the first petal, you will use the side of the brush, curving it wide for the stroke, and then bring it in toward the center to finish the stroke. Your second stroke will begin at the base again and you will bring it in toward the middle of the petal to close it off. Your third stroke will be the widest, achieved by completing a structure that resembles a wide full-belly compound stroke (page 31). Your last petal will be the highest point on the flower, achieved with a thinner compound stroke.

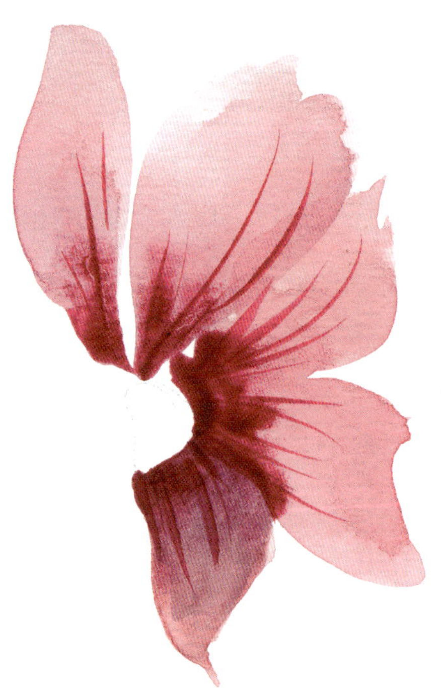

Note: You'll notice that my second and third petal look a bit different than the first petal; this is because I put all the steps together in one seamless motion versus pausing to scan each step as I moved forward. Yours will likely be closer to the later petals.

Step 5B.

Again, create two more petals, following Steps 2 through 4. Your fourth petal will overlap the third just slightly, and your fifth petal should be the highest petal on the flower, pointing almost straight up to the top of the page.

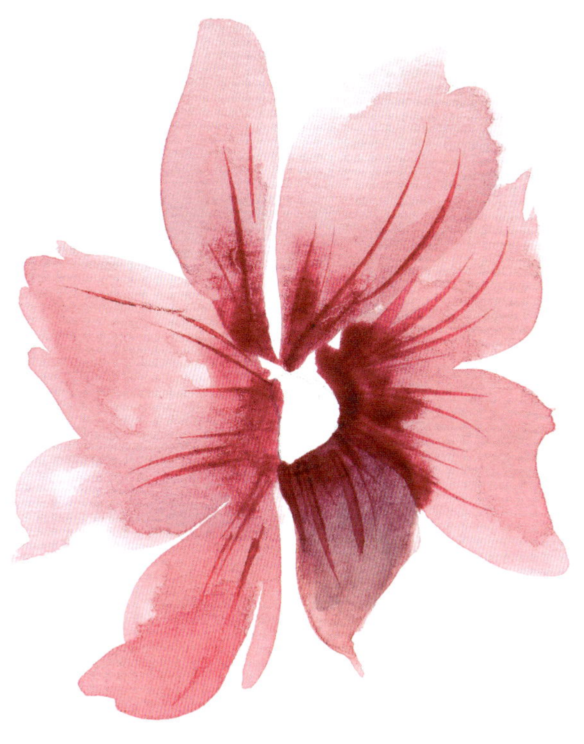

STEP 6A.

Using your size 4 filbert brush, finish the flower with the last three petals following the steps we've covered. Allow the next two petals to merge so there is no visible separation. While the petals are wet, reload your size 6 brush with Helios Purple in CSC and drop it in at the base of the flower so it runs through both petals.

STEP 6B.

For the final petal, leave a bit of white space between so there is a clear separation.

STEP 6C.

Add a small upward stroke on the right side of the final petal to indicate where it's shorter. This extra stroke is important in that it helps to add structure to the flower, making it seem as though the petal is almost on its side.

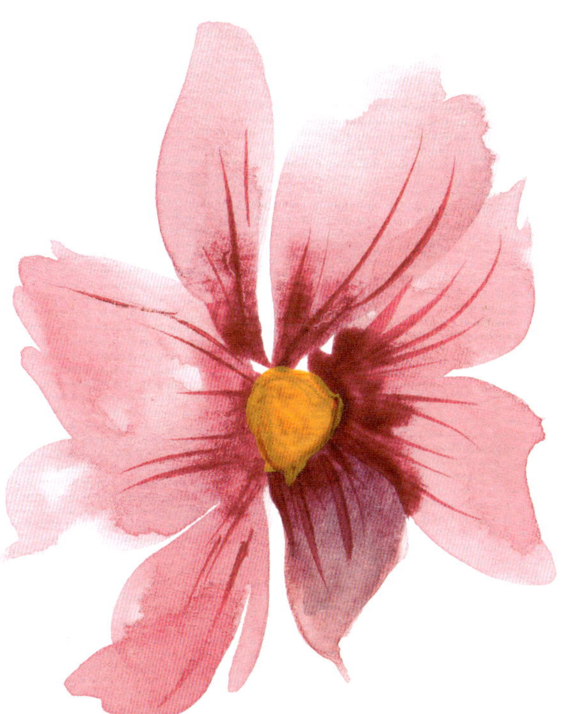

STEP 7.

Be sure your petals are dry and then, using your size 6 round brush, mix Cadmium-Free Yellow to CSC and paint the center of the flower. You're welcome to proceed with this step while the petals are still wet for wet-into-wet technique (page 29) The yellow will run into the pink and create a peach hue.

Tip: If you've lost a bit of the gumball shape while painting, just reshape the center as it was prior so it overlaps the petals.

Step 8.

Be sure the center is fully dry. Mix Sepia to CSC and, using your size 6 round brush, add small, fine lines to the center near the top. To do this you'll use the toe of the brush, applying light pressure.

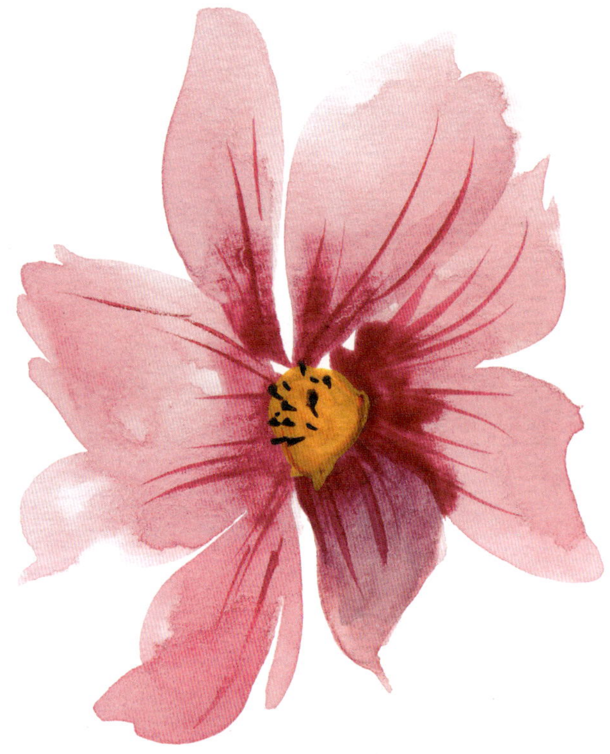

Step 9.

Mix together Helios Purple and Sepia to CSC, and using your size 6 round brush, add shading to the bottom four petals. These will be slightly thicker downward strokes.

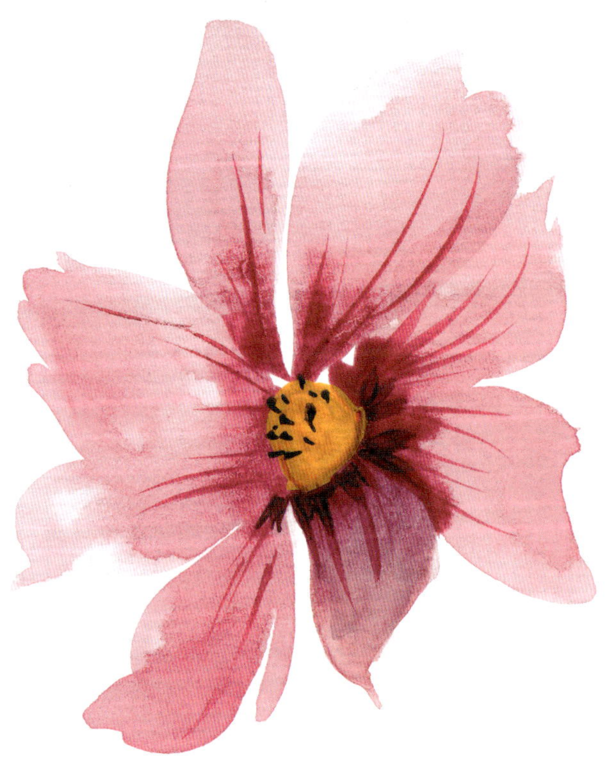

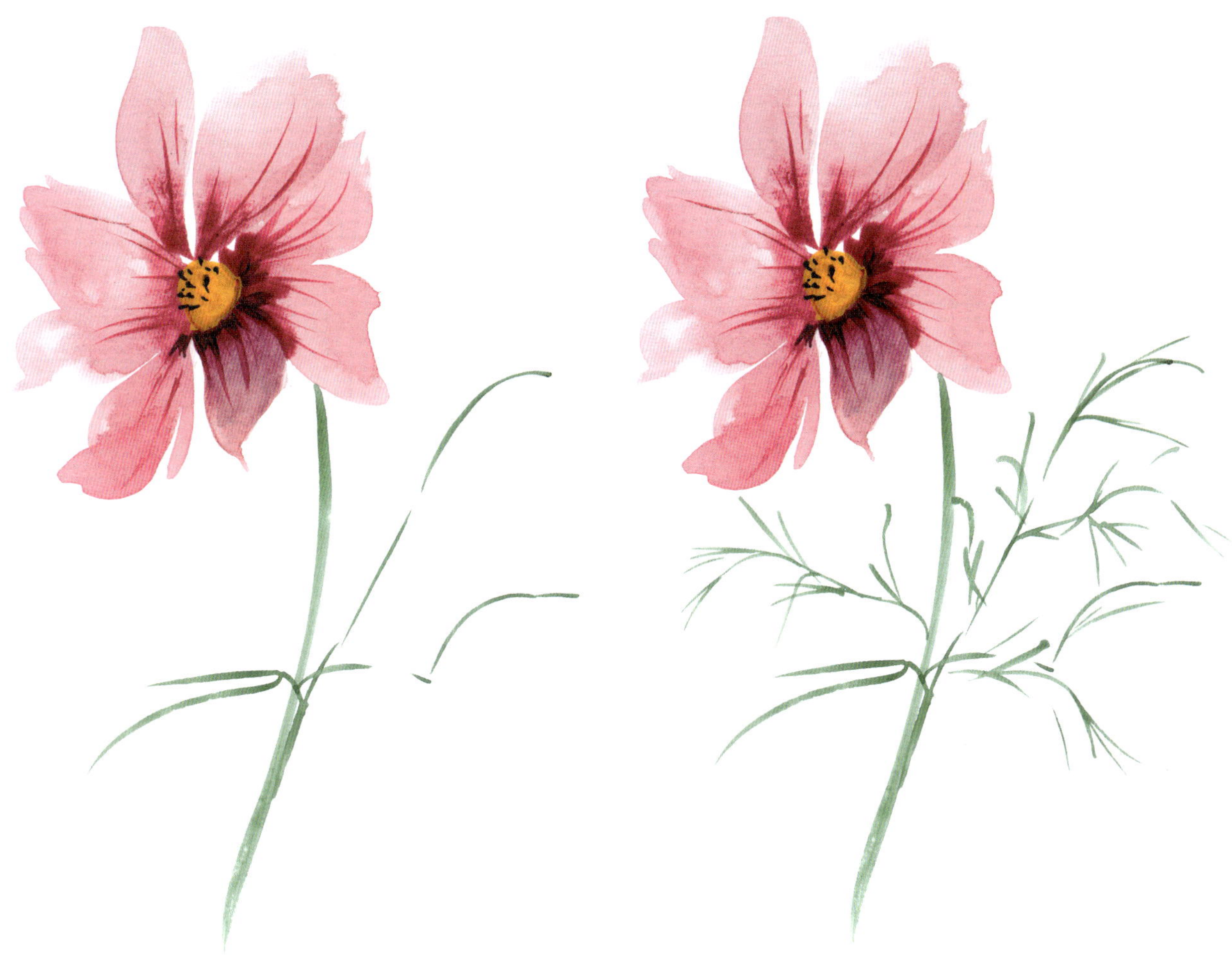

Step 10a.

Mix together Sap Green and Sepia to BC, and using the toe of the brush, paint a stem extending from the second petal we painted so there is a severe curve.

Step 10b.

Paint a few finer lines extending from the stem to serve as branches for your leaves. Come up on the toe and apply light pressure.

Step 11.

Using the same mixture and brush, add gestural leaves (page 34). You can wait until your branches are dry if you like, or for a looser look, proceed with this step while they are still damp. These are twiggy in nature, almost like blades of grass, and look best very loose. Again, utilize the toe of the brush and flick it around somewhat wildly to create a variety of long and short fine lines. Movement is key here, so really access full wrist mobility to be sure your leaves are pointing in different directions.

Alstroemeria

Alstroemeria, sometimes called Peruvian lily, is one of my favorite flowers for its ability to be a focal or filler flower depending on how it's used. Its clustering nature may tend toward a filler element, but as a feature flower, it is a showstopper with beautiful spotted petals and unique petal shape. Its pinwheel shape makes it feel approachable, yet there is something intrinsically special about the way alstroemeria open as though in embrace. If you're not already familiar with this bloom, I believe you are about to find a new favorite flower to paint!

Supplies

Three size 6 round brushes

Canson 140-lb (300-gsm) cold-press paper

Palette

Naples Yellow (petals)

Green Gold (petals)

Permanent Rose (petals)

Burnt Umber (petal details)

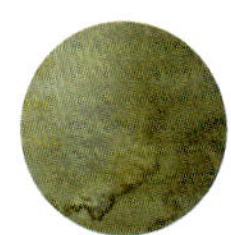

Undersea Green (leaves)

Preparing the Palette

Using a size 6 brush, mix Naples Yellow to BC (page 16).

Using a second size 6 brush, mix Green Gold to CSC (page 16).

Using the third size 6 brush, mix Permanent Rose to BC.

Please note: Now that we have thoroughly studied wet-into-wet technique (page 29), I'll be performing all of Step 1 in one fluid progression while the media is wet, so as to correctly achieve the end result.

Step 1a.

Prime your first size 6 brush and load it with Naples Yellow in BC. Paint your first petal near the top of the page. It should be about the size and shape of half a thumb. We'll be using five-petal pinwheel flower structure (see page 37) and modifying it slightly by creating a tip in the middle of the petal.

Step 1b.

Using your second size 6 brush loaded with Green Gold in CSC, immediately create a merge of color at the base of the petal while the media is wet.

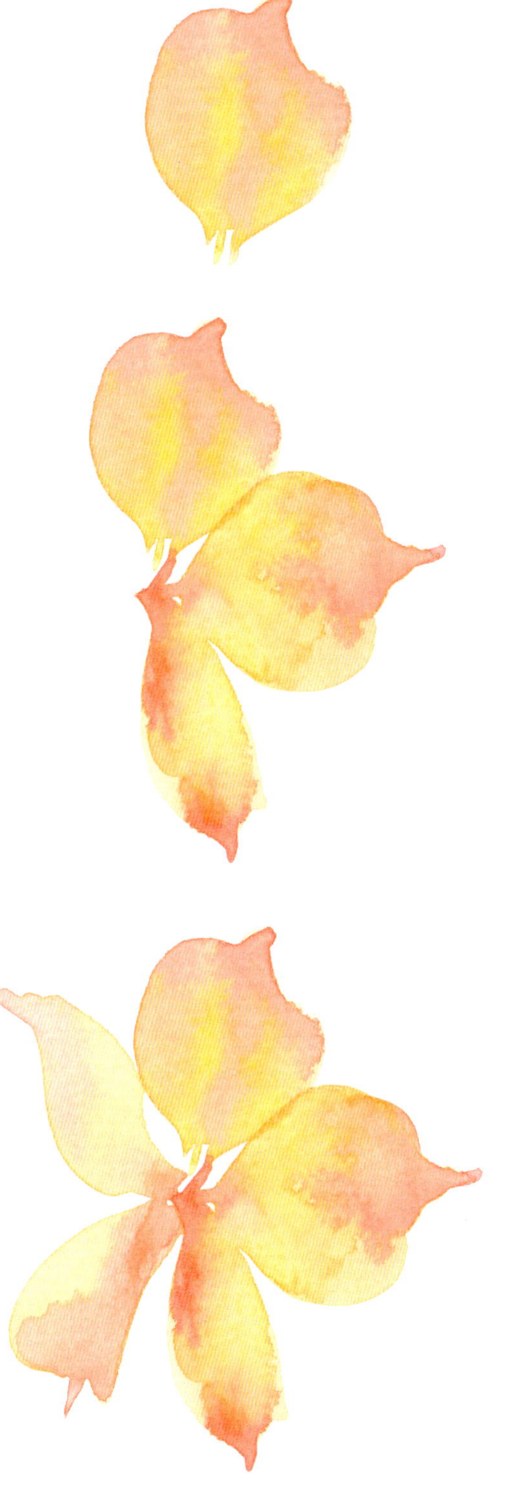

Step 1c.

Using your third size 6 brush loaded with Permanent Rose in BC, immediately touch the tip of the wet petal to flood the petal with a streak of pink while the media is wet. Shape to create the point. To do this, you will graze the toe of your brush along the outer edge of the petal.

Step 2a.

Repeat Step 1 for the next two petals.

Step 2b.

Once you've made both petals, and the media is damp but not overly wet, touch the middle of the flower with the tip of your size 6 brush loaded with Permanent Rose in BC to create a pink center.

Step 3.

Repeat Steps 1 and 2 to create the next two petals. This time, however, decrease the value of the Naples Yellow BC first, so that it is one shade lighter. This will create a range of light throughout your flower so that it appears to be in the shade on the right and in the sun on the left. Do not add the Green Gold at the middle. Instead use the Permanent Rose in BC. For a review on color value, see page 38.

STEP 4.

Repeat Steps 1 through 3 again to create the next flower directly to the right. This time, you can elect to make the petals on the left a bit darker so they appear to be shaded by the first flower. It doesn't need to be drastic—just a slight difference is enough here to provide the flower with variation. You can also play with how much pink you want to drop in, flooding the base of the flower or leaving it mostly Green Gold. Feel free to take liberties here!

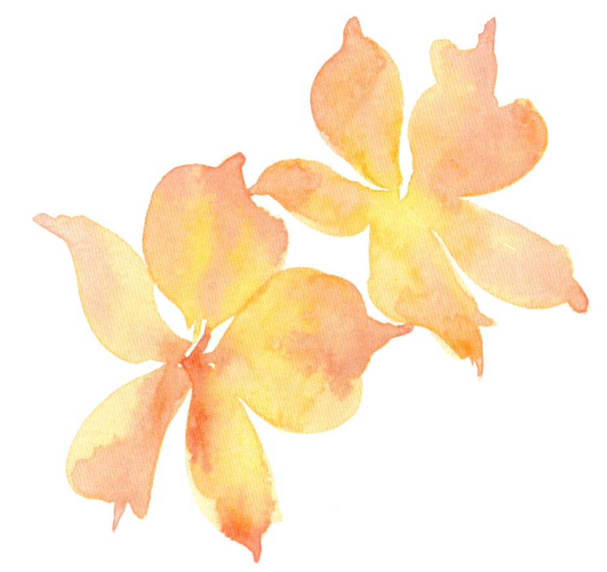

STEP 5.

Repeating Steps 1 through 3 once more, create one final main flower to the bottom left of the center flower. This time we will only be painting the three lower petals extending from the main center flower; this is to gesture that this flower is partially hidden and on its side. You'll use the same progression here: Naples Yellow in BC, Green Gold in CSC in the center and Permanent Rose in BC at the tip. Be sure to play with variety of shapes (see page 32 for a refresh) here so that each petal feels like its own unique moment.

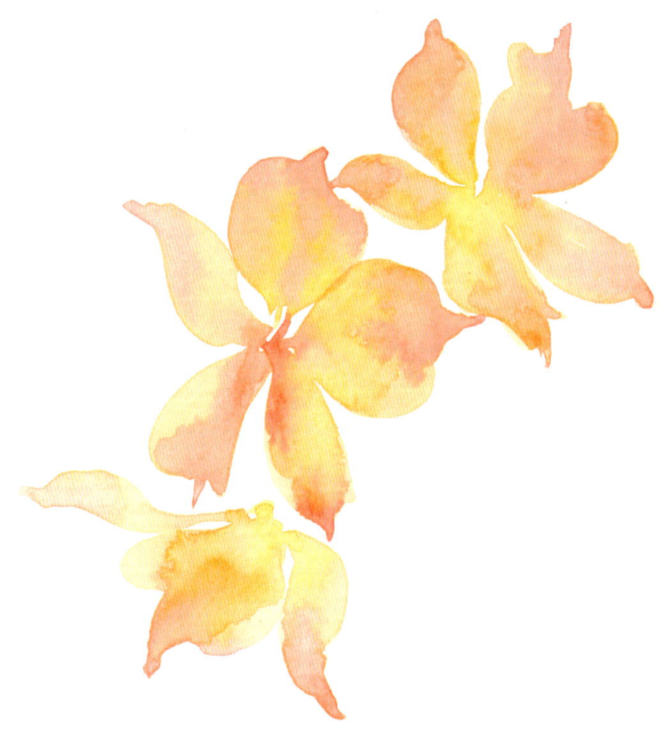

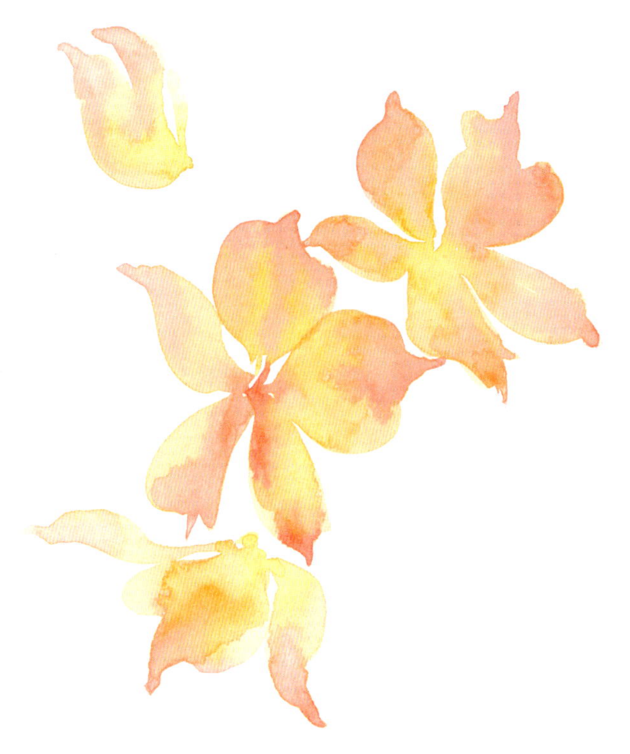

Step 6.

In the top left corner, create a flower just on the verge of opening, using bud structure (see page 40). These petals will be clasped together and be the same colors we've used for our main flowers. To do this, you can use a series of simple and compound strokes (pages 30 and 31). Paint the body of the petals in Naples Yellow at BC, Green Gold at the base and Permanent Rose at the tip.

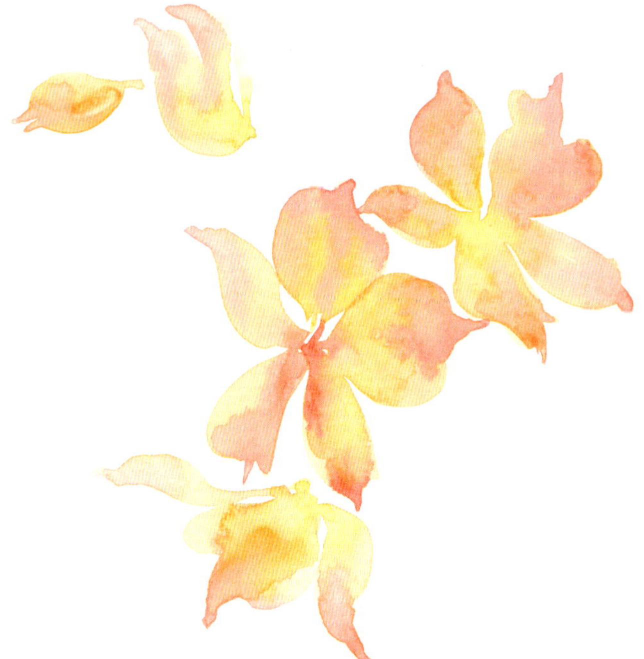

Step 7.

Create one more bud, this time slightly smaller to show it's not quite as close to opening. Paint it sideways to give some movement to the piece. Later, we will attach leaves and it will all flow together. Allow all the petals to fully dry before proceeding to the next step.

Step 8.

Using a size 6 brush, mix Burnt Umber to CSC and add detail lines to the middle of the petals. The key to getting these lines to not feel like an afterthought but rather part of the flow of the flower is using the toe of your brush in moderately quick flicks. You don't need to rush it, but you also don't need to spend more than half a second between lines. Find that balance and groove that feels right to you and don't overthink this step! Variety is also key. Allow some of your lines to be lines, and some to be nothing more than a dot.

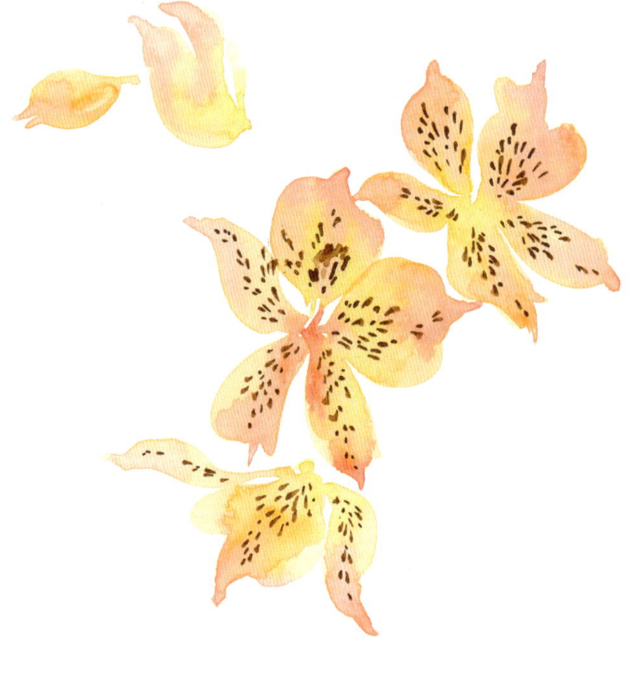

Step 9a.

Mix Permanent Rose and Burnt Umber to CSC, and add gestural outlining (page 41) to the tips of the petals.

Step 9b.

Optional: You can use Undersea Green to create a stamen in the center of the flowers. I opted not to because I like the loose look of the flowers and the detail lines provide plenty of intricacy.

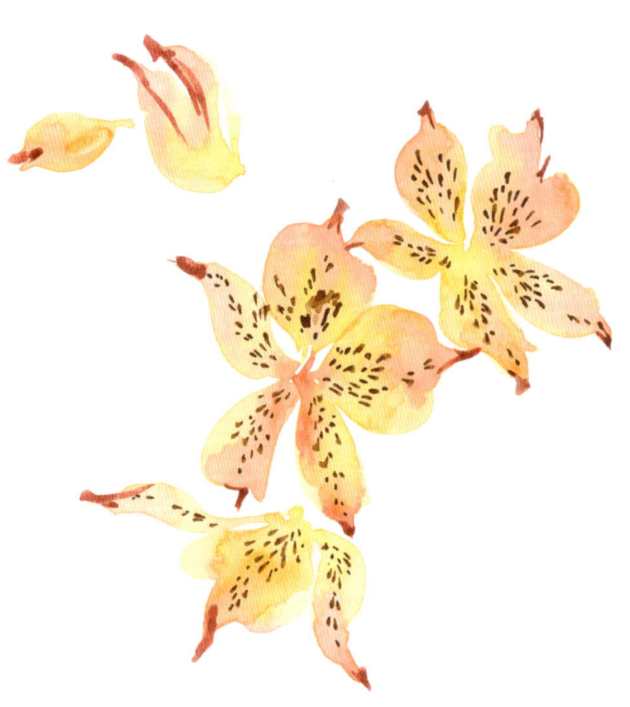

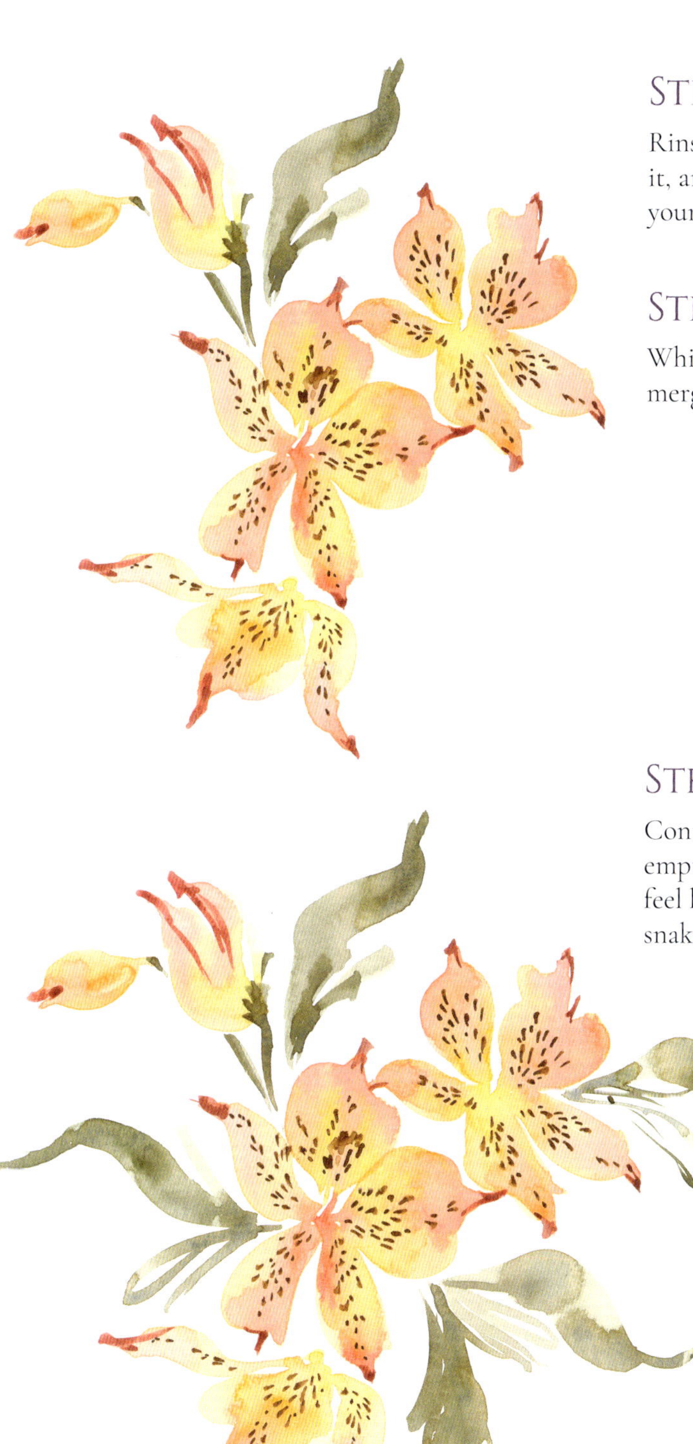

Step 10a.

Rinse a size 6 brush until there's no trace of pink on it, and mix Undersea Green to BC and CSC. Paint your first two gestural leaves (page 34) using BC.

Step 10b.

While the leaves are still wet, use CSC to create a merging of consistencies.

Step 11.

Continue to paint gestural leaves, filling in the empty space around the flowers so that the leaves feel like a moving part of the piece, slithering snakelike throughout the bouquet.

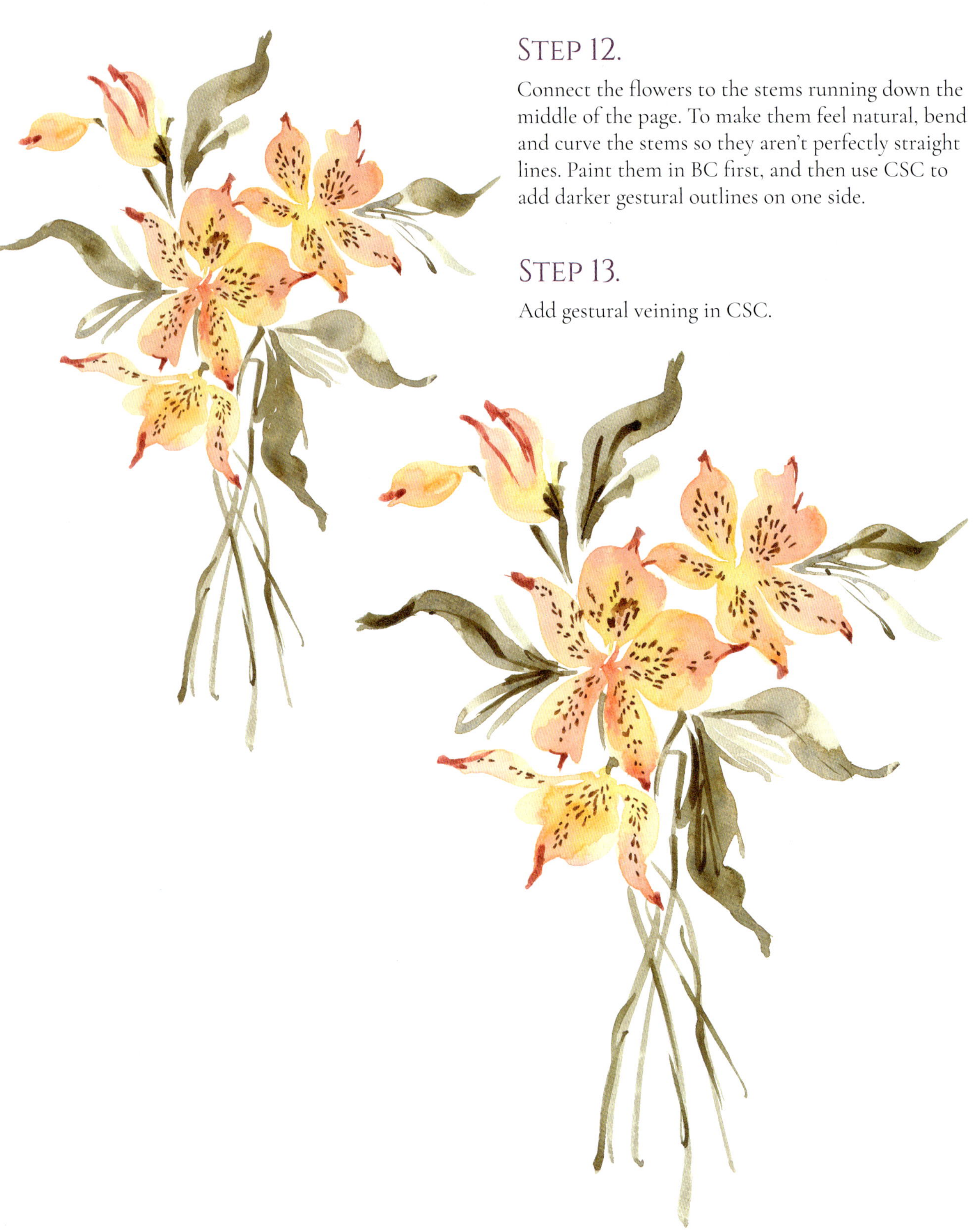

STEP 12.

Connect the flowers to the stems running down the middle of the page. To make them feel natural, bend and curve the stems so they aren't perfectly straight lines. Paint them in BC first, and then use CSC to add darker gestural outlines on one side.

STEP 13.

Add gestural veining in CSC.

Agapanthus

Is it just me, or does the name of this flower present the vision of some demigod holding dominion over panthers? Perhaps I've been watching too much sci-fi . . . but beyond its interesting name, it's quite eye-catching. There are many varieties of this flower and a range of colors; however, I've chosen my favorite for us today, a shade of blueish-purple I've lovingly dubbed blurple. Here's something fun—we'll be creating our first mixture consisting of three colors in this project! Let's get to it!

Supplies

Two size 6 round brushes

One size 2 round brush

Canson 140-lb (300-gsm) cold-press paper

Palette

French Ultramarine (Flowers)

Smalt (Flowers)

Lamp Black (Flowers)

Sepia (Stamens)

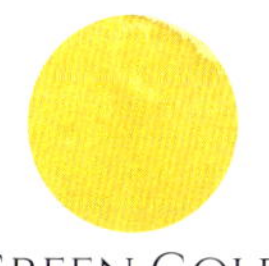
Green Gold (Stamens)

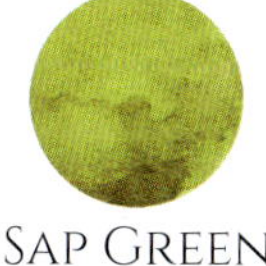
Sap Green (Stems)

French Ultramarine + Smalt + Lamp Black

Preparing the Palette

With one size 6 brush, mix together French Ultramarine and Smalt to CSC (page 16).

Next, add Lamp Black to that mixture until you've achieved a swatch similar to mine. Go slowly, adding just a bit at a time or you may have to start over again. Once you're satisfied with the color, set that brush off to the side.

With your other size 6 brush, begin a new pile of the French Ultramarine, Smalt and Lamp Black mixture on the palette and decrease the value of the mixture by adding water until you've reached the same color in BC (page 16).

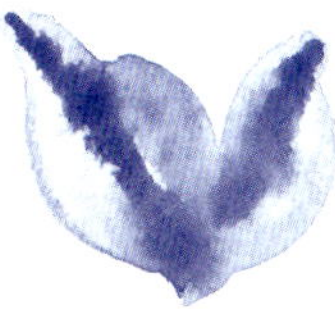

Step 1A.

Using your size 6 brush loaded with our French Ultramarine, Smalt and Lamp Black in BC, begin by painting an open-faced flower in the center of the page. The structure is a six-petal pinwheel flower. We'll start with the first petal and use the compound stroke method here (see page 31 for a refresh). Begin the stroke with medium pressure at the base of the flower and then pulling the brush upward, gradually lighten pressure by lifting up to finish the tip.

Step 1B.

While the petal is still moist but not wet, use your other size 6 brush loaded with our flower mixture in CSC to paint a line straight down the middle of the petal for wet-into-wet technique (page 29). Get down at eye level with the paper to check how damp it is. It should be glistening but not saturated with water. The result should be a blurry line slightly darker than the outside of the petal.

Tip: *If your dark line spread through the entire petal, your media was too wet. If the dark line didn't spread at all, your media was too dry. Try to improve the timing in the next petal, and take note that it doesn't need to look like a defined line every time. A slight disruption of color is what we're hoping to achieve.*

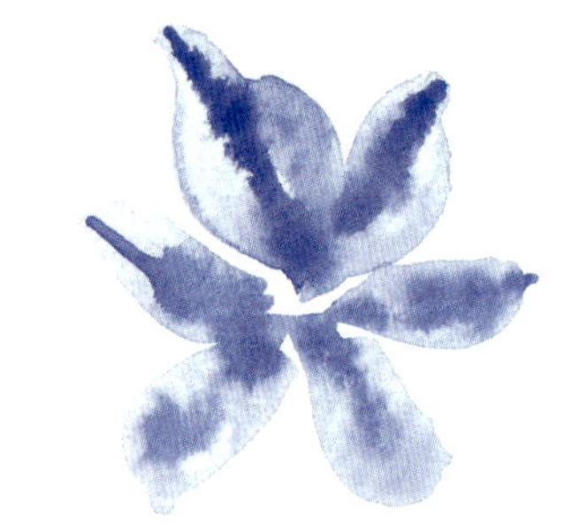

STEP 2.

Repeating Step 1, finish the flower by painting the other five petals.

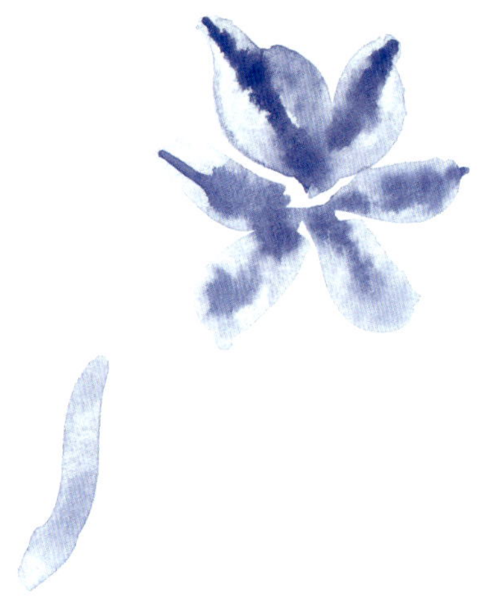

STEP 3.

Using your size 6 brush with the BC mixture, paint a flower directly to the lower left. This time, we'll begin by painting the smallest petals that extend into the rear of the flower. Use the simple stroke technique (page 30) beginning at the tip of the petal and maintaining pressure through the end of the backside. It should resemble a worm about an inch (2.5 cm) long.

STEP 4.

Glaze (page 28) the tube shape with another layer of color in BC so that it's slightly darker than the petals. Add an extension to the petal by painting a kernel-sized stroke to the right side of the petal. This serves as the opening of the flower.

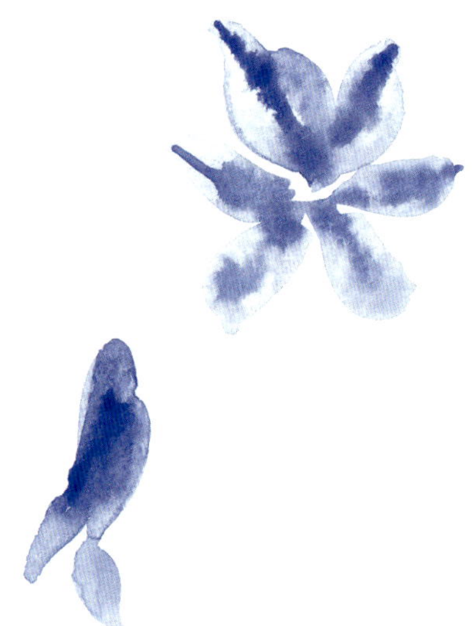

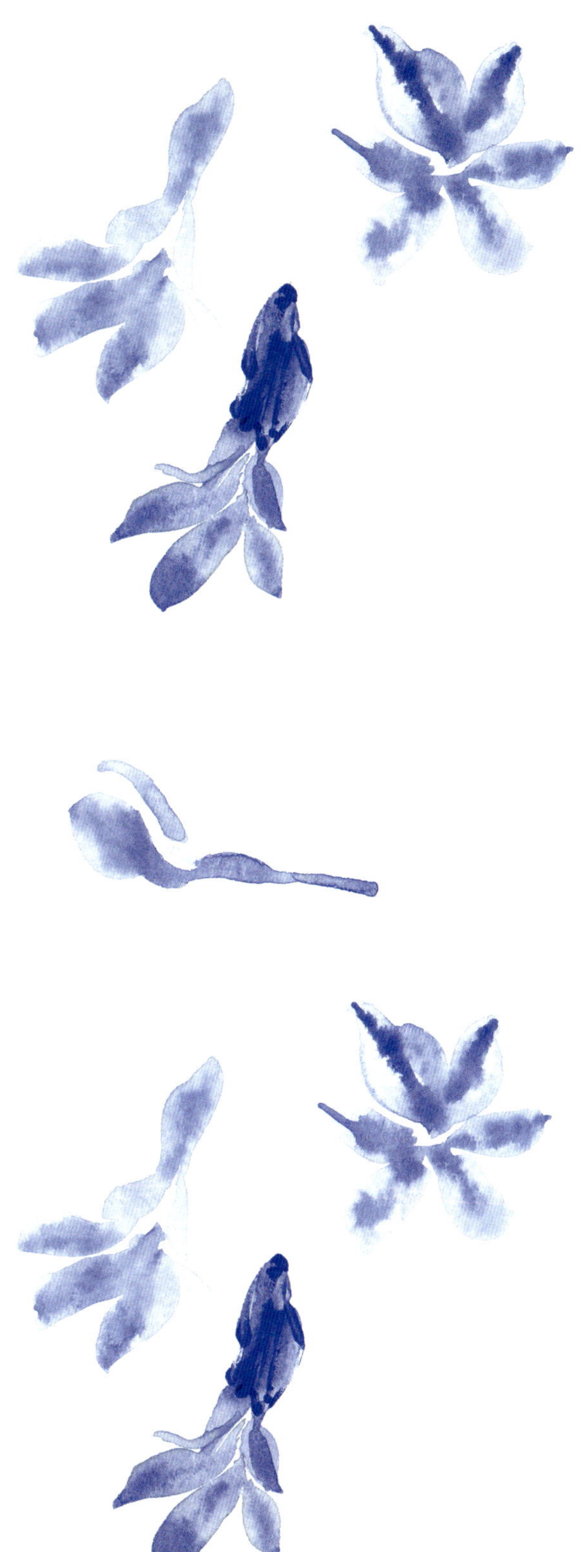

STEP 5A.

Finish the flower by painting the other four petals.

STEP 5B.

Be sure the tube part of the flower is completely dry and then load your size 2 brush with French Ultramarine, Smalt and Lamp Black in CSC and paint a gestural stroke just big enough to create separation between the front two petals and the tube. Give the tube gestural outlining. For more on gestural outlining, see page 41.

STEP 5C.

Paint the third flower, using the same techniques in Steps 3 through 5b.

STEP 6A.

Paint the fourth flower, using the same techniques; however, this time we'll be painting it from behind, so rather than the first two petals being the smallest, they will now be the largest. Begin the same way as we did before, starting with the tip of the petal and increasing pressure as you pull the brush towards you to complete the tube.

STEP 6B.

Repeat on the other side.

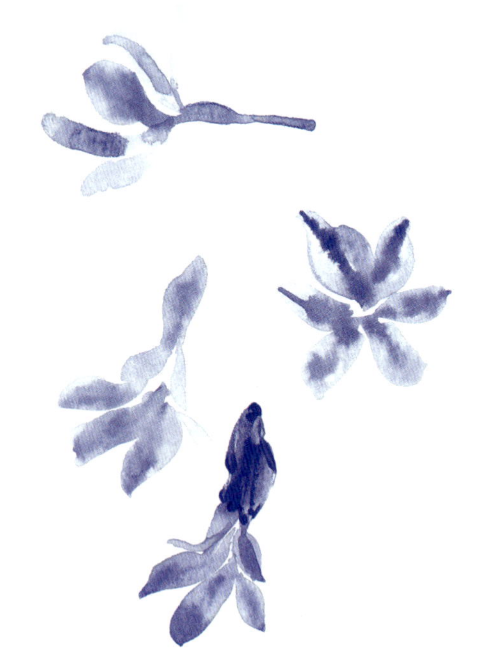

Step 7.

Finish the flower by painting the other four petals, using the same methods in Steps 3 through 5b.

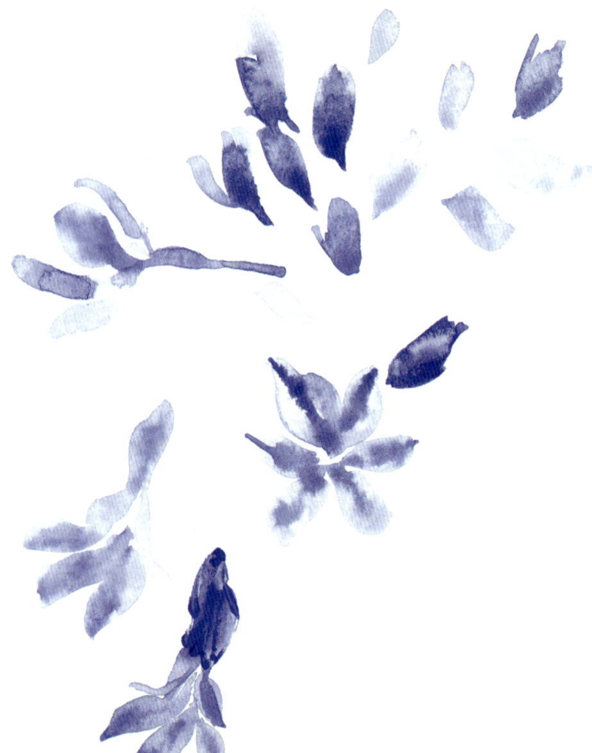

Step 8.

Begin forming buds at the center of the main flower. These are simply slender compound strokes. Using your size 2 brush loaded with French Ultramarine, Smalt and Lamp Black in BC, start at the base of the flower, where we will later attach stems, and paint two strokes so they are closed at the tip. The important thing to remember here is to play with color value and size. Some of the buds should be darker—not nearly CSC, but in between BC and CSC, and other buds should be very pale. This is done by decreasing and increasing the value (i.e., adding water to dilute, or more paint for a thicker, darker mixture). For a thorough refresh, you can see page 21. In the same way, some buds should be small, just starting to sprout, and others should be close to opening to bloom. These buds should point in a variety of directions, but mainly aiming upward.

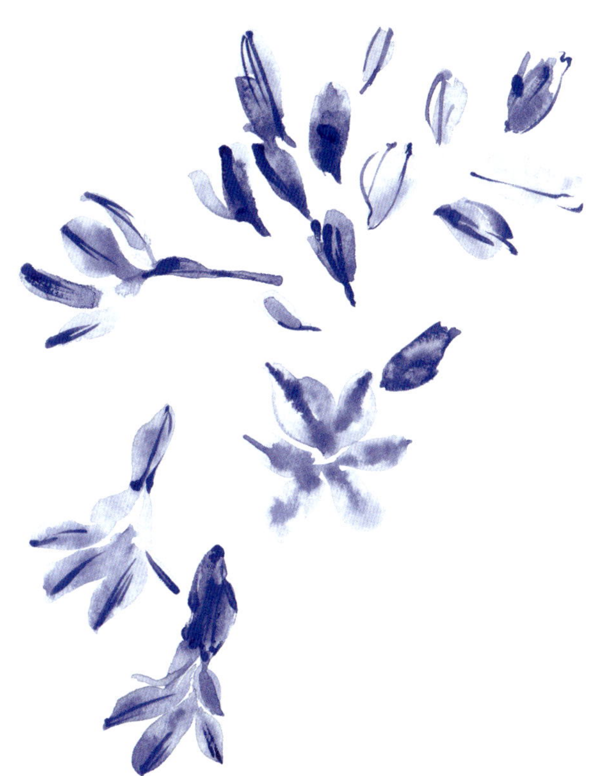

Step 9a.

Referring to Step 5b, add the gestural outlining to the flowers the same way as we did for the second flower.

Step 9b.

Darken the center of the petals with a gestural vein.

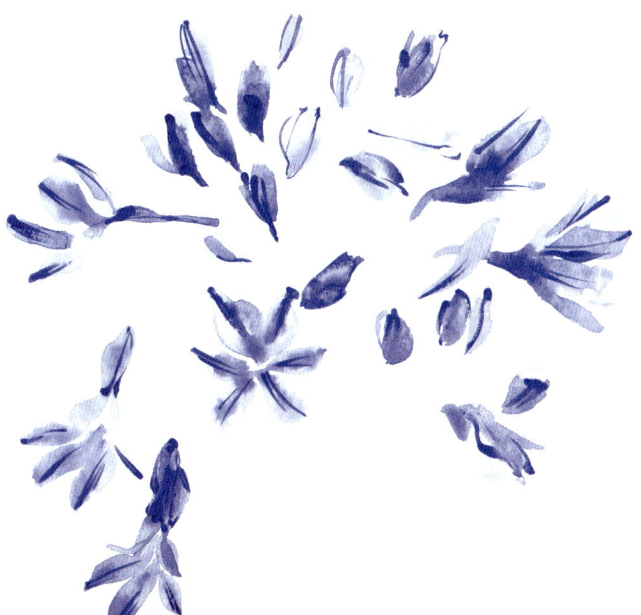

Step 10a.

Move to the right side and finish off the main flower by adding three more large flowers, using the same steps we've previously covered.

Step 10b.

Fill in the empty area with more buds to round out the entire flower as a whole.

Step 10c.

Refer back to Step 5b and repeat. Be sure all flowers are completely dry before proceeding to the next step.

Step 11a.

We'll conclude the petal portion of the project by adding stamens to the center of the partially open flowers. Load a size 6 brush with Sepia in CSC. Come up on the toe of the brush at the center of the flowers and make a very fine line that curves outward.

Step 11b.

When the stamens are dry, using your size 2 brush, mix Green Gold to CSC. Add a small dot on the end of each stamen.

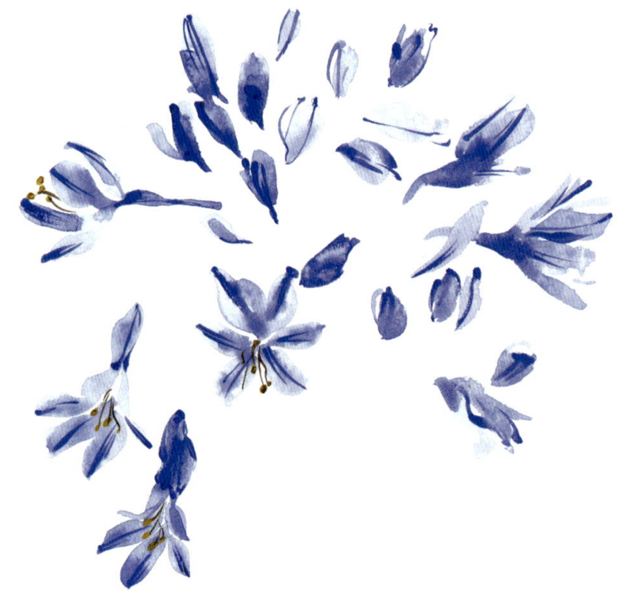

Step 12.

Rinse your size 6 brushes thoroughly and load one with Sap Green in CSC and the other in Sap Green in BC. Paint a stem in BC directly beneath the middle flower.

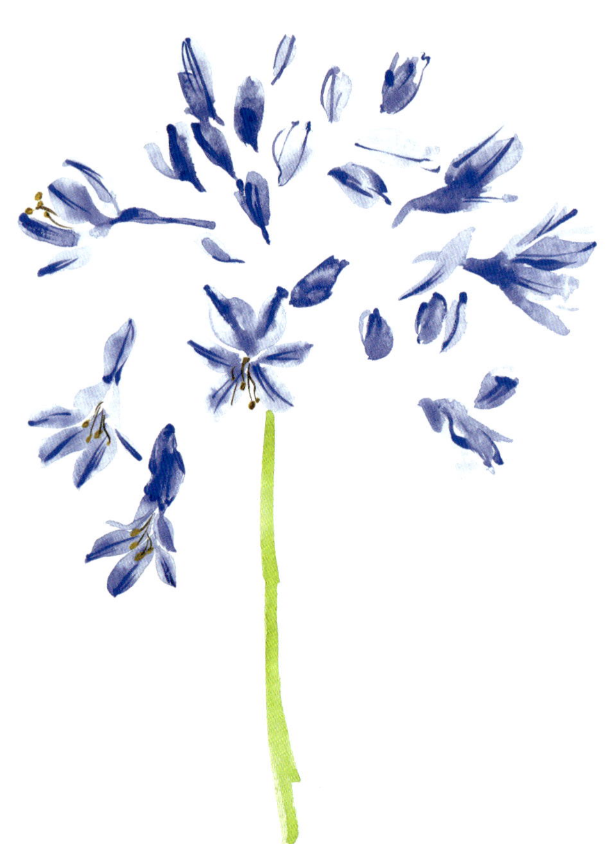

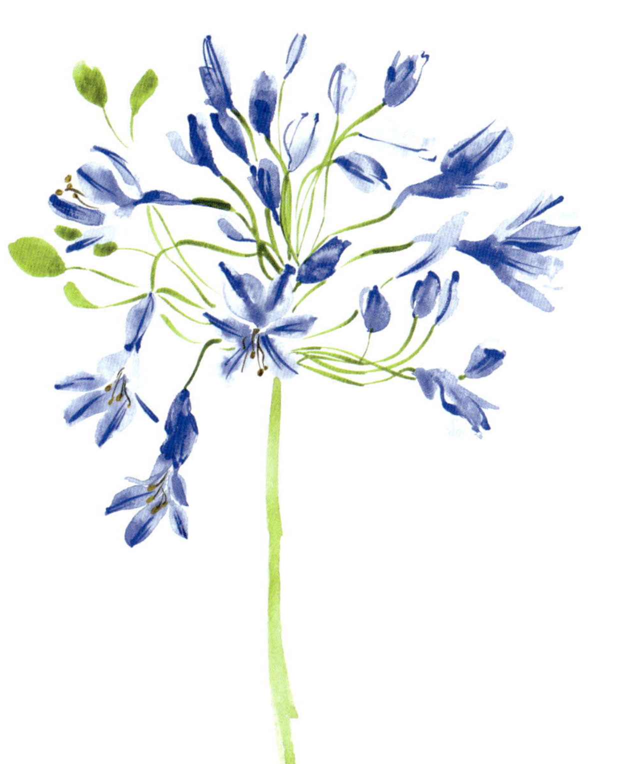

Step 13a.

Using your size 6 brush loaded with Sap Green in CSC, attach smaller stems to the flowers that lead back to the main stem.

Step 13b.

Using your size 6 brush loaded with Sap Green in BC, round off the flower as a whole by painting a few green unopened buds the same way you painted the purple buds.

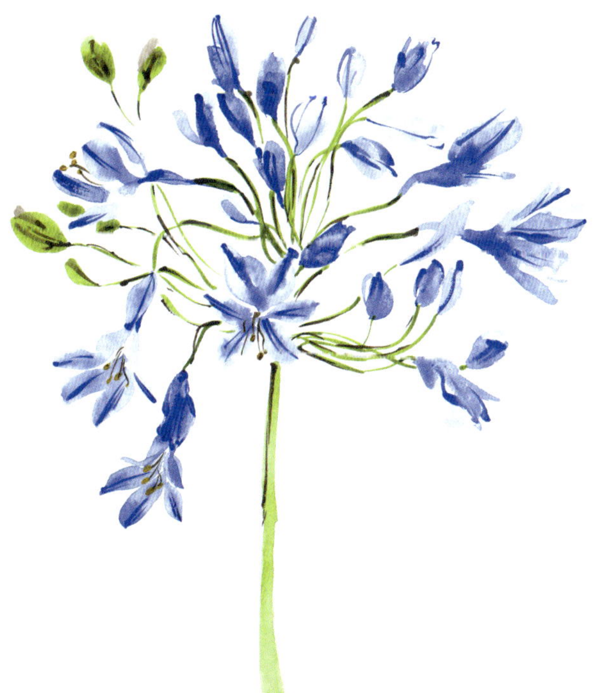

Step 14a.

Be sure the stems are fully dry, then, using a size 6 brush loaded with Sepia in CSC, add lines of contrast to the main stem and smaller stems by running the toe of the brush along the edges.

Step 14b.

Using the same brush, add gestural lines to the buds.

Zinnia

Of all our projects, this could be one of the more challenging, simply due to the voluminous nature of this flower. Whenever we are working with flowers that have many petals, the tendency is to want to control the structure, which can lead to overworking. Our goal will be to give a nod to the intricacy of the zinnia without feeling as though we need to capture every single detail to get it right. Using the filbert brush will help us stay loose because it has neither a toe nor or belly, though we can utilize the side of the brush for a slightly thinner stroke. I'm excited about this one, so let's get to it!

Supplies

Two size 6 round brushes
One size 2 round brush
One size 4 filbert brush
Canson 140-lb (300-gsm) cold-press paper
HB pencil
Dust-free eraser

Palette

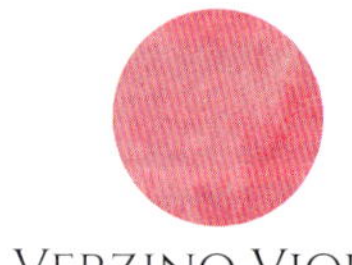

Verzino Violet (petals)

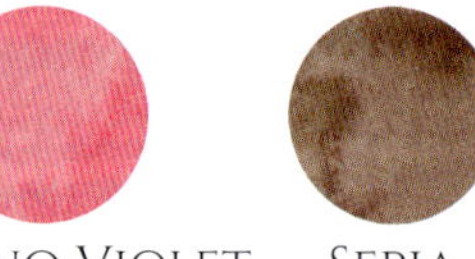

Sepia (petals)

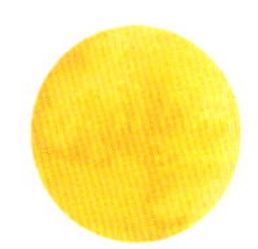

Cadmium-Free Yellow (petals)

Green Apatite Genuine (leaves)

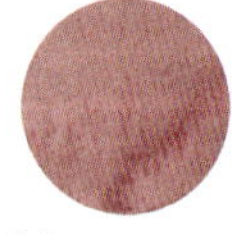

Verzino Violet + Sepia

Cadmium-Free Yellow + Sepia + Verzino Violet

Preparing the Palette

Mix Verzino Violet and Sepia together to BC (page 16).

Using that mixture, begin a new pile on the palette and add Cadmium-Free Yellow until you've arrived at a peachy hue.

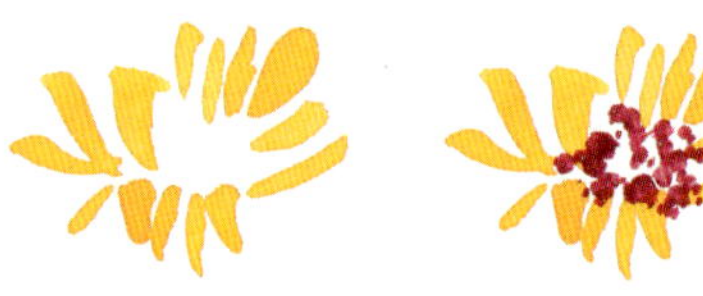

Step 1.

Load a size 6 round brush with Cadmium-Free Yellow in BC and paint the first layer of small petals (about the size of a staple), taking care to leave negative space in the middle where we will later add the center of the flower. To do this, you'll use the small simple stroke technique covered on page 30.

Step 2.

Load the size 2 round brush with Verzino Violet in CSC (page 16) and paint the middle of the flower by using the toe of the brush to press down on the page light to firm to create a variety of small circles ranging from pinprick to berry-sized.

Tip: *To best capture the looseness of this flower, we will be employing gestural stroke (page 32), using a series of small dots to convey the appearance of a busy center of the flower. Consider leaving a bit of white space so there is some distinction of shape.*

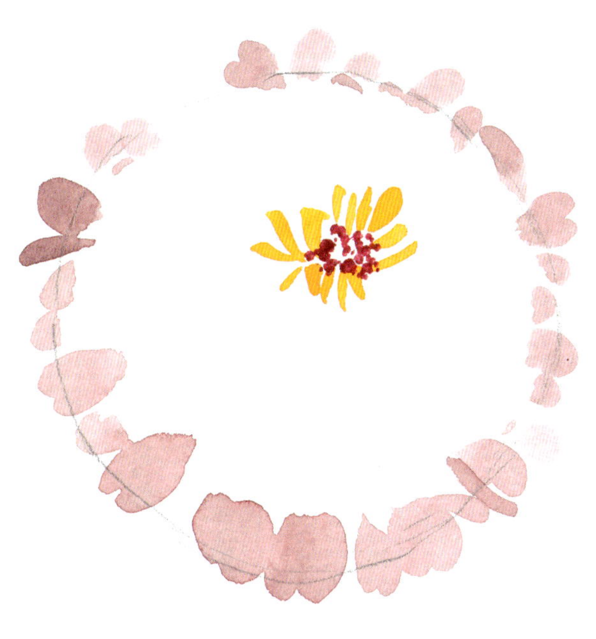

Step 3.

Using a pencil, lightly sketch a boundary line around your flower 3 inches (7.5 cm) in diameter. We are going to begin with the outside petals and work our way toward the center; this ring will ensure our flower doesn't lose its balance and proportion. This ring should be longer toward the bottom and shorter toward the top. Later, you can erase it with an eraser.

Step 4.

Using your size 4 filbert brush, load it with the Verzino Violet and Sepia mixture in BC and paint the outer ring of petals. If you need a refresh on filbert strokes, see page 43. As you work your way around, your bottom petals should be longer and wider, and gradually get smaller. For these small petals, remember to use just the tip of the filbert brush.

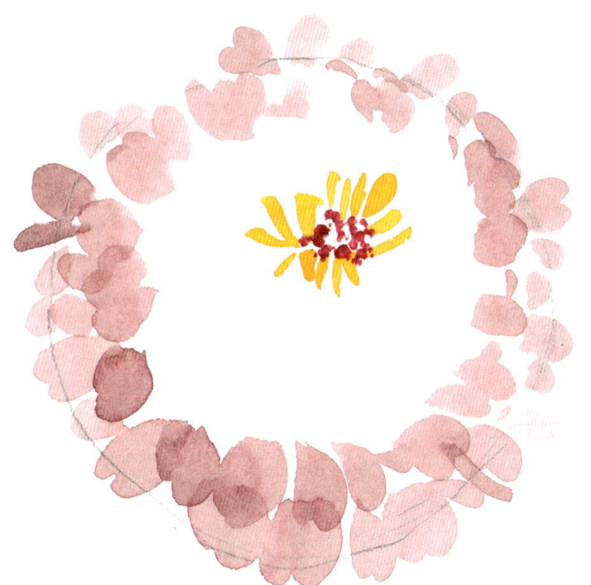

Tips: *What helps me is to turn my paper upside down and paint the strokes by pulling the brush toward me in a downward stroke, rather than fighting the tension of an upward stroke.*

It would be best if you wait until each ring of petals is dry before creating a new ring. Damp is okay, though if they are too wet, the petals will merge and become indistinguishable.

Step 5.

Repeat Step 4; however, this time slightly increase the value of your mixture by adding a bit more Verzino Violet. If you need to do a test swatch before you make the petals to be sure the colors aren't too unalike, that might be helpful.

Step 6.

Repeat Step 5; however, you will not need to increase the color value.

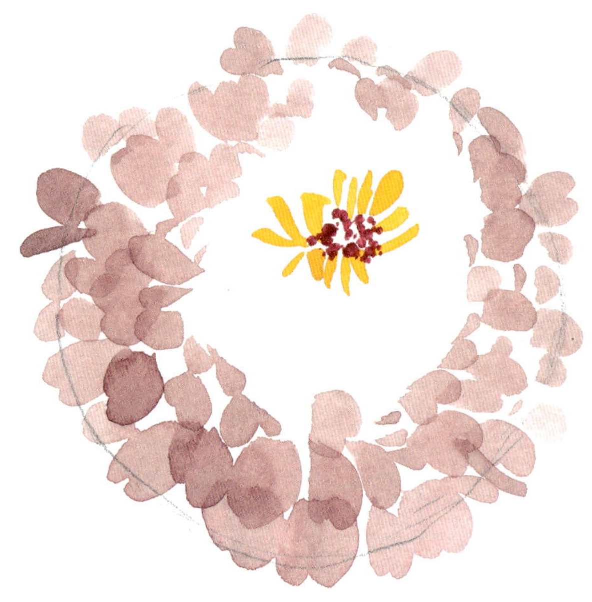

Step 7.

Be sure the previous ring is dry and erase the pencil lines. Again, repeating Steps 4 through 6, we'll make one change by rinsing off the filbert brush and loading it with the Cadmium-Free Yellow, Sepia and Verzino Violet mixture in BC. Paint your third, fourth and fifth ring of petals, leaving a bit of space between the layers, where we will later add a few more intentional strokes in CSC. The color should be the darkest version of BC and gradually lighten as it reaches the center of the flower.

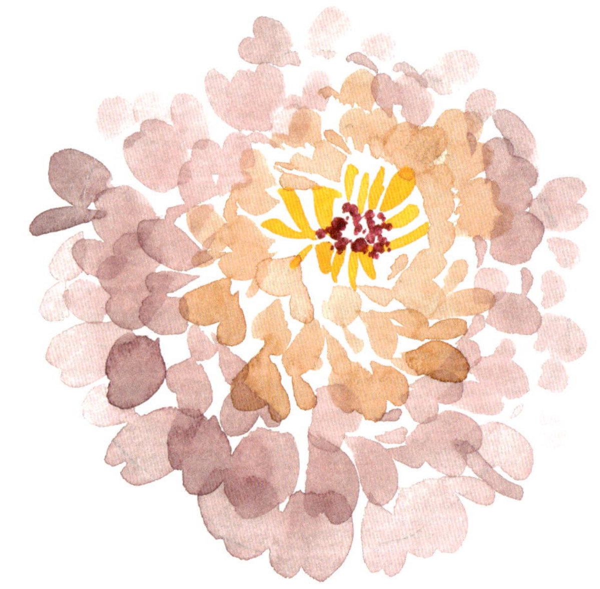

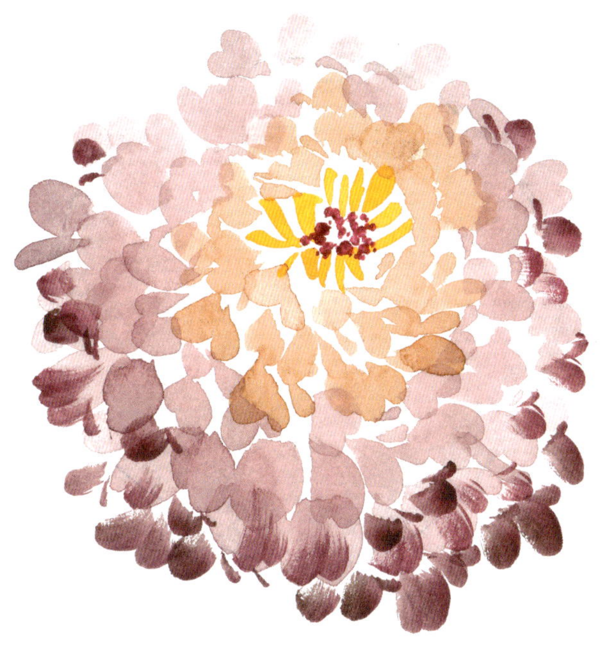

Step 8a.

Load your filbert brush with the Verzino Violet and Sepia mixture in CSC and add another layer under the bottom ring of petals. This should be your darkest layer, leaning more toward Sepia than Verzino Violet.

Step 8b.

Rinse off a bit of the Verzino Violet and Sepia mixture, and reload your brush with the same mixture at 50-50 color. This time, add a layer to the top of the outer petals. For this technique, really make sure your consistency is at CSC. You want very little water on the brush so that the stroke is nearly dry, leaving only a few lines behind on the petals. Go slow, and if the effect isn't what you're hoping for, blot and reload again. This is where the flower really comes to life with depth and texture and it's worth doing right!

Tip: To ensure success, first blot the brush on a paper towel to remove excess water and then load the brush with the paint on the palette. Consider making a few test strokes on a scrap piece of paper to be sure the stroke is thick but not opaque. You want to see white space between the bristle marks.

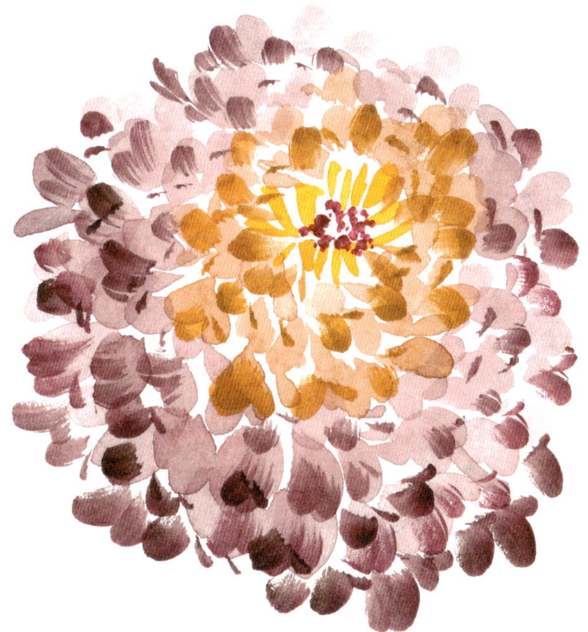

Step 9.

Repeat Step 8a until the Violet petals are finished and then do the same thing as in step 8b, this time with the Cadmium-Free Yellow, Sepia and Verzino Violet mixture.

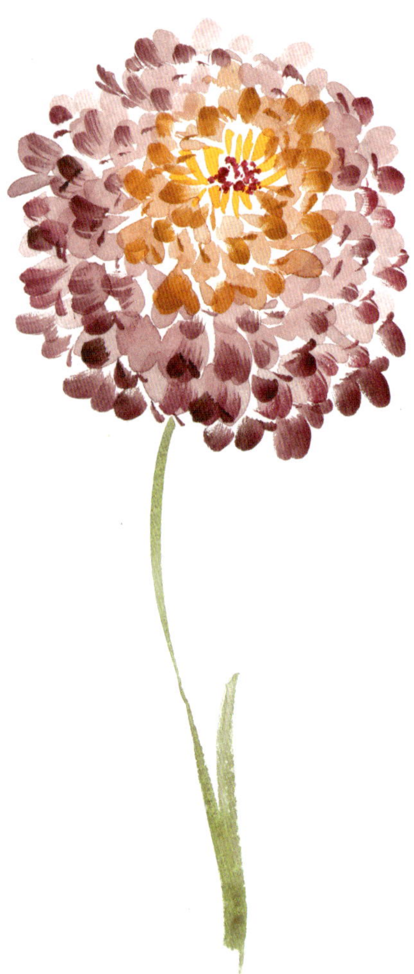

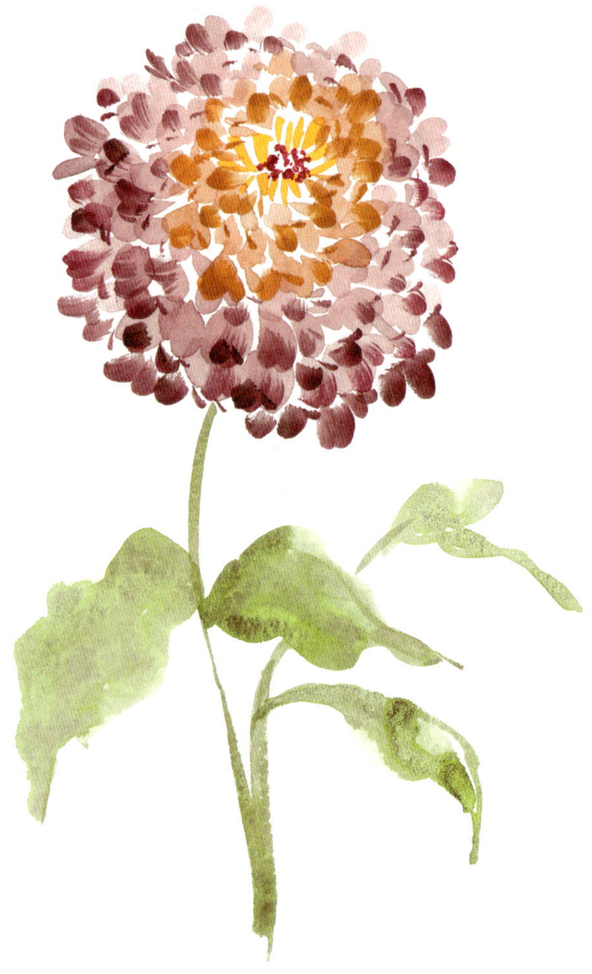

Step 10.

Be sure your size 6 brushes are rinsed and mix Green Apatite Genuine to BC on one brush and to CSC on the other. Paint your stem using BC.

Tip: This color is super fun. It has properties that cause the pigment to separate, which results in a color that ranges from intense gemstone green to dark gray-green, leaving behind a texture akin to fine sand. Try not to fight the color by smoothing it out; allow it to spread as it likes.

Step 11.

Paint your leaves in BC, using the compound stroke method (page 31). While they are wet, run the brush along the edges to give a little more zigzag structure to the leaves.

Step 12.

Using your size 6 brush loaded with CSC, add some gestural outlining (page 41) to your leaves and a darker line of contrast along the edge of the main stem. Try to allow your strokes to remain loose and somewhat careless. Do what you can to give yourself room to play without much expectation.

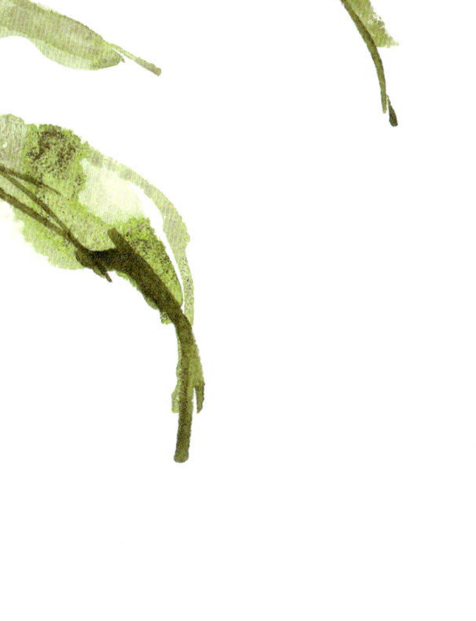

Striped Flaming Flag Tulips

Bouncing off our previous project, I've chosen a striped flaming flag tulip for us to do next, and while it is likely going to be more challenging than a solid colored tulip, I know you have it in you to step up and show up to this project. My hope is not to give you lessons you nail 100 percent on the first go, but rather give you ones you can revisit again and again, each time learning something new and intriguing about watercolor and honing your style. As far as structure goes, the tulip is probably one of the simplest; however, we shouldn't allow simple to be confused with easy. It takes thoughtfulness to create a flower consisting of only a few petals. It means we need to be intentional about our strokes and, though keeping loose, maintaining intentionality with the marks we make. We're going to be using another white tone consisting of two colors (which will continue to warm us up for the final chapter, where we work solely with white watercolor!) and creating some really beautiful bleeds. For a refresher on bleeds, see page 26.

Supplies

One size 6 round brush

One size 10 round brush

Canson 140-lb (300-gsm) cold-press paper

Palette

Verzino Violet (Flower)

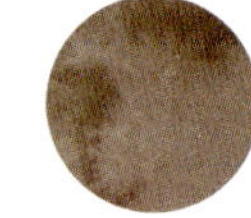

Sepia (Flower & Leaves)

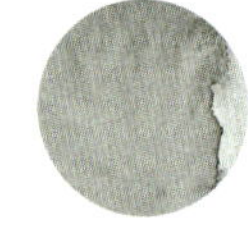

Lamp Black (Flower)

Green Gold (Leaves)

Sap Green (Leaves)

Verzino Violet + Sepia

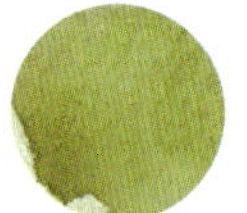

Sap Green + Sepia

Green Gold + Lamp Black

Preparing the Palette

Mix Verzino Violet and Sepia to BC and CSC (page 16). This hue falls under "muted colors"; refer to page 22 if you'd like a refresh.

Load your size 6 brush with BC and set off to the side.

Mix Green Gold and Lamp Black to BC, and then dilute one step further by adding water to decrease the value. (Refer to page 16 for a refresh about consistencies.) This is essentially a watered-down version of BC. It doesn't need to be exactly the same shade as mine; as long as there is a slight difference, that will be enough. We'll refer to this consistency as LC.

Load the size 10 brush with this mixture and set it off to the side.

Please note: We will be working wet-into-wet (page 29) here, so the first steps will be combined to show the proper result. To set yourself up for success, take the time to load your brushes with enough water so that when you make the stroke, there is enough moisture on the paper to then add the next color. Be sure you have enough of the white tone on your brush to execute a damp stroke. Get down at eye level with the paper and check it for dry areas or pockets of excess moisture. If dry, dip into your pile and rewet the area. If too wet, take a clean brush, blotted off on a paper towel, and lift a bit of the moisture from the paper. This step is well worth the effort and ultimately decides the success of the project.

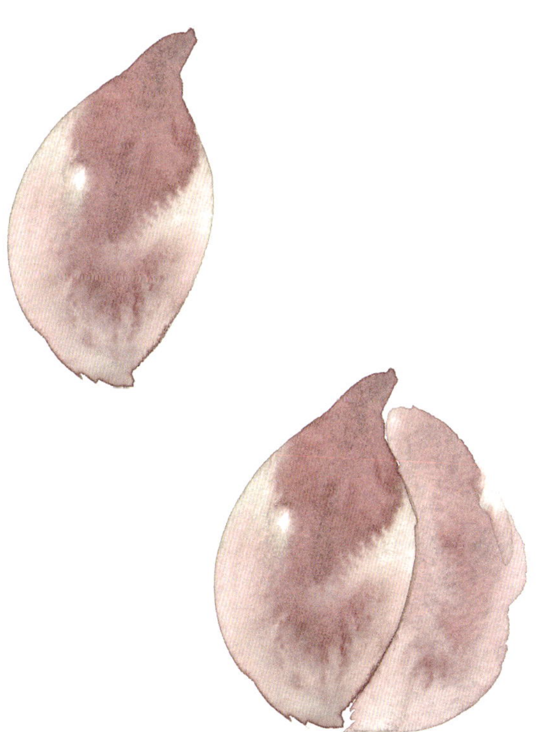

Step 1a.

Using your size 10 brush loaded with Green Gold and Lamp Black in BC, paint the first petal of the tulip near the top of the page, slightly off to the left. This is done by using the compound stroke technique (page 31). Begin at the top and curve your brush outward as you pull down and conclude by bringing it inward to create the base. Repeat on the other side.

Step 1b.

Using your size 6 brush loaded with the Verzino Violet and Sepia mixture in BC, immediately touch the toe of the brush to the tip of the flower while it's still wet. Pause and study how the paint moves through the petal. Results will vary here depending on how wet the media was: too wet and the color may run through the entire petal; too dry and the paint won't move. Still working wet-into-wet, touch the toe of the brush to the base of the petal. Repeat this step until the color has saturated both the tip, base and middle of the petal.

Step 2.

Repeating Step 1, create your next (middle) petal. This time, drop in the Verzino Violet and Sepia mixture at the right side of the petal while wet. Carefully work your way toward the first petal until there is no white space between them.

Step 3.

Create the third petal, on the far right, by repeating Steps 1 and 2. This time, allow the white tone to dry a bit (roughly 30 seconds to 1 minute) so that when you drop in the colored mixture, it is more controlled and doesn't spread throughout the entire petal. You can also get down at eye level with the paper to ensure it is damp but not pooling with water. Ideally, the top and the bottom of the petal have a bit of the white mixture revealed.

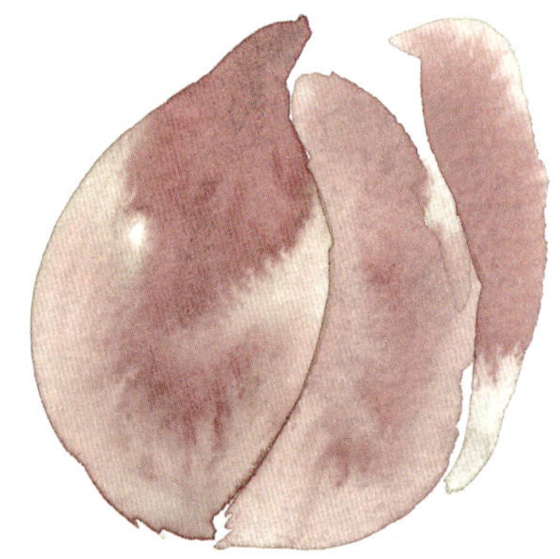

Step 4.

Using your size 6 brush in Verzino Violet and Sepia in CSC, begin to add the detail veining through the first petal. This is done by coming up on the toe of the brush and painting fine lines in a downward stroke. Keep these lines loose and irregular. Think of these as the birthmarks of the flower: no two exactly alike. Carefully darken the areas where the petals are folded beneath the other petals.

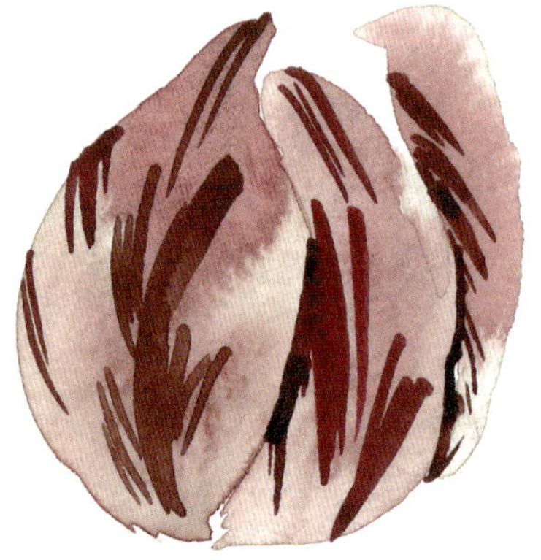

Step 5.

Add one last gestural stroke (page 32) at the back of the flower to indicate a shadowed, dark petal.

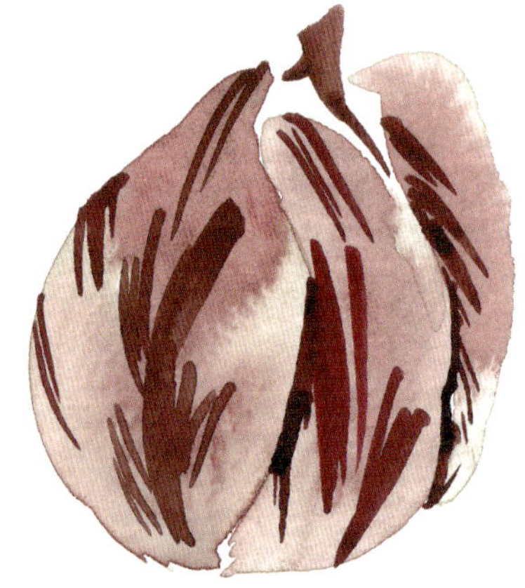

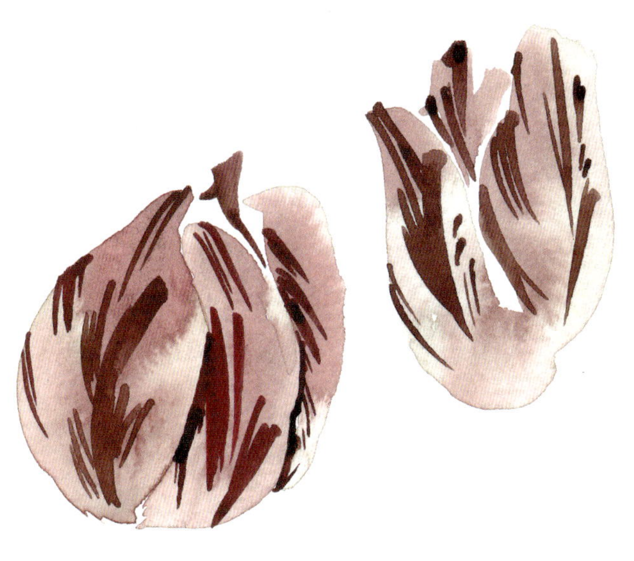

Step 6.

Create your next tulip by repeating Steps 1 through 5; however, take new liberties with the shape of the petal so that it is not an exact copy of the first flower. My petals are simple strokes (page 30) using the full belly of the size 10 brush. I also opted to let my larger petals not overlap and for this flower to consist of more white tone, meaning I allowed the Green Gold and Lamp Black mixture in BC to dry a bit longer (1 to 2 minutes) and then added the Verzino Violet and Sepia mixture.

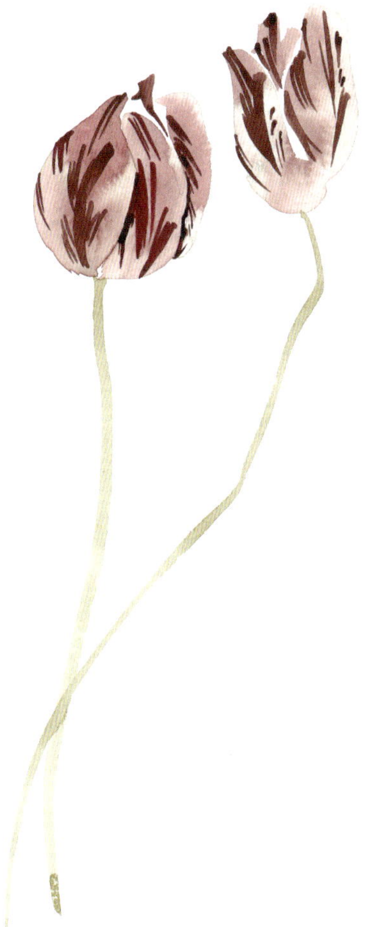

Step 7.

Rinse your size 10 brush until no pink remains. Mix together Sap Green and Sepia and attach stems to the tulips. These stems should have a curvy, almost noodle-like feel to them.

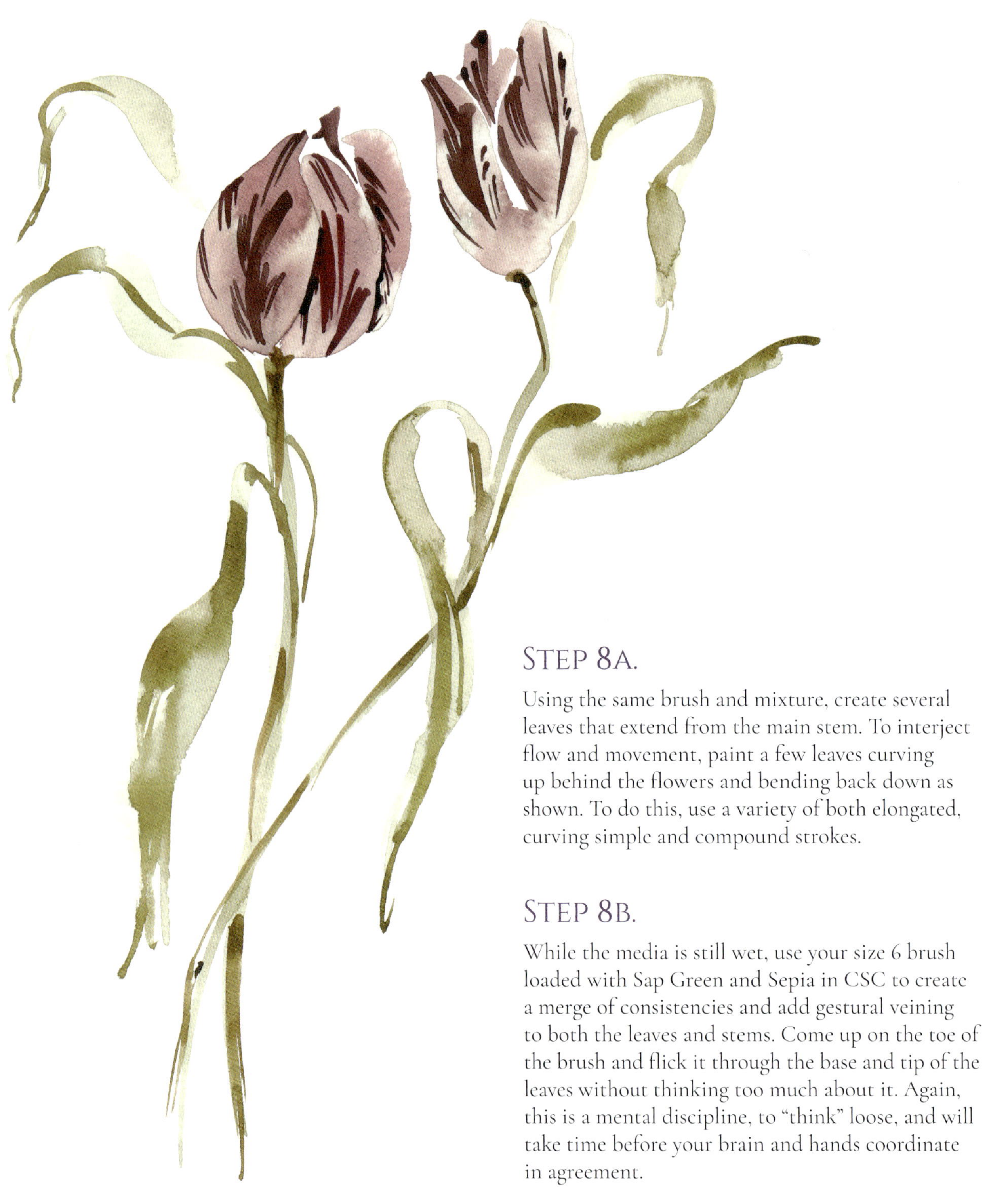

Step 8a.

Using the same brush and mixture, create several leaves that extend from the main stem. To interject flow and movement, paint a few leaves curving up behind the flowers and bending back down as shown. To do this, use a variety of both elongated, curving simple and compound strokes.

Step 8b.

While the media is still wet, use your size 6 brush loaded with Sap Green and Sepia in CSC to create a merge of consistencies and add gestural veining to both the leaves and stems. Come up on the toe of the brush and flick it through the base and tip of the leaves without thinking too much about it. Again, this is a mental discipline, to "think" loose, and will take time before your brain and hands coordinate in agreement.

Chrysanthemum

This is another one of those flowers that can seem a bit overwhelming at first if we were to approach it with a strictly botanical intention. Rather than trying to pin down every detail with paint, instead we'll lean on gestural stroke (page 32) to give our petals plenty of movement and give ourselves the freedom to play with the details. Mums come in a variety of colors, so be sure revisit this project again in the future, using a different palette. For this project, I've selected a beautiful earthy pink, another muted color, keeping the pink vivid but not bright. Brushes ready—let's head in!

Supplies

Two size 6 round brushes

Canson 140-lb (300-gsm) cold-press paper

Palette

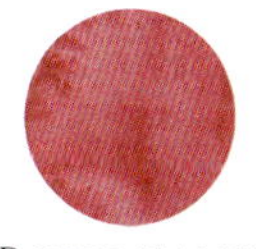

Bordeaux (Petals)

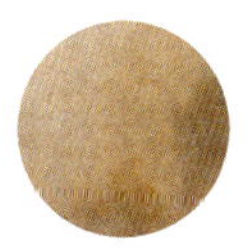

Van Dyke Brown (Petals, Stem & Leaves)

Naples Yellow (Center)

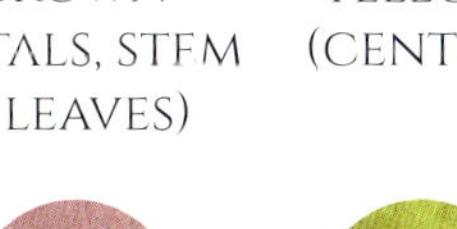

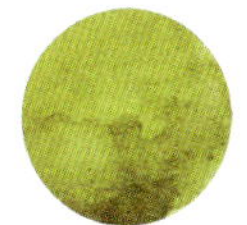

Sap Green

Bordeaux + Van Dyke Brown

Sap Green + Van Dyke Brown

Preparing the Palette

Mix Bordeaux and Van Dyke Brown to BC and CSC (page 16). Load a size 6 brush with the BC mixture and set it off to the side.

Using your other size 6 brush, mix Naples Yellow to BC and set it off to the side.

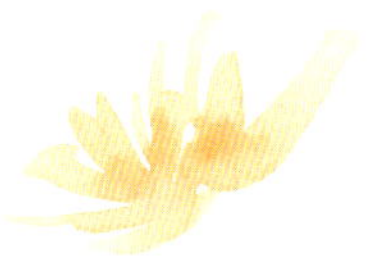

Step 1.

We will be using a variety of simple and compound strokes (pages 30 and 31) to create this flower.

Begin with the center, using your size 6 brush loaded with Naples Yellow at BC. This should be a series of fine lines, very gestural; this is mainly to allow the petals to have a place from which to extend. Allow the media to dry completely.

STEP 2.

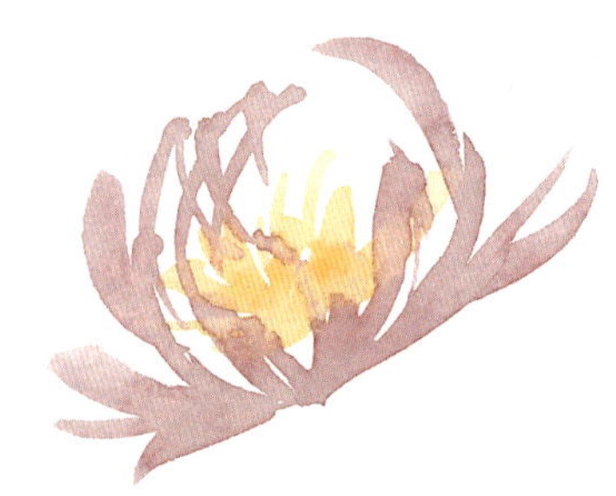

Use your size 6 brush loaded with Bordeaux and Van Dyke Brown in BC to create the first ring of petals. If you look at your reference picture, you may notice how the inner petals curl toward the center. To recreate this loosely, you will use the toe of your brush to paint fine lines that crisscross through the center. Think of a C shape. You may find it easiest to use downward strokes for the petals, beginning with the tip of the flower and gradually increasing pressure as you work toward the base. Wait until the petals are fully dry before proceeding to the next step.

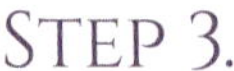

STEP 3.

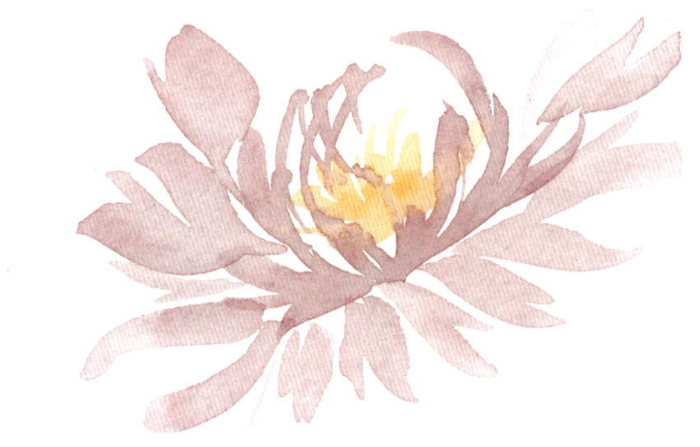

Create the second ring of petals. These should be slightly bigger than the first ring and, as always—variety is key! Take liberties here to implement a combination of simple, compound and gestural strokes (pages 30-32), as you work your way from left to right (or right to left if you're left-handed) to avoid smearing the work. As you reload the brush with more paint, allow some petals to be somewhere close to light consistency. This can be done simply by using the very last bit of paint on the brush before reloading again.

STEP 4.

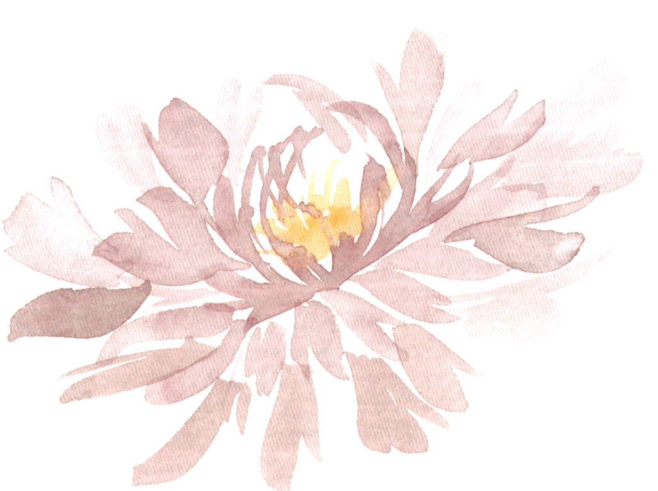

Repeat Steps 1 and 2 to create the third and fourth ring of petals.

Tip: *Look for the space between two petals on the second ring and place your petals for the third ring in there.*

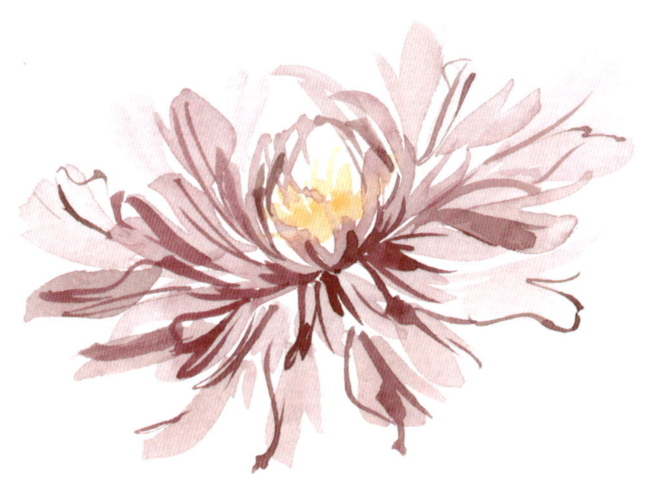

Step 5.

Load your size 6 brush with the mixture you mixed in CSC. Add gestural veining and outlining to the petals. Just outside the first ring of petals should be the darkest marks, as this is where the flower changes position and the petals fold outward. From there, take liberties to place marks where they feel right and natural to you. You can make this step as detailed or simple as you like! Be sure all of the petals are dry before proceeding to the next step.

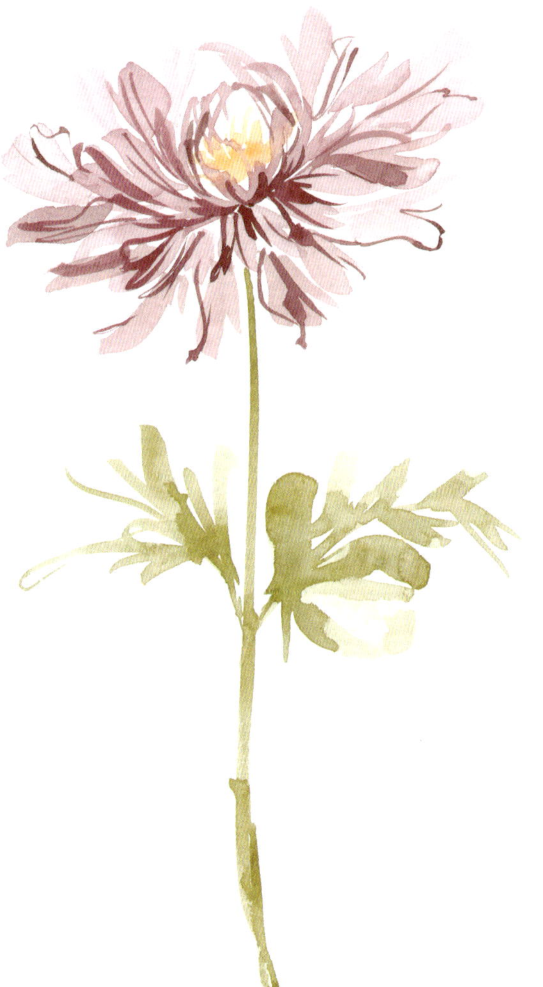

Step 6a.

Rinse your brush and mix together your pile of Sap Green and Van Dyke Brown to reactivate it. Paint a stem in BC extending from the bottom middle of the flower.

Step 6b.

Add leaves to both sides of the stem. These leaves are created by first painting a line to serve as the middle or the vein of the leaf, and then attaching simple strokes to it to shape the leaf. The leaves turn gestural when you add in the fine lines extending from the vein.

Step 6c.

Optional: While the media is still wet, load the brush with the mixture in CSC and work wet-into-wet on the leaves and stem (page 29).

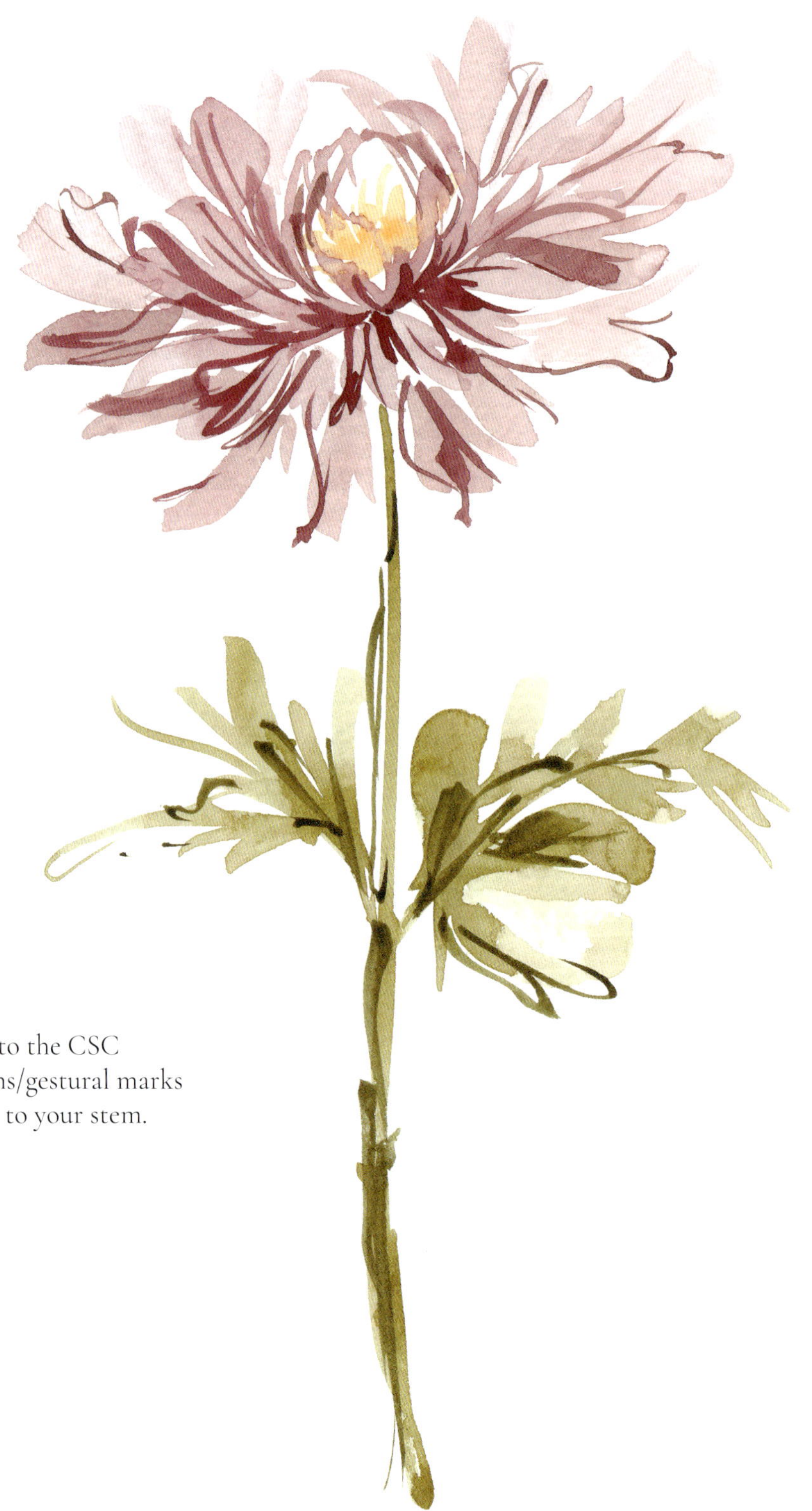

Step 7.

Add a bit more Van Dyke Brown to the CSC mixture and add a few darker veins/gestural marks to the leaves and a darker shadow to your stem.

Wild Rose

Wild roses have appeared in my work throughout all my artistic evolutions. For some reason I never tire of painting them, I think, because there is something inherently approachable about the pin-wheel structure that instantly puts me at ease. The center of the flower, too, feels very interpretable so that I manage not to lose myself in the details. There will be room for you to take liberties, which I always encourage, and although I've thrown in a bit of a twist with the way we will paint our petals (always with a goal of conditioning those muscles), it's going to be a lot of fun.

Supplies

Two size 6 round brushes

One size 10 round brush

One size 2 round brush

Canson 140-lb (300-gsm) cold-press paper

Palette

Bordeaux (Petals)

Permanent Rose (Petals)

Naples Yellow (Center)

New Gamboge (Center)

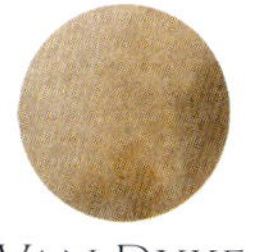

Van Dyke Brown (Center)

Greenish Umber (Stem & Leaves)

Greenish Umber + New Gamboge

Bordeaux + Permanent Rose

Preparing the Palette

Using your first size 6 brush, mix Bordeaux and Permanent Rose to BC and CSC (page 16) and set it off to the side.

Using your second size 6 brush, load it with Naples Yellow in BC.

Some Real Talk Before We Begin

To continue evolving in our skills, we are going to be creating our rose petals a little differently than we have in previous projects. We will first use clean water to wet the area we intend to paint and then, using our size 6 brush loaded with Bordeaux and Permanent Rose in BC, we will drop in the color onto the paper.

Sound easy enough?

It *isn't*.

This is not meant to discourage you; this is meant to *assure you* that it's supposed to be a challenge. It will be. I want you knowing that going in. Many of the projects in this book, you will conquer on the first or second try. But I wouldn't be doing my job if I didn't stretch you with these lessons, and this project will be one you revisit again and again as your muscles get stronger and your instincts fine-tuned. Try to keep in mind that the structure is nothing more than a five-petal pinwheel flower (page 37). It's by adding nuances that we elevate the flower and give it room to become what it is.

Step 1.

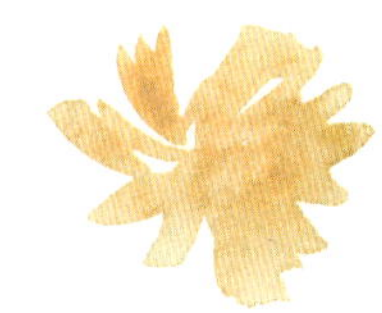

Using your size 6 brush loaded with Naples Yellow in BC, make a quarter-sized (1-inch [2.5-cm]-diameter) center in the middle of the page. This is a circle that has been shaped on the ends with the toe of the brush to resemble a star shape. Be sure this area is fully dry before proceeding to the next step.

Step 2A.

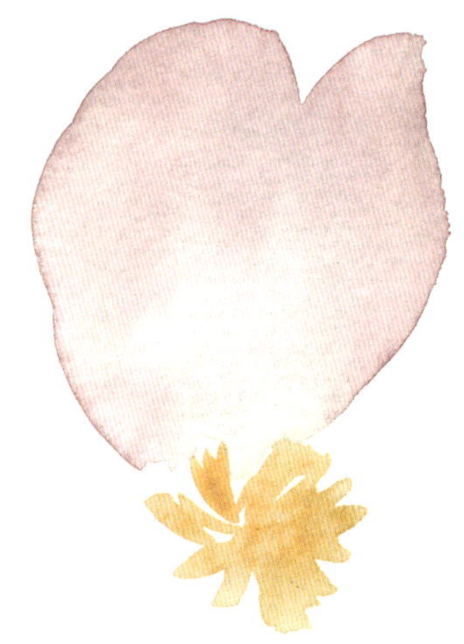

Note: Steps 2A and 2B need to be combined for the best results. With the size 10 brush and clean water, shape the first petal, using the compound stroke technique (page 31). Instead of long, thin strokes, think wider strokes. The entire petal should resemble a heart shape.

Tip: *Take your* time *with this step. The following step's success depends on it. Get down at eye level with the paper to be sure it's evenly damp. You need to account for the time it takes you to pick up your brush, swirl it through the pink mixture and drop it in. It can feel overwhelming at first, but I promise it becomes second nature as you practice.*

Step 2B.

Using your size 6 brush loaded with the Bordeaux and Permanent Rose in BC, drop in the color at the tip of the petal and along the edges. Gently guide the color in downward strokes, stopping halfway down the petal, then use your size 10 brush damp with clean water to fill in the rest of the petal. We want the color to gradually fade to a very light pink as it reaches the center of the flower.

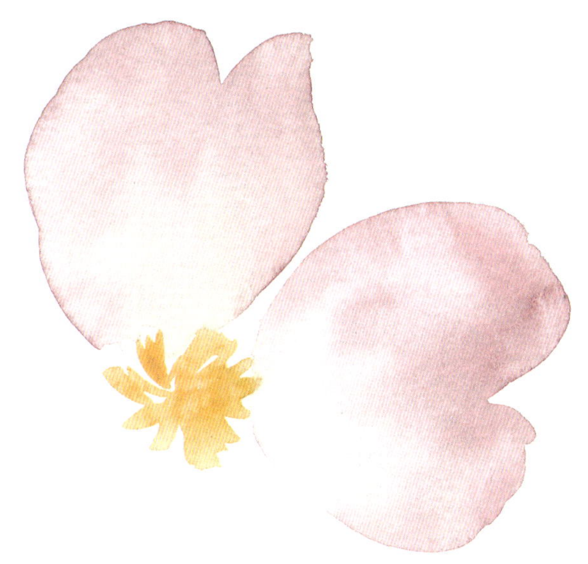

Step 3.

Repeat Step 2 to create your second petal. Again, this should resemble a sideways heart.

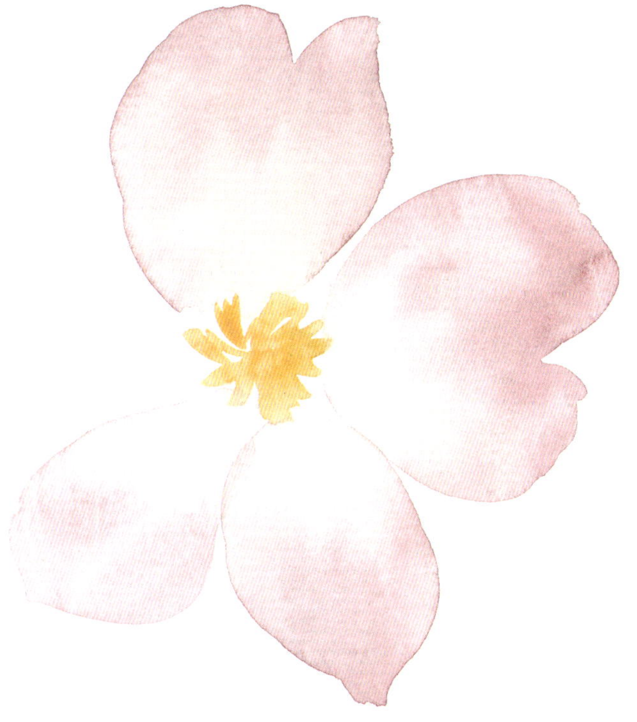

Step 4.

Repeat Step 2 to create the third and fourth petals. These petals should be significantly smaller than the first two and more leaf-like in structure. We are attempting to give the flower as a whole the perspective of tilting slightly on its side.

Step 5.

Paint your last petal, taking care to shape it so that it curves up slightly, maintaining the perspective we're aiming for. One side should be higher than the other. Allow the area to dry fully.

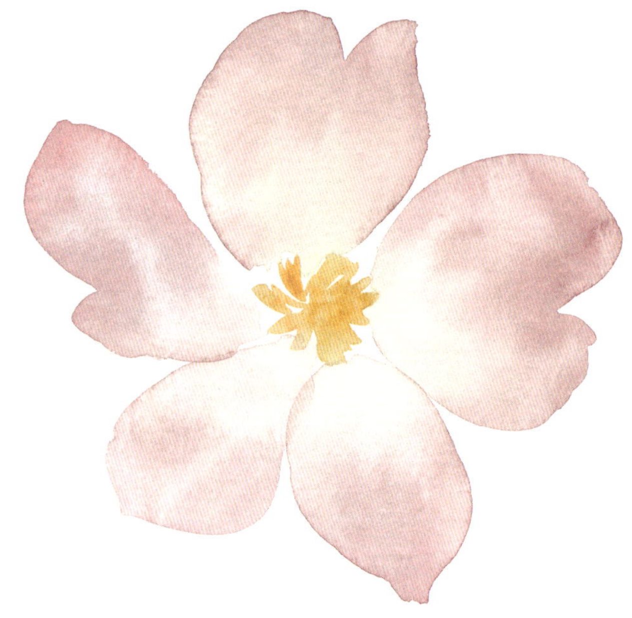

Step 6A.

Load a size 6 brush with New Gamboge in CSC and add an outer ring of gestural dotting to cover up where the petals and the center meet.

Step 6B.

Using the toe of your brush, paint the filament (these are the fine lines extending from the center). No need to wait until things are dry.

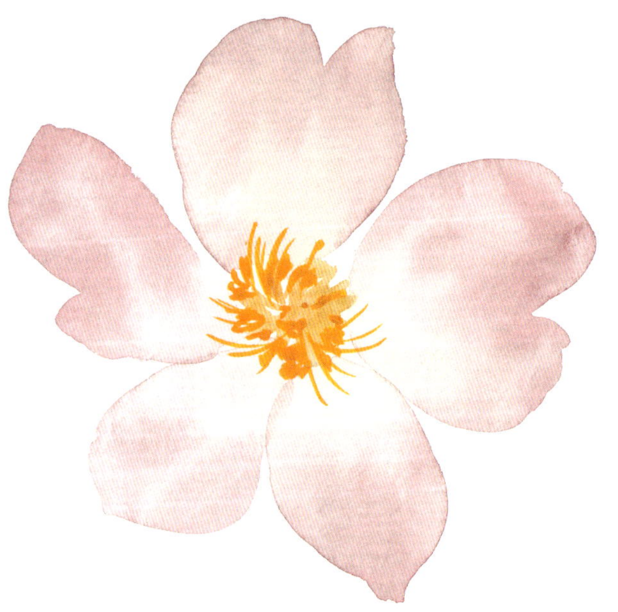

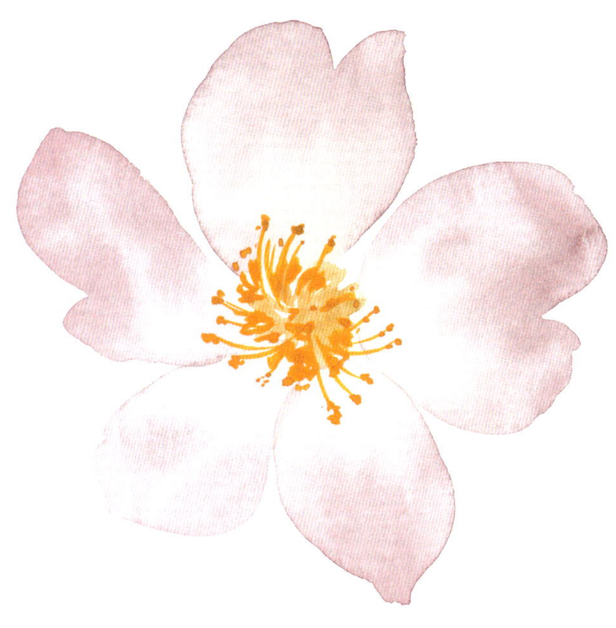

Step 7.

Be sure the area is fully dry. Add the anther (the small bean shapes at the end of the fine lines) by painting gestural dotting at the ends of the filament.

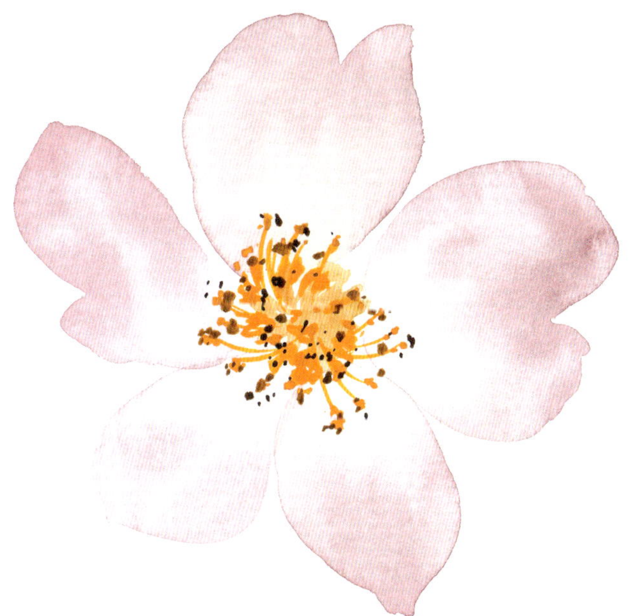

Step 8.

Make sure the previous layer is dry. Next, mix Van Dyke Brown to CSC, and add another layer of gestural dotting on top of the anther.

Step 9.

Now, we will add some shading to the petals. Load a size 6 brush with Bordeaux and Permanent Rose in BC, and use the toe of your brush to pull down, in a stroke, from the tip of the petal toward the middle of the petal.

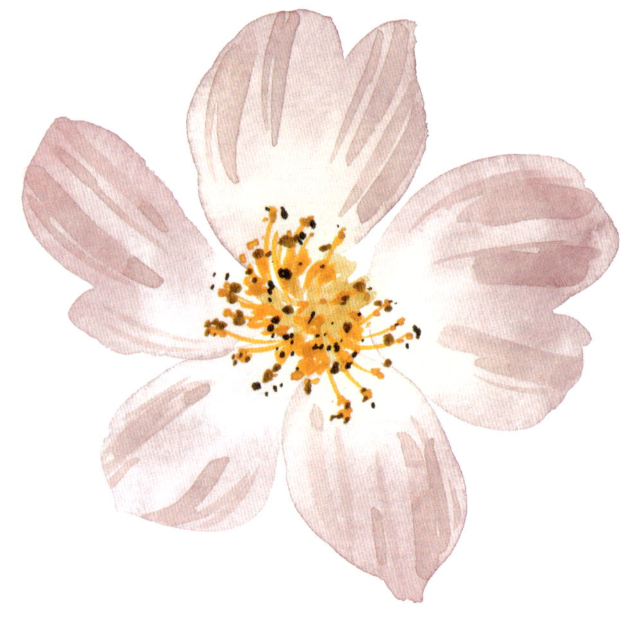

Step 10.

Repeat Step 9, except increase the value of the color by one shade. This consistency should not be quite CSC, but halfway between BC and CSC. This ratio would look something close to 65 percent paint and 35 percent water.

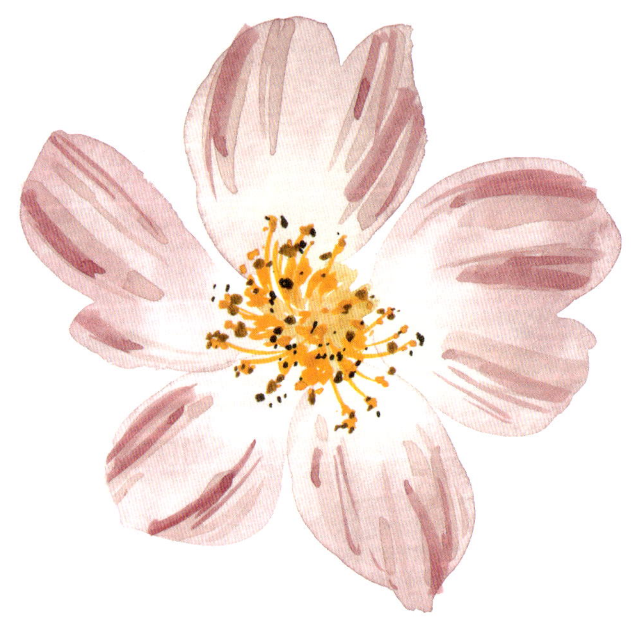

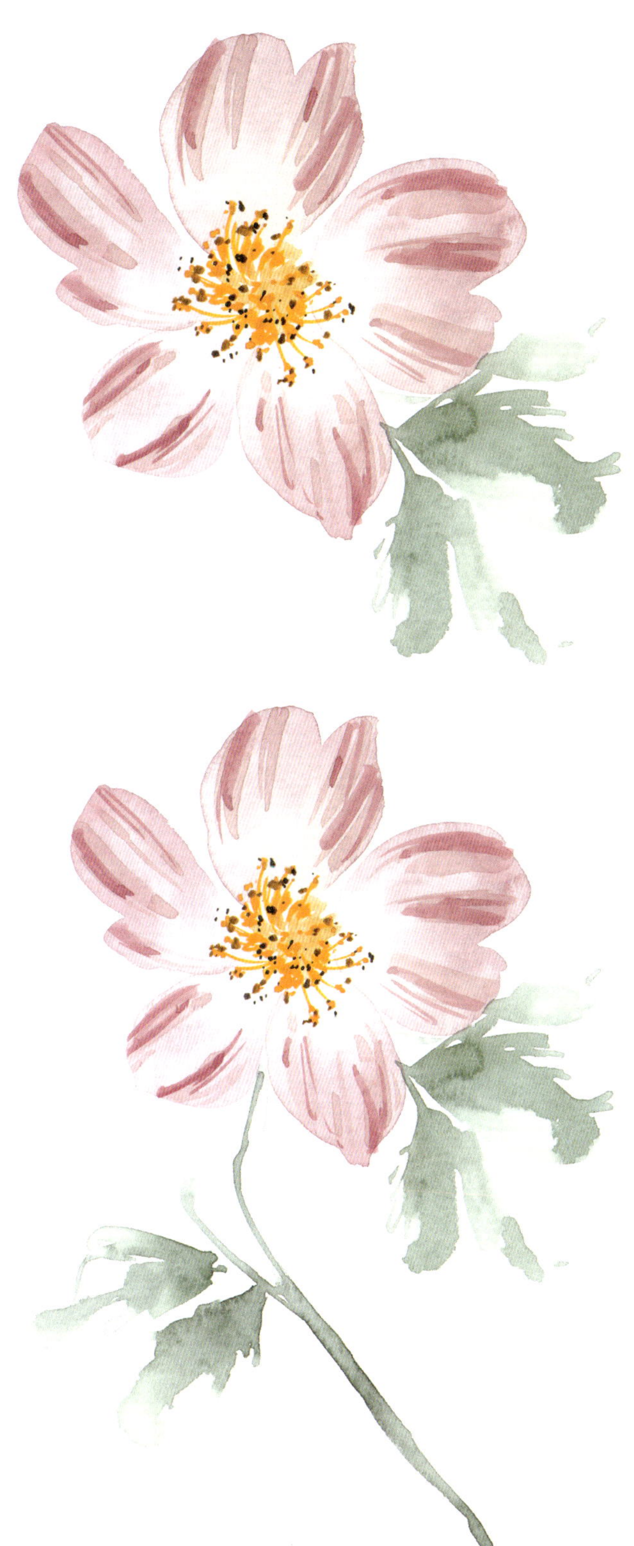

Step 11.

Load your size 10 brush with Greenish Umber and New Gamboge in BC and paint three leaves extending from the right side of the flower. Use the compound stroke technique for the basic shape and then use the toe of the brush to shape accordingly. *Optional:* While the leaves are wet, drop in the Greenish Umber mixture at the base of the leaf in CSC for more interest.

Note: It may appear as though there is white pigment in my leaf; however, that effect was achieved when I was shaping the leaf and that part of my brush had mostly water in it. Although it would be nice to have an a + b = c recipe every time, this isn't true or possible for watercolor. We are not measuring and weighing each gram of paint and water, so there is no way to have repeated identical results—this is true for professional artists, too! Keep this is mind as you work and know that results will vary. The important thing is to keep exploring and taking risks. By now you know exactly how to use the strokes we've learned. Consider alternating them by flicking your brush at the edges of the leaf to create rough edges. Use the toe on one leaf and full belly on another. I encourage liberties here.

Step 12a.

Paint a stem and finish with two more leaves. For this severe angle, you will bring the brush straight down and then turn it and drag it to the right to create a diagonal stem.

Step 12b.

For a more detailed leaf, you could add gestural veining. I've opted not to because the petals are fairly ornate and I like balance between complicated and simple.

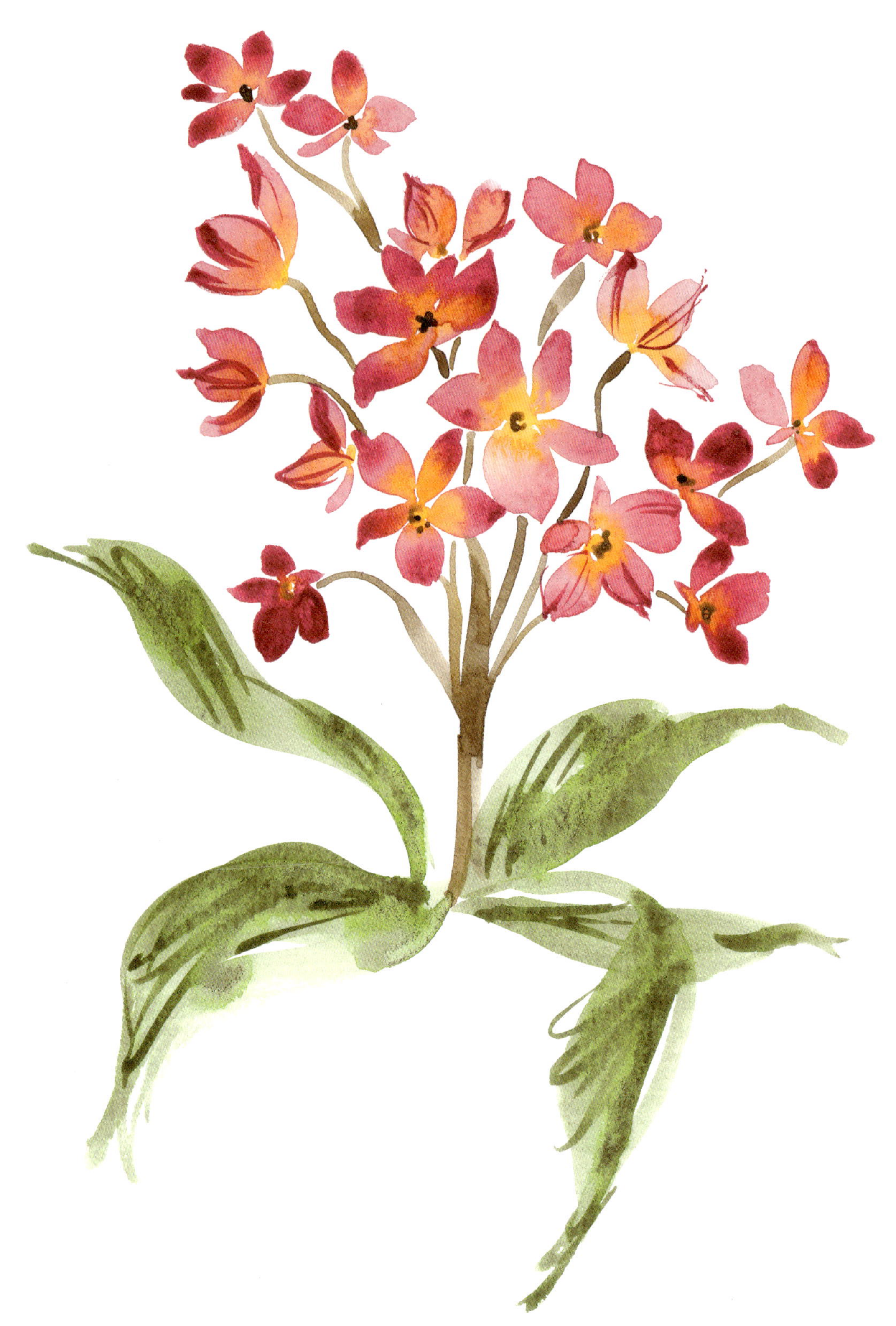

A Hint of Paradise

If you've ever visited a tropical destination and took a moment to observe the local flora, you may have wondered, *What kind of flower is that?* If so, there's a possibility we'll be painting it in this section featuring tropical flowers! These exotic blooms are an expert way of adding a bit of flair and personality to calmer compositions and tend to be more conducive to an expressive nature—meaning we are going to use color and gestural strokes (page 32) to convey a sense of wild abandon. You'll love these flowers for their anything-but-plain appearance and ability to draw attention. Let's head in now and have a look at our first project together!

Bluebird Hibiscus

Kicking off this chapter, we have one of the prettiest flowers I have yet to stumble upon. Talk about a showstopper! Again, we'll call on the five-petal pinwheel flower (page 37) to serve as a groundwork structure, with a few new modifications. The colors we will be mixing are some of my very favorite muted colors (if you find yourself drawn to them, similar hues can be found in the Midnight Series from the Color Guides on my website), which will pave the way for some stunning bleeds. More on muted colors on page 22.

Supplies

Two size 10 round brushes

One size 6 round brush

Canson 140-lb (300-gsm) cold-press paper

Palette

Indigo (petals)

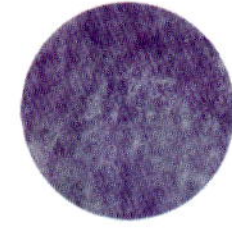

Cobalt Violet Deep (petals)

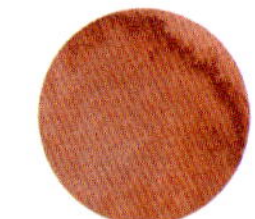

Quinacridone Burnt Scarlet (petals)

Naples Yellow (center)

Greenish Umber (leaves)

New Gamboge (leaves)

Indigo + Cobalt Violet Deep

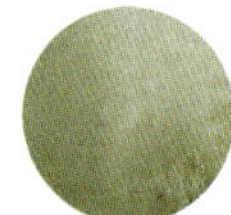

Greenish Umber + New Gamboge

Preparing the Palette

Using your size 10 brushes, mix together Indigo and Cobalt Violet Deep to BC and CSC (page 16) and set it off to the side. Load each one with a different consistency.

Step 1a.

Using your size 10 brush loaded with Indigo and Cobalt Violet Deep in BC, create this first petal in the pinwheel flower. Note that these petals have a ruffly edge and you will need to use the toe of your brush and wiggle it along the edges to create some structure.

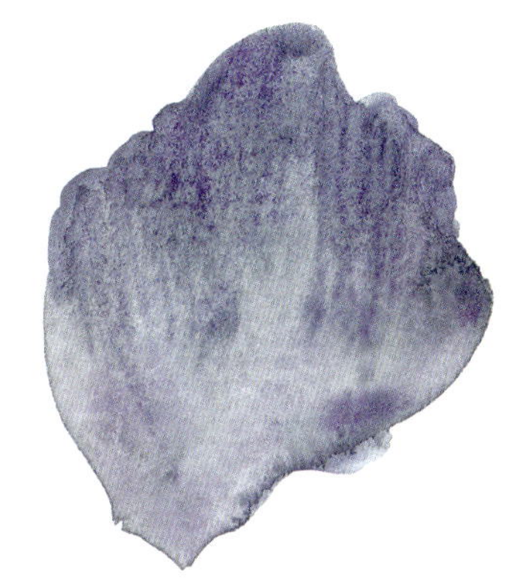

Step 1b.

While the petal is still wet, use your other size 10 brush to drop in the mixture in CSC along the tip and edges of the petal. As it dries (get down at eye level with the paper to check how moist it is), use the toe of the brush to paint fine lines in CSC through the petal, starting at the top and pulling them down toward the middle of the petal. As with our Wild Rose (page 137), we are aiming for the darkest color at the tips of the petals and then gradually seeing it fade toward the center. Depending on how your versions are mixed, you may need to repeat this step two or three more times to achieve the darker edges.

Note: The colors we are working with have beautiful natural properties that will work in your favor as you blend consistencies. If you're using the same brand (Daniel Smith, for instance), you may notice some separating of the pigment. Also note that your mixture may favor a bluer tint if you're adding more Indigo, or purple tint if adding more of the Violet. There is no incorrect ratio here and I invite you to modify the mixture to your liking.

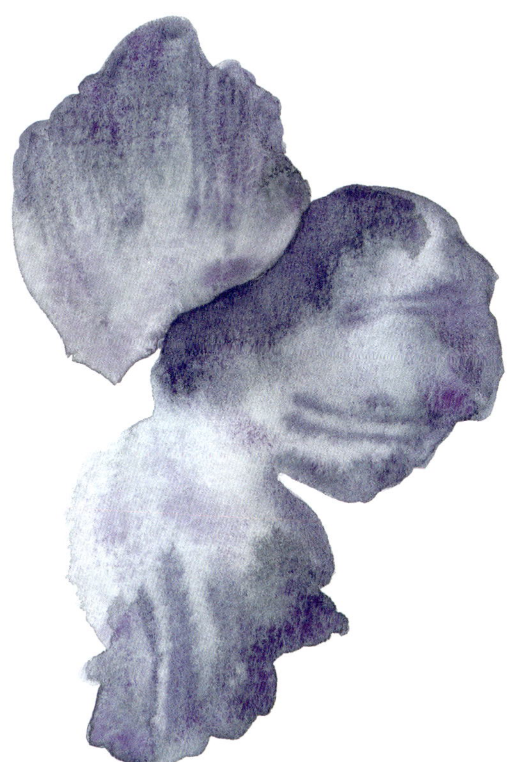

Step 2.

Repeat Step 1a to create the second and third petals. To create the shadow behind the first petal, first be sure the first petal is completely dry. Then, run the toe of the size 10 brush loaded with the Indigo and Cobalt Violet Deep mixture in CSC along the edge of the first petal. If your media is wet, the color will flow dark. Use the other size 10 brush loaded with the Indigo and Cobalt Violet Deep mixture in BC to guide it gently to fill in the remainder of the petal.

STEP 3.

Repeat Step 1 to create the fourth and fifth petals. As always, I'd love for you to take liberties here, noting the most exciting details to you, which make this flower your own. You'll see I opted not to include additional shadows behind the petals; I feel there is enough separation between each one. You can absolutely add more shadowing if you like or even gestural outlining (page 41) as we have done in previous projects.

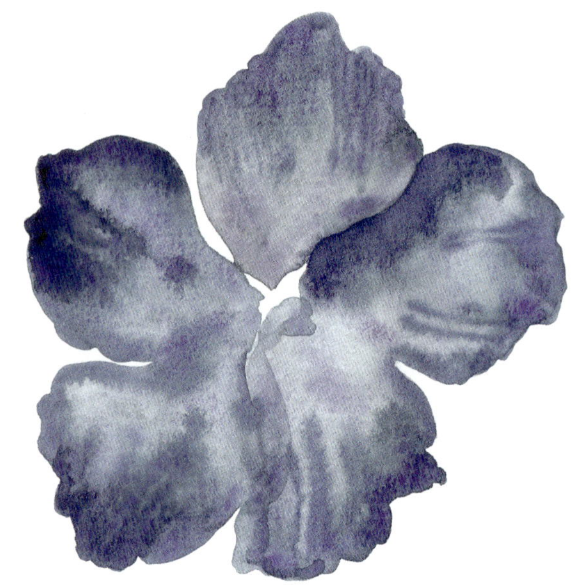

STEP 4.

Be sure all your petals are completely dry before attempting this next step. Using your size 6 brush, mix Quinacridone Burnt Scarlet to CSC. You will now add a dark layer on top of each petal extending from the center of the flower. Use the toe of the brush and light pressure to create fine lines (the filament) into the middle of the petals.

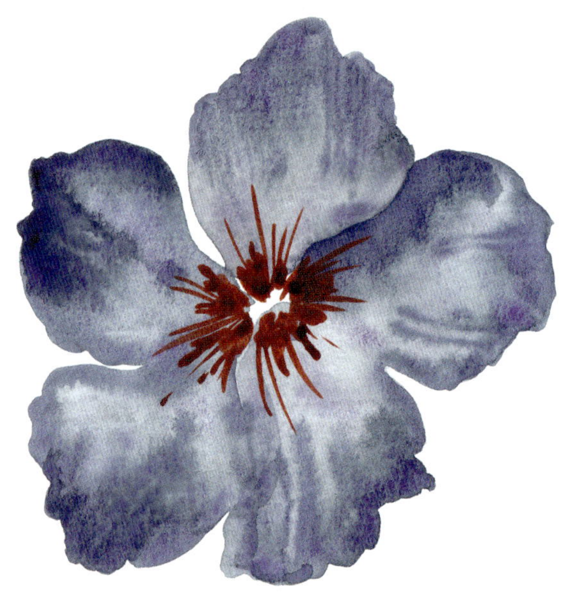

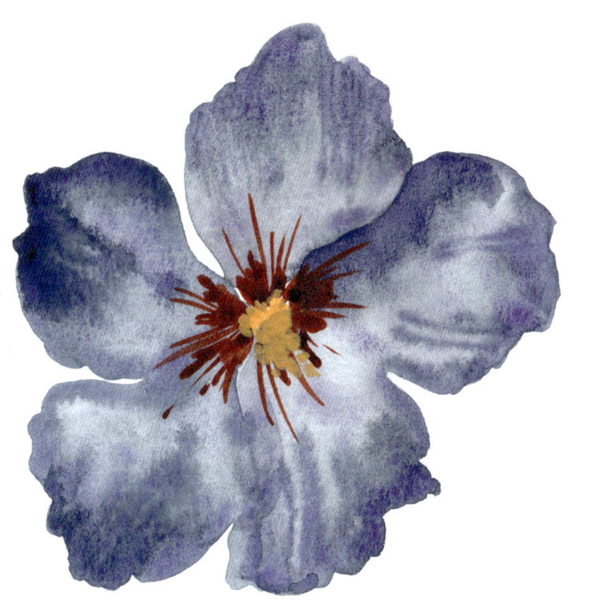

STEP 5.

Clean your size 6 brush thoroughly and mix Naples Yellow to HRC. You want this consistency to be at its very thickest, like paste. We will now add a third layer in the middle of the petal to serve as the style and anther. To do this, take the tip of the brush and poke it gently on the paper in small dots. You may need to do one layer, allow it to dry and then repeat it so that the color is solid.

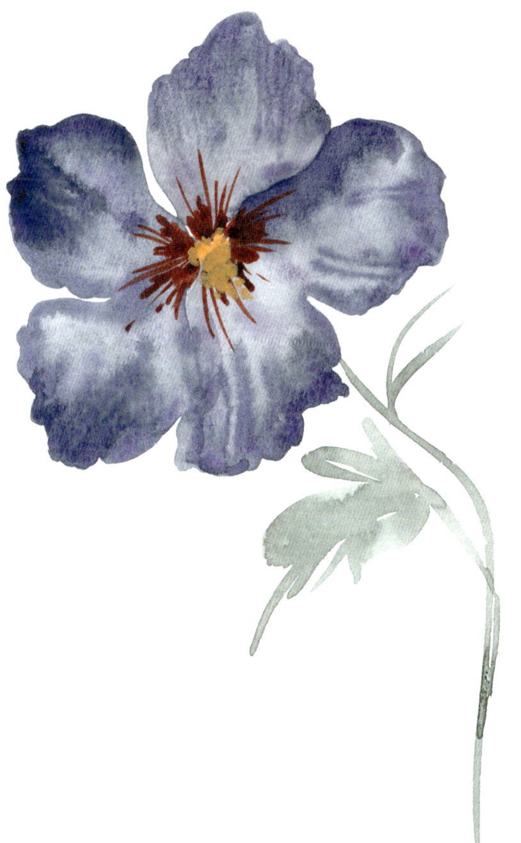

STEP 6A.

With a clean size 10 brush, mix together Greenish Umber and New Gamboge to BC and CSC. Using BC, paint a stem extending from the bottom petal of the flower. It should curve severely to the right and then drop down to run parallel with the paper.

STEP 6B.

In BC, paint your first leaf, using the compound stroke technique (page 31) and then use the toe of the brush to shape the ends of the leaf. Add two stems on the right to act as guide points for more leaves.

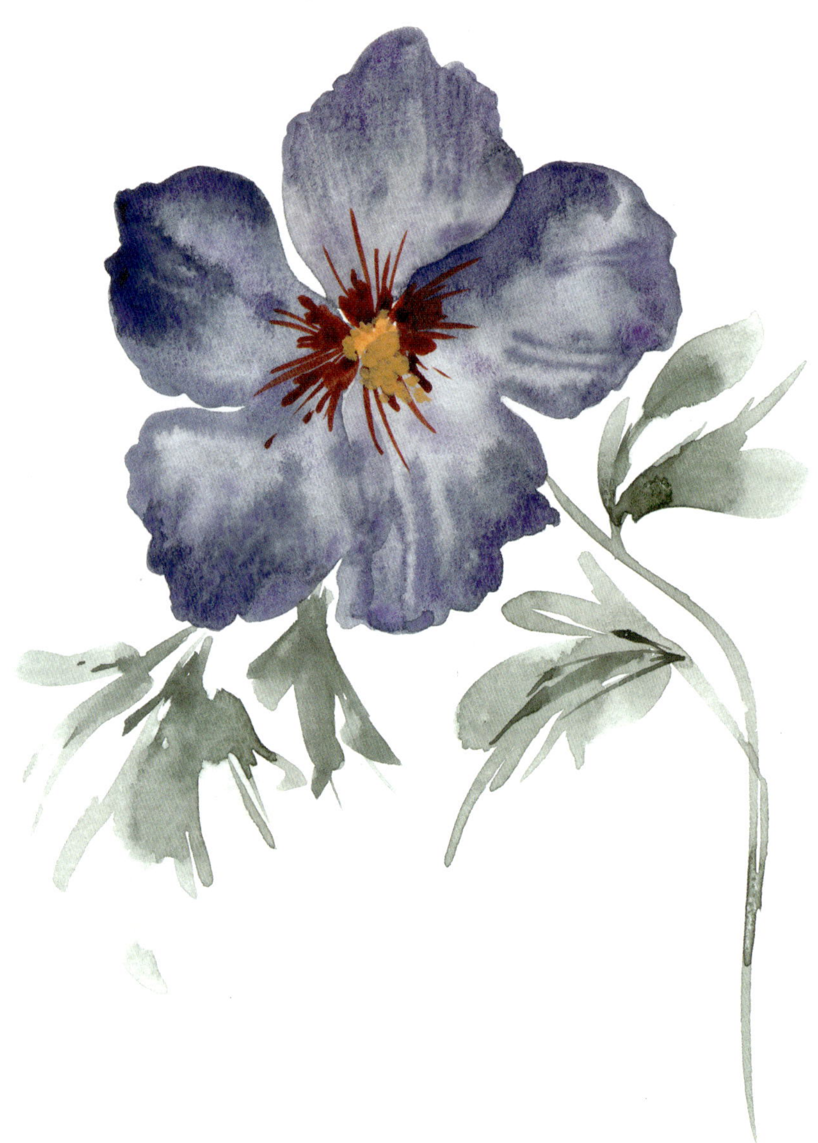

Step 7a.

Finish the piece with a few more leaves where they feel most natural to your composition. If room is tighter on one side of the page, you are welcome to place your leaves elsewhere so they suit the flow of the piece. Always feel free to add more or less leaves as well.

Step 7b.

Optional: While the media is wet, add gestural veins to the leaves in CSC. You can add them while wet, and this will result in loose, watery veins. Or you can wait until the leaves are dry for a bit more structure and clearer veins. I chose to wait until the leaves on the main stem were dry before adding darker veins. For the leaves extending from the petal, I added them while the leaves were still damp.

Plumeria

Plumeria wins the award for Most Looks like an Actual Pinwheel. Of all our pinwheel flowers, the structure is nearly identical! When I think of plumeria, I can't help but think of my only experience with tropical destinations, Hawaii, where these blooms can be found decorating nearly every hotel landscape and oftentimes stitched into leis. If the scent doesn't draw you in, perhaps the way these darling flowers huddle closely like chilly starfish will.

Supplies

Two size 8 round brushes

One size 10 round brush

Canson 140-lb (300-gsm) cold-press paper

Palette

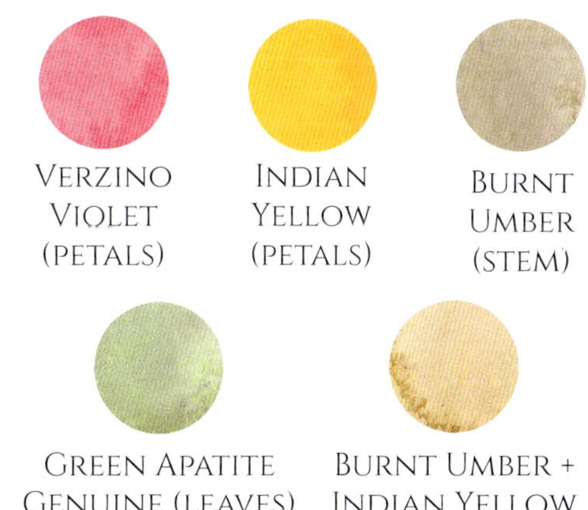

Preparing the Palette

Using one size 8 brush, mix Verzino Violet to BC and CSC (page 16). Load the brush with BC and set it off to the side.

Using the other size 8 brush, mix Indian Yellow to CSC and set it off to the side.

Note: *Although these flowers follow the five-petal pinwheel structure, we will use size, variety and positioning to prevent a stagnant-looking cluster. We will also be using wet-into-wet technique. See page 29 for a refresh.*

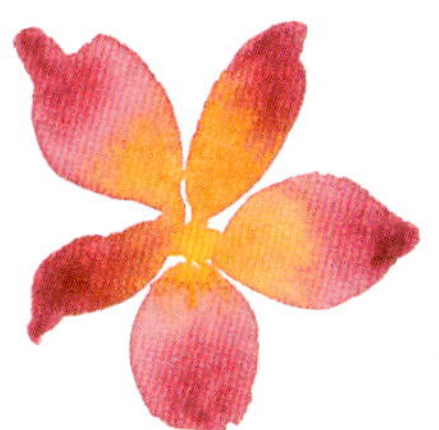

Step 1A.

Using your size 8 brush loaded with Verzino Violet in BC, paint your first pinwheel flower, about the size of a quarter (1 inch [2.5 cm] in diameter), near the middle of the page. Position it so it appears to be slightly on its side, pointing up. This is done by painting the top three petals close together and the bottom petals slightly bigger and spread apart.

Step 1B.

Using your other size 8 brush loaded with Indian Yellow, while the petals are still damp, add color to the center of the flower.

Step 1C.

Get down at eye level with the paper and observe how wet your flower is, and when it's damp but not sodden, use your size 8 brush loaded with Verzino Violet in CSC to add another layer of color on the tips of the petals.

Step 2.

Next, we will paint a larger version of the flower—closer to its actual size—and position it just above the first flower. Paint the top three petals roughly the same size, the fourth petal smaller and the fifth petal larger. I'll also rinse off a bit of my Verzino Violet in BC so it's paler than the first flower. You can choose to follow along or use the darker consistency. Repeat Step 1.

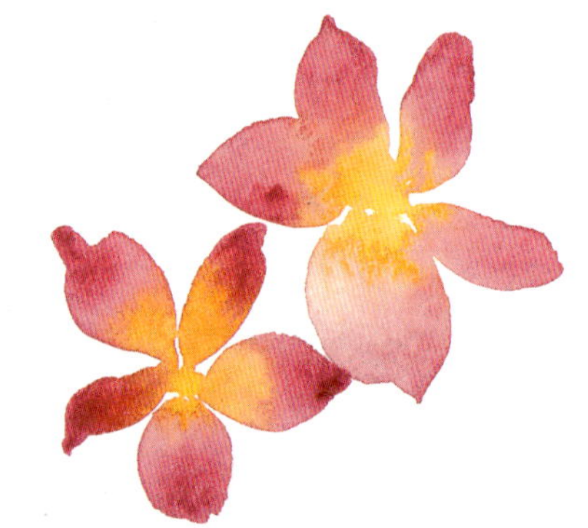

Step 3.

Now, we'll paint a closed pinwheel in Verzino Violet BC just above the second flower. Only three petals should be visible. While the petals are still wet, using your size 8 brush loaded with the Indian Yellow mixture, add it to the bottom where the flower will meet the stem.

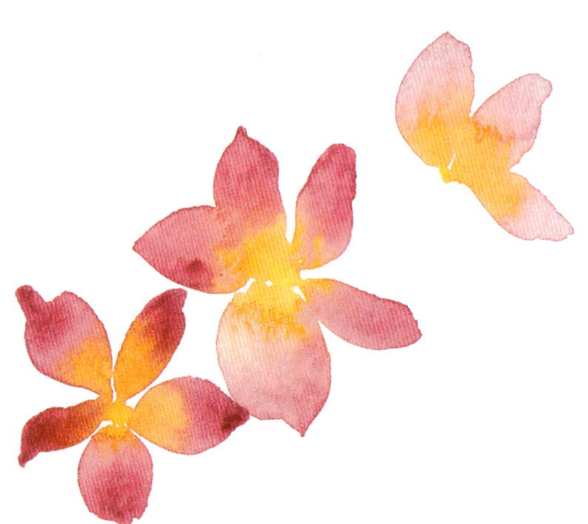

Step 4.

Next, we'll paint a downward facing pinwheel below and slightly to the right of the second flower. If you need a refresh on flower positions, see page 39. For this flower, you'll invert the steps, painting the bottom three petals largest and the top two petals small. Repeat Steps 1a and 1b but not 1c.

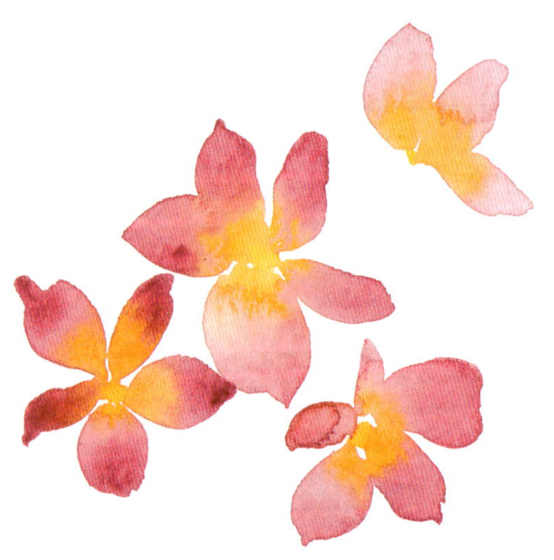

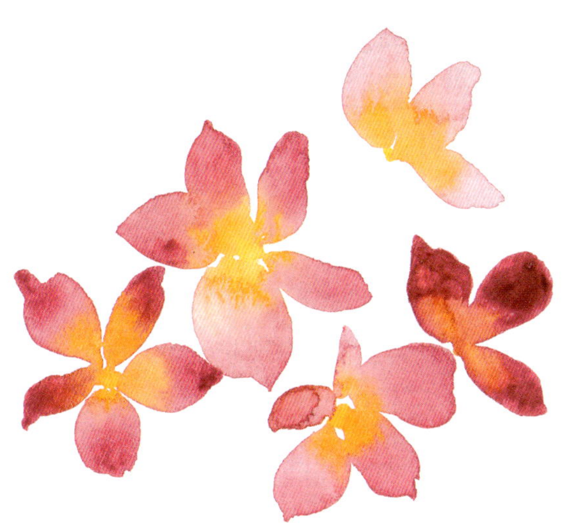

Step 5.

This time, we will paint another three-petal pinwheel, giving it the appearance of peeking out from behind our fourth flower. These petals will all be similar in size. I opted to use the BC version at a bit of a darker color, and then added CSC at the tips.

Step 6.

Now that we have explored multiple positions and consistencies, I'd like you to begin filling the remainder of the cluster, using the steps and suggestions provided. If you wish to deviate from my exact flower placement, please feel free! Take liberties where you like, using both consistencies for darker or lighter elements.

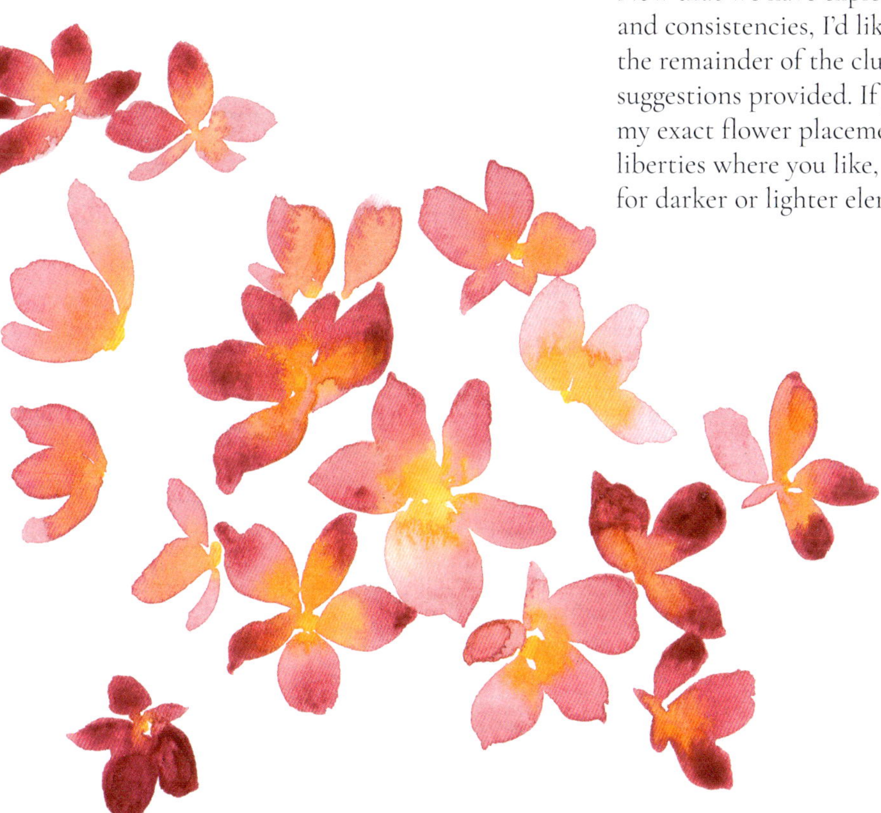

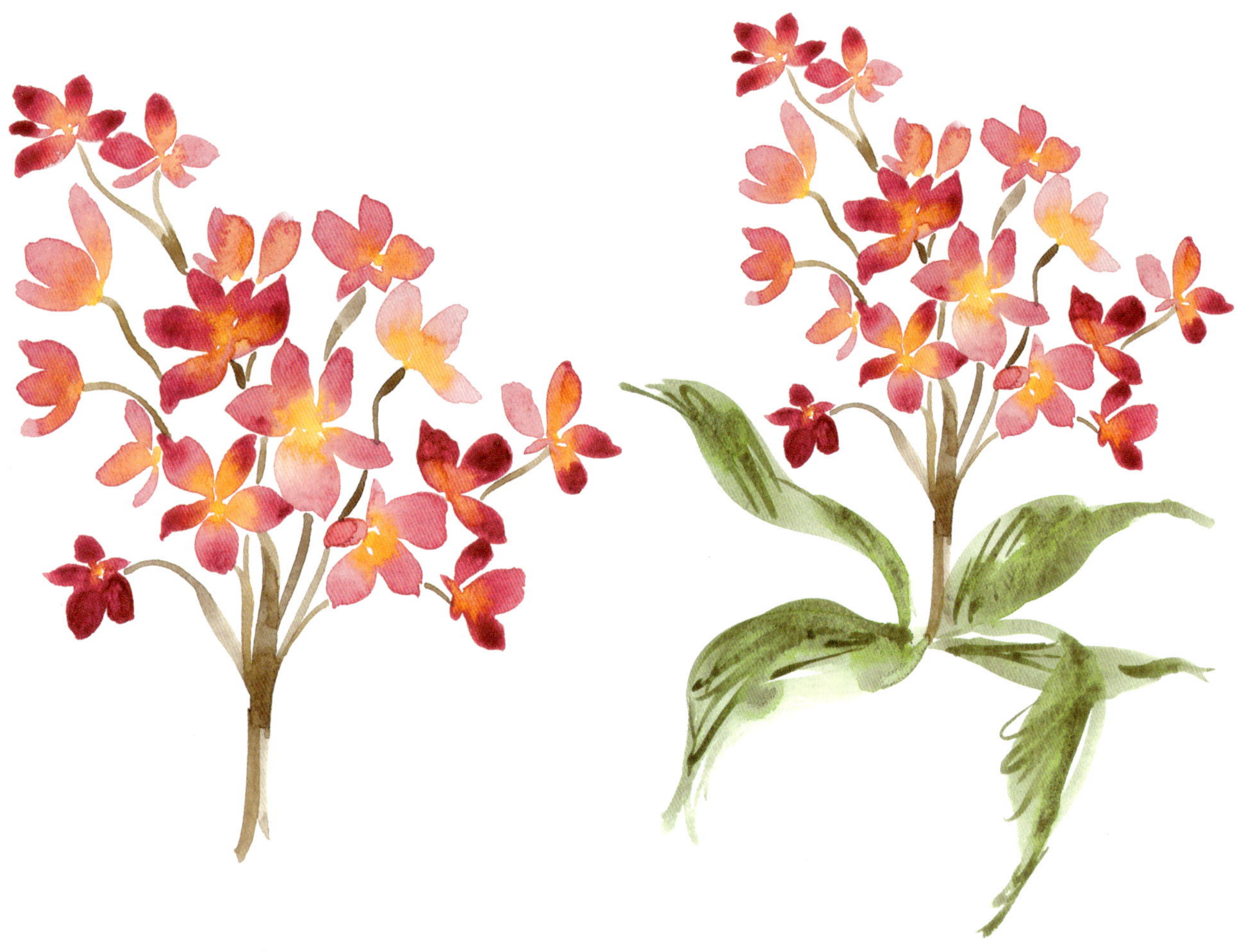

STEP 7.

Rinse off a size 8 brush and mix Burnt Umber to BC. Paint a thick stem (about the size of a linguine noodle) running down the middle of the cluster. Attach the flowers to smaller stems that connect to the large stem. No need to wait until things are dry.

STEP 8.

With your size 10 brush, mix Green Apatite Genuine to BC and CSC. Using the compound stroke technique (page 31), paint large leaves extending from the bottom of the cluster in BC. While the leaves are still wet, add gestural veins in CSC.

STEP 9A.

Rinse a size 8 brush and mix together Burnt Umber and Indian Yellow. Add a dark center to the flowers roughly the size of a pea.

STEP 9B.

Optional: Using your size 8 brush loaded with Verzino Violet in CSC, add gestural outlining (page 41) to some but not all of the flowers, for an added layer of interest.

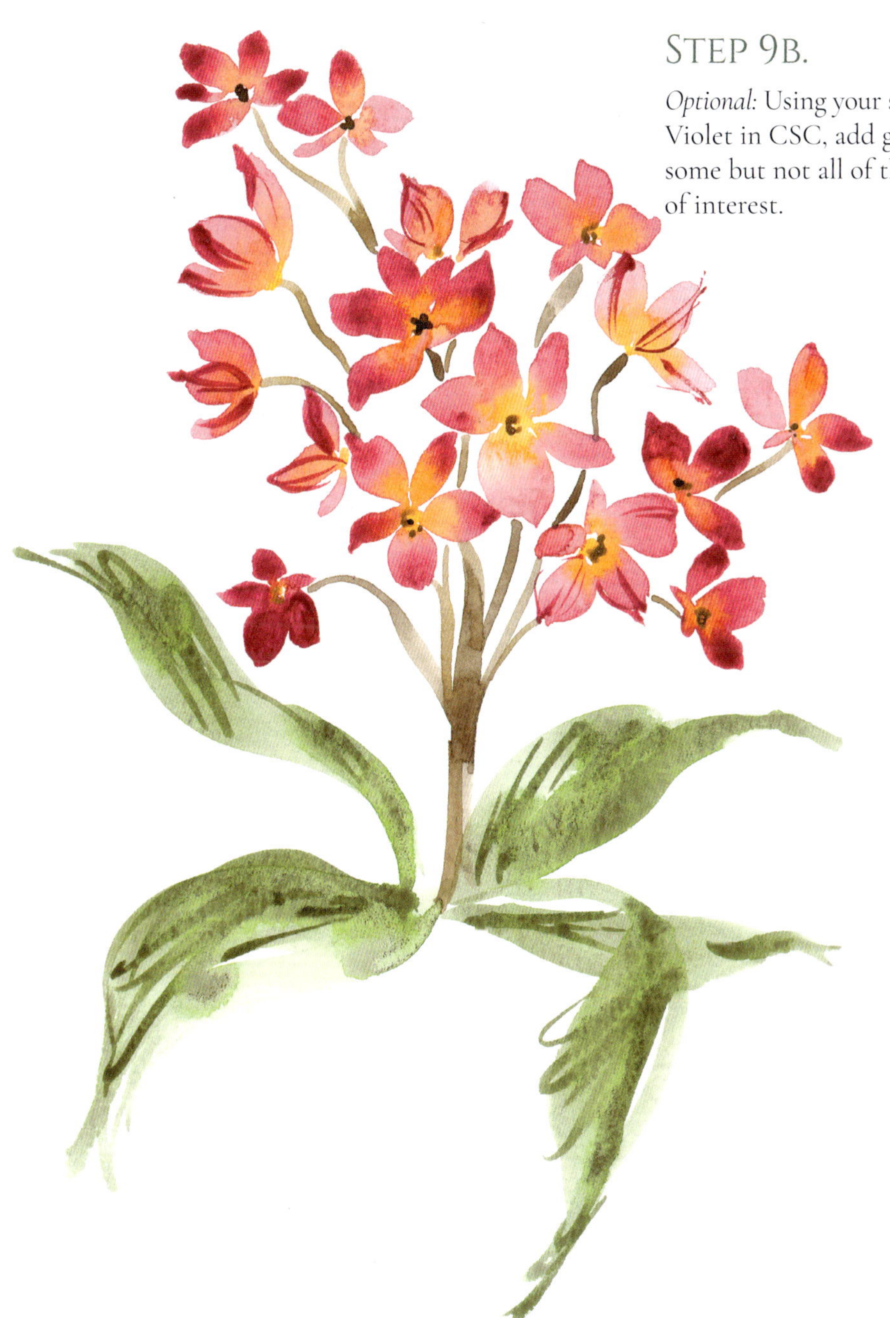

Tiger Lily

The burnt orange color I've selected for this flower is one of my very favorites and highly versatile as both a focal and supporting hue. Tones of these colors can be found in the Sunset Series Color Guide on my website. This is one of those flowers where I feel like the details are what make it shine, so we're going to have fun and play with that!

Supplies

Two size 10 round brushes
One size 6 round brush
Canson 140-lb (300-gsm) cold-press paper
HB pencil
Dust-free eraser

Palette

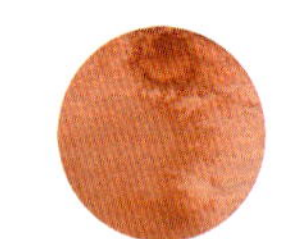
Quinacridone Burnt Scarlet (petals)

Yellow Ochre (petals)

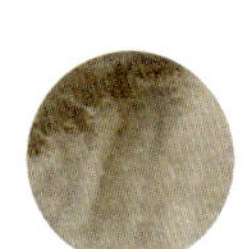
Sepia (petals & leaves)

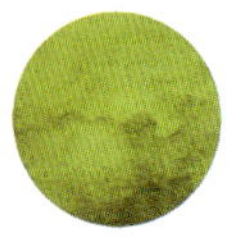
Sap Green (leaves)

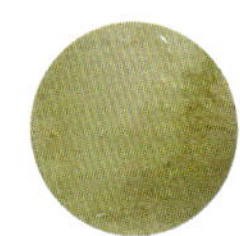
Sap Green + Sepia

Sap Green + Yellow Ochre

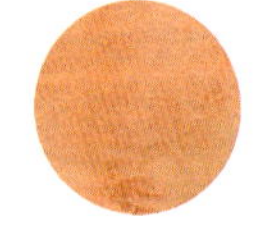
Quinacridone Burnt Scarlet + Yellow Ochre

Quinacridone Burnt Scarlet + Sepia

Preparing the Palette

With one size 10 brush, mix Quinacridone Burnt Scarlet and Yellow Ochre to BC.

With a second size 10 brush, mix Quinacridone Burnt Scarlet and Sepia to CSC.

Note: *We'll be using the abbreviation QBS for Quinacridone Burnt Scarlet.*

Tiger Lily Sketch

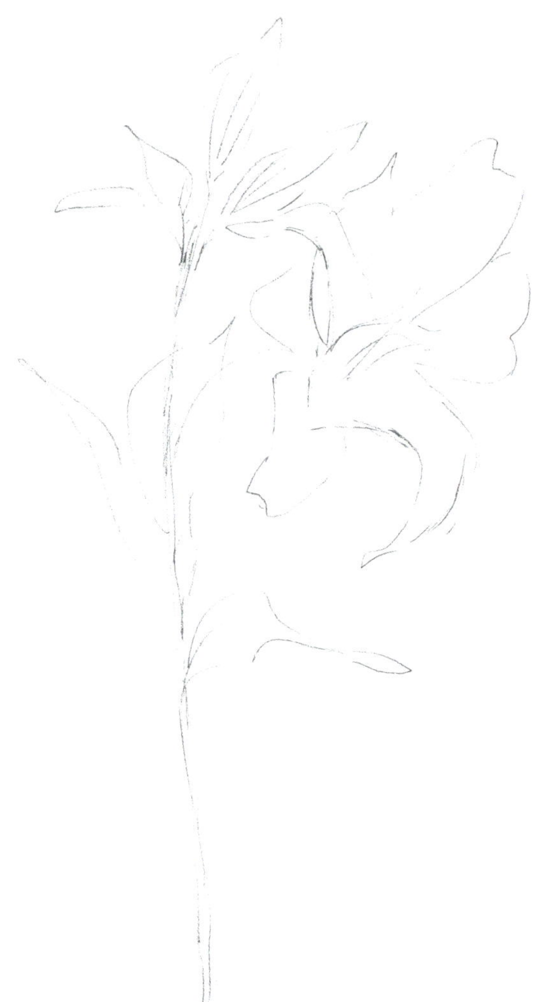

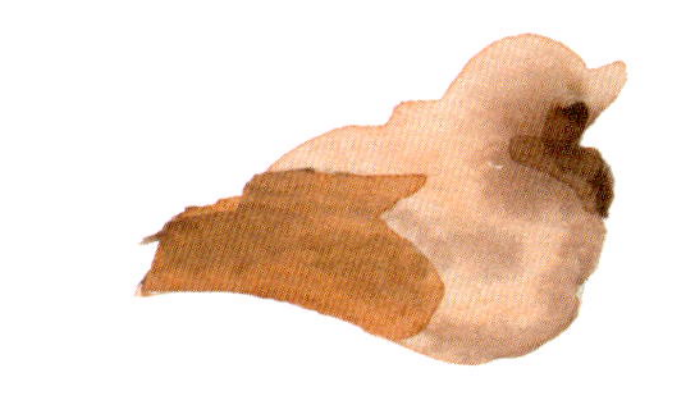

Step 1.

Referencing the sketch, use an HB pencil to lightly draw the design on a piece of watercolor paper.

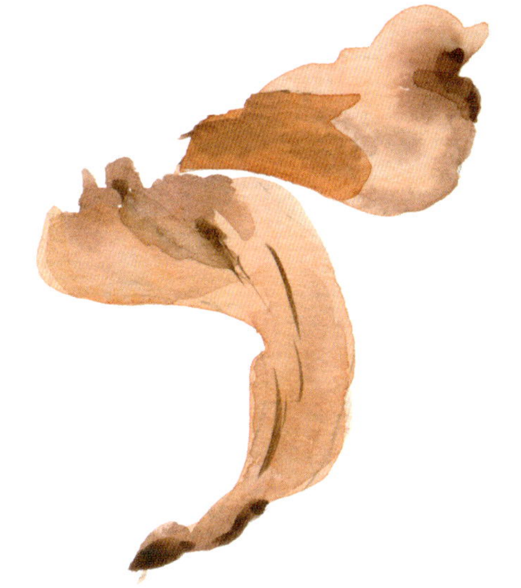

Step 2a.

With your size 10 brush loaded with QBS and Yellow Ochre in BC, paint the first petal using the compound stroke technique (page 31). You'll start at where the center would be and bring your petals to a rounded shape.

Step 2b.

Once the media is dry, continue to use your size 10 brush loaded with QBS and Yellow Ochre to add a darker layer extending from the center.

Step 2c.

When the media is dry or slightly damp, use your second size 10 brush loaded with QBS and Sepia in BC and add a small marking to indicate shadowing at the tip of the petal.

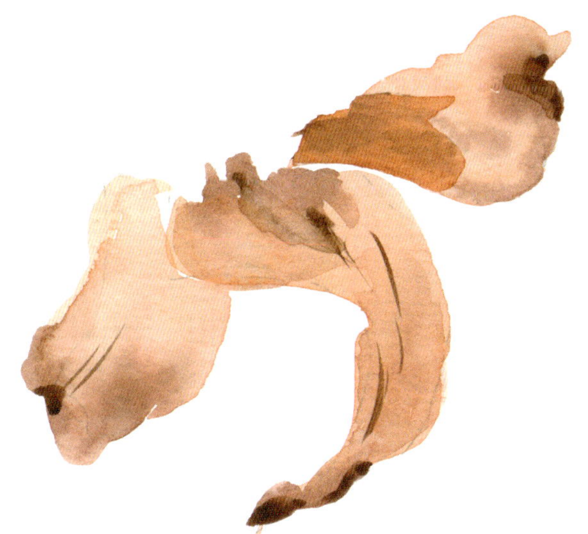

Step 3a.

Creating the second petal, repeat all of Step 2.

Step 3b.

Once the petals are dry, use the toe of your size 10 brush loaded with QBS and Sepia to add a couple of gestural strokes (page 32) to the petals, to serve as veins.

Step 4a.

Repeat Steps 2a and 2c but not 2b to create the third petal.

Step 4b.

Repeat Step 3b.

STEP 5A.

Add the fourth and fifth petals. You might find it easiest to begin with the top and largest petal and then work your way back down to the fifth petal, allowing them to merge so they appear as one giant petal. While the media is still wet, use your size 10 brush loaded with QBS and Sepia to drop in color at both ends of the petal.

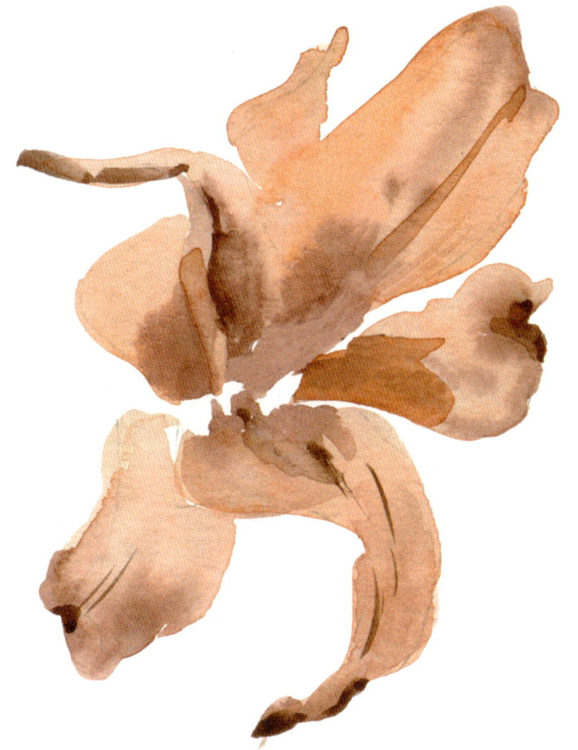

STEP 5B.

Using your size 10 brush loaded with QBS and Yellow Ochre, paint a stripe down the middle of the largest petal.

STEP 5C.

Using your size 10 brush loaded with QBS and Sepia, use the toe of the brush to add outlining to the fifth petal.

STEP 5D.

Paint the sixth petal so it appears to be beneath the fourth and fifth petal. Drop the color in CSC at the beginning of the petal where the center will be.

STEP 6.

Rinse your size 6 brush and load it with Sepia in CSC. Using the toe of the brush, create the filament and anther: the curved slender lines and the sideways ovals at the ends.

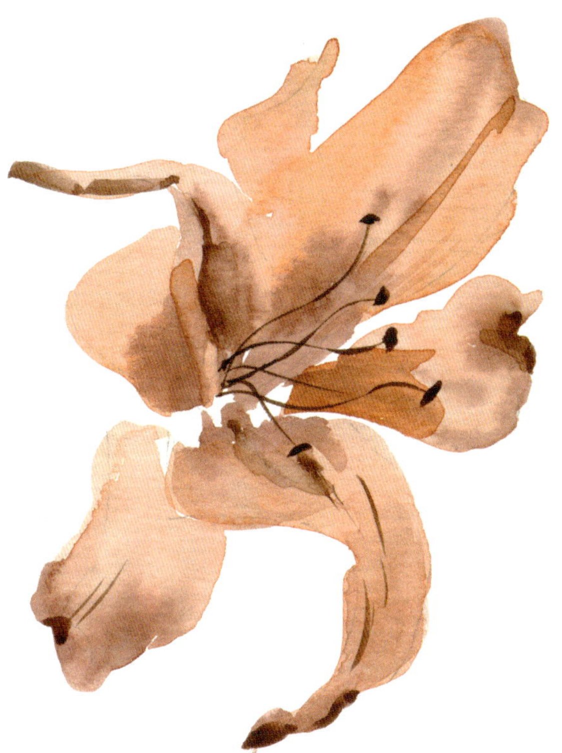

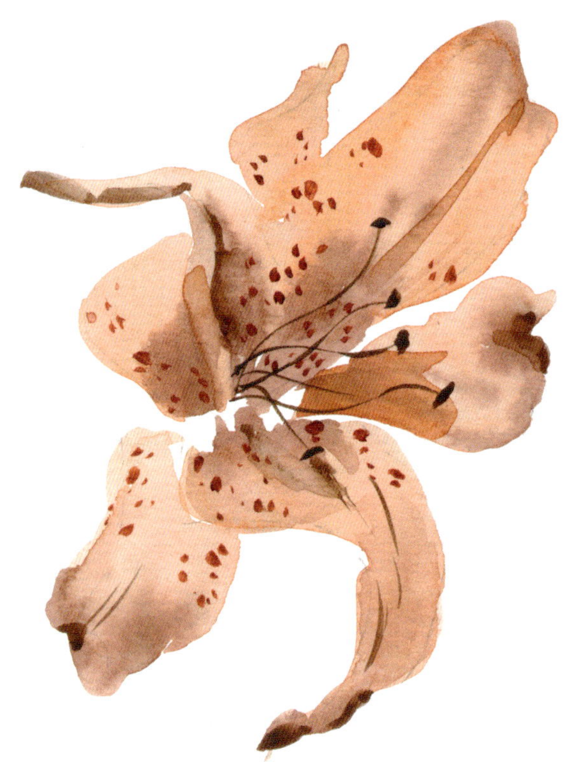

Step 7.

Using your size 6 brush loaded with QBS in CSC, use the toe of the brush to make small dots inside the petals. There is no specific pattern or structure. Place them arbitrarily and where they feel most organic to you.

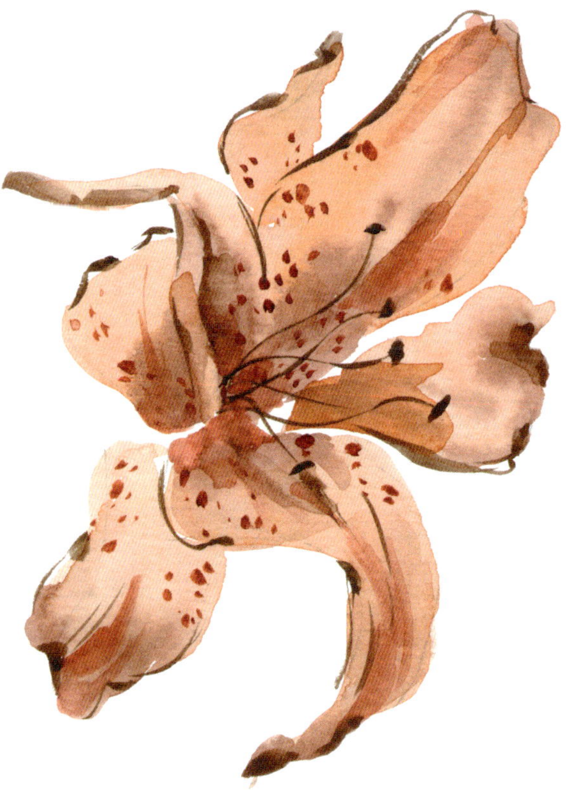

Step 8.

Going back to the size 6 brush loaded with Sepia in CSC, give the outside of the petals gestural outlines (see more about that technique on page 41). Keep them loose and flowy.

Step 9a.

Rinse a size 10 brush and load it with Sap Green in BC. Rinse another size 10 brush and load it with Sap Green and Sepia in BC. With Sap Green, paint the main stem that ends pointing toward the upper right side of the paper. Come back to the stem and paint a thinner stem to connect to the flower.

Step 9b.

Using the same brush, paint two lily buds at the very top of the main stem. These are achieved by executing a rounded-off compound stroke. While they are wet, drop in Sap Green and Sepia in BC at both ends.

Step 9c.

Take liberties here and add however many leaves you'd like to the main stem. Use both the simple and compound stroke techniques, painting the leaf first using Sap Green in BC, and then while wet adding the Sap Green and Sepia in BC for a darker contrast.

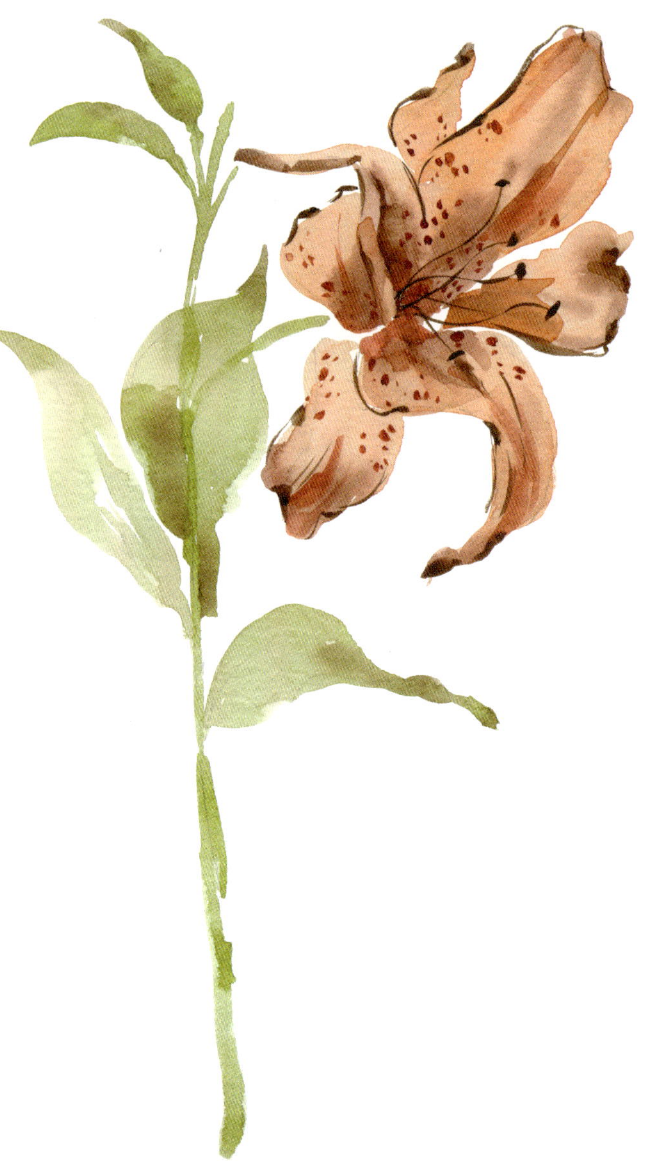

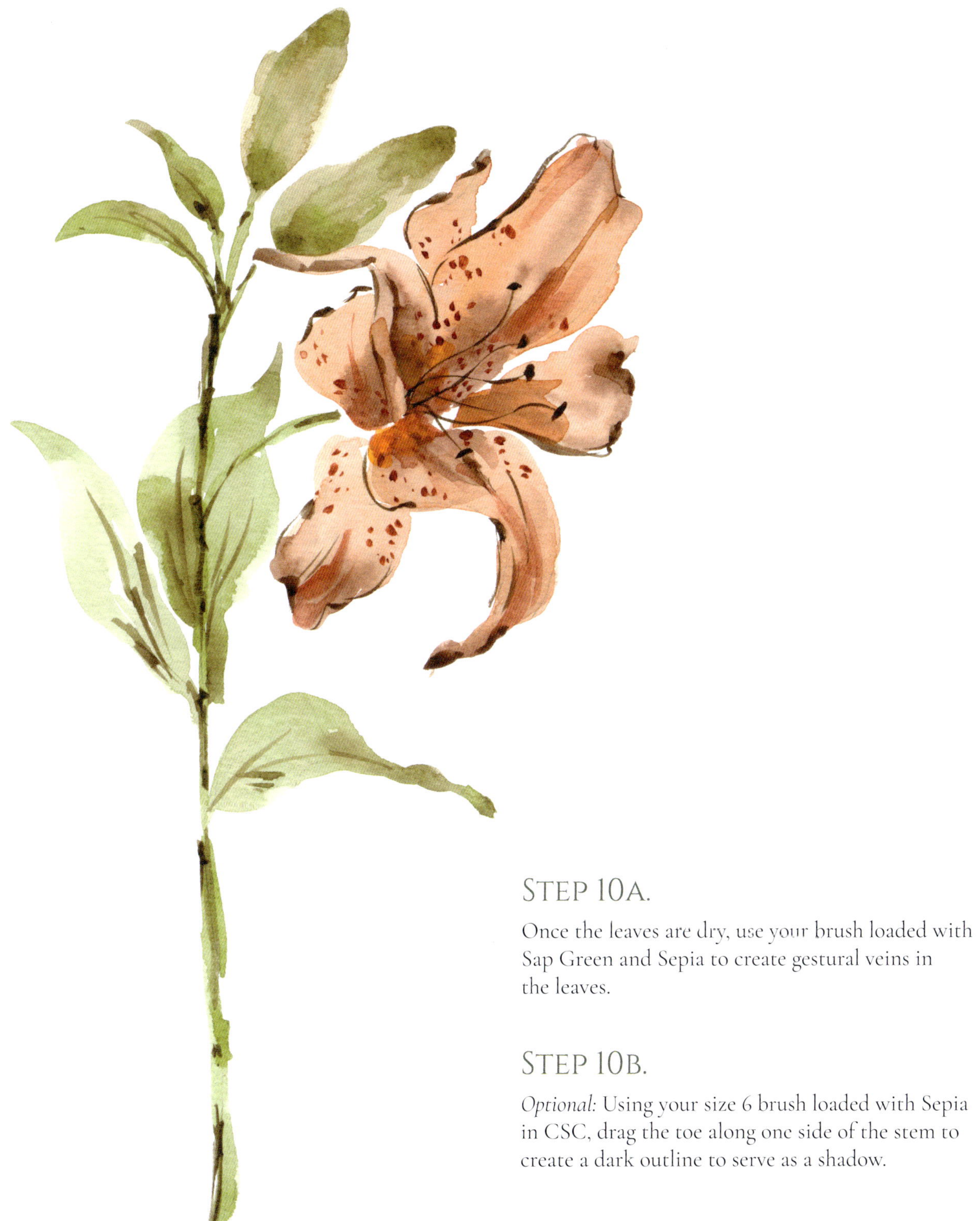

Step 10a.

Once the leaves are dry, use your brush loaded with Sap Green and Sepia to create gestural veins in the leaves.

Step 10b.

Optional: Using your size 6 brush loaded with Sepia in CSC, drag the toe along one side of the stem to create a dark outline to serve as a shadow.

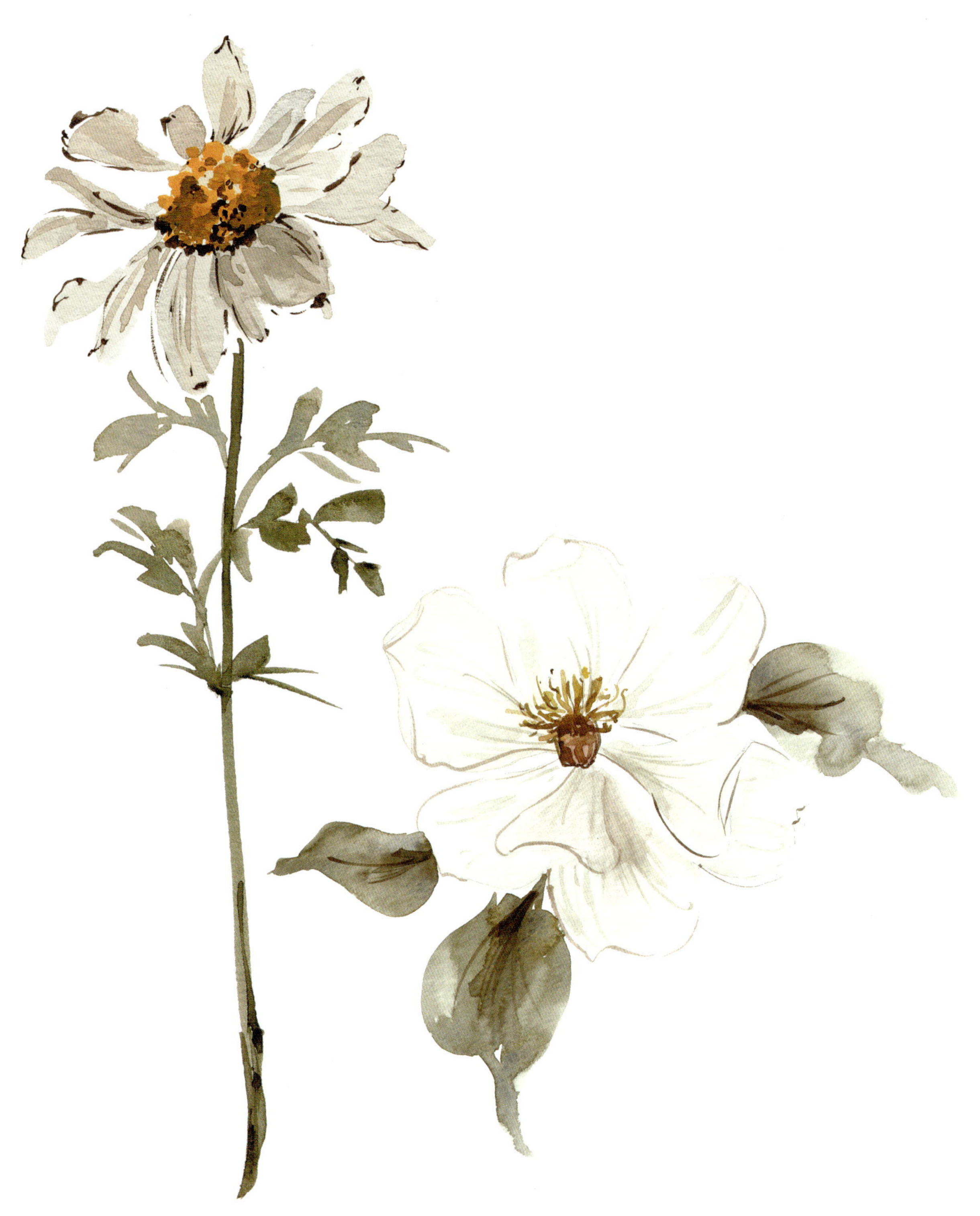

Enchanting, Snowy Blooms

How to paint white watercolors continues to be the number one question I'm asked from new watercolorists (and sometimes experienced ones!). It *can* be tricky and somewhat overwhelming at first figuring out how to create white without using white paint—which is not how it's done, by the way! Have no fear; I will be walking you through step by step, and placing you directly on the path to success!

Mastering white in watercolor is important not only because white florals are especially enchanting and some of my personal favorites and best sellers, but because so *many* flowers are white and we run the risk of limiting ourselves if we omit them. Because white flowers can easily get lost or turn drab if not mixed carefully, we'll rely heavily on color value (see page 21) to convey a sense of fresh and clean atmosphere. Lastly, because this is an area of such avid interest, I created a whole line of colors in my Color Guide series, called the Enchanted Series (which can be found on my website), where I provide 20 different recipes to create white in watercolor.

A note before we begin: *Please be advised if you purchased the ebook edition of this book that certain colors will appear more brown, yellow or green depending on your e-reader's color settings. I've done what I can to color correct the imperfect nature of a scanner, so that what I see in real life is what you see here, but there will inevitably be slight and minor discrepancies as we work with white tones.*

Chamomile

I could not have possibly put this book into the world without including perhaps my favorite flower of all. There is an innocence and playfulness chamomile possesses that fills my soul with such joy. I think because they remind me of children—my own, anyway—their lack of personal boundaries, the way they run, all arms and legs, as though they are laughing for no other reason than because they want to. Roses are nice, but give me a bouquet of chamomile any day, and I'm a happy girl.

If you haven't much experience with these happy little blooms, you're in for a treat. I love adding them to compositions to give the painting immediate movement and personality.

Supplies

Two size 6 round brushes

One size 2 round brush

Canson 140-lb (300-gsm) cold-press paper

Palette

Van Dyke Brown (center & petals)

Lamp Black (center & petals)

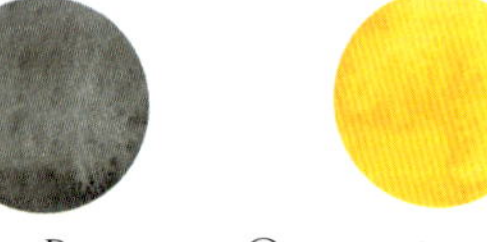

Cadmium-Free Yellow (center)

Undersea Green

Lamp Black + Van Dyke Brown

Van Dyke Brown + Cadmium-Free Yellow

Preparing the Palette

Using a size 6 brush, mix together Van Dyke Brown and Lamp Black to BC (page 16) and then dilute it further by adding water to decrease the value—95 percent water to 5 percent paint. As we did with an earlier lesson, we'll call this lightest consistency (LC). Load this brush and set it off to the side.

Using your other size 6 brush, mix together Cadmium-Free Yellow and Van Dyke Brown to BC and CSC. Load it with BC and set it off to the side.

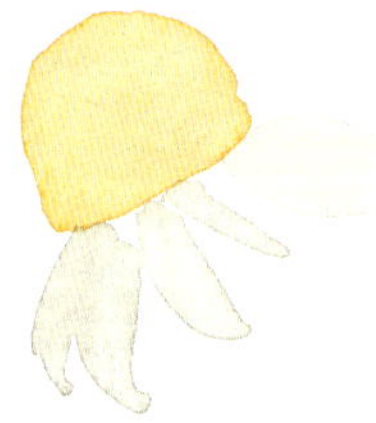

Step 1.

Using the size 6 brush loaded with Van Dyke Brown and Cadmium-Free Yellow in BC, make a sideways gumdrop shape in the upper middle section of the paper. This should be roughly ¾ inch (1.8 cm) in diameter. Wait until your media is fully dry before proceeding to the next step.

Step 2.

With your size 6 brush loaded with Lamp Black and Van Dyke Brown in LC, begin adding petals at the bottom of the center, using both the simple and compound stroke techniques (pages 30 and 31). This is simply a pinwheel flower with some petals omitted. For the best variety, utilize different sizes and shapes of the petals, using a small simple stroke for some petals and fuller compound strokes for others. Starting from the left, I used compound, simple, gestural, compound. Feel free to take liberties here.

Note: *Depending on whether your center is still damp when you add the petals, you may see some wet-into-wet results. This is fine, and even encouraged if you are drawn to this effect; however, you may want to allow some centers to fully dry simply so that some of the elements are separate.*

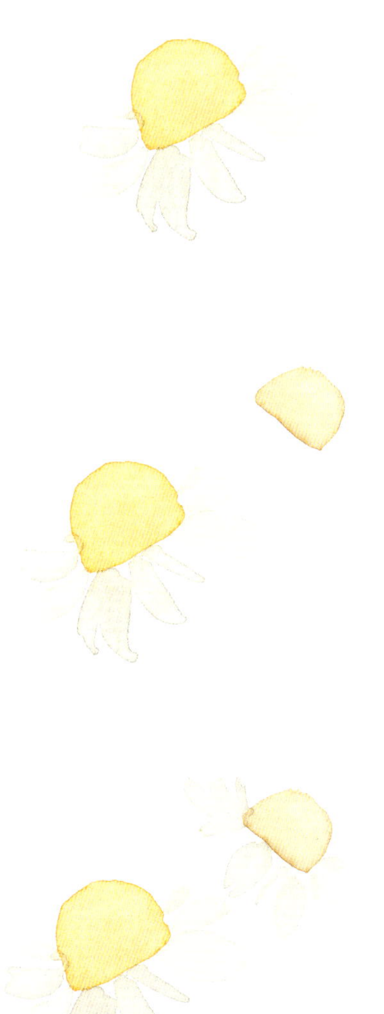

Step 3.

Continue working your way around the center, avoiding the very top where the petals would be hiding from this angle. This is what will essentially give your flower movement—the sideways center, plus the petals arranged to gesture the angle. Consider leaving small gaps between the petals, and don't be concerned if your petals are lining up perfectly with the center. We are going to add details along the outside that will cover up this area and add great depth to the chamomile.

Step 4.

Begin again, this time painting the center facing the other direction, toward the upper right side of the page. Paint it slightly smaller than your first gumdrop shape.

Step 5.

With a combination of the strokes used in Step 2, add the petals so they are working with the angle of the flower. Aim for variety here, so that there are minor differences between your first flower and the second. This really lends to giving your composition a satisfying balance and invites the eye to travel across the painting.

Step 6a.

Let's paint three chamomile flowers this time. The idea is to build up a cluster of tiny blooms, which we will eventually add to stems. The goal is to give each flower its moment—meaning, again, *variety*. I'll sing it until the cows come home because it's *important*! Let's play with some different angles, painting the flower above our first flower at a severe side angle. You'll begin the same way, with a sideways gumdrop and then painting the petals around the perimeter, avoiding the top side. Also, I will begin to use wet-into-wet here (page 29) allowing my centers and petals to merge. Follow along or choose your own path; either is wonderful!

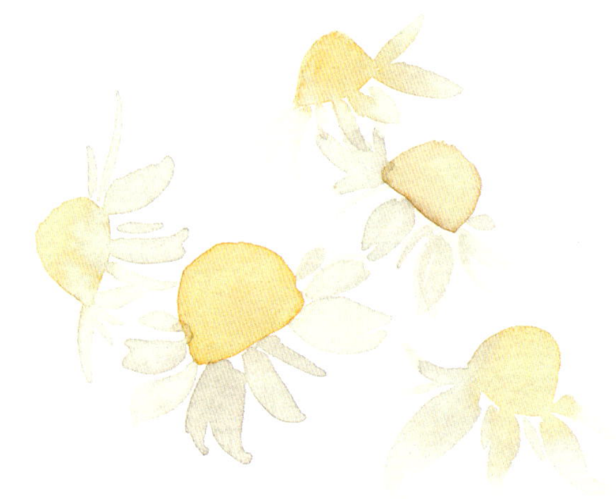

Step 6b.

For the next flower, placed just above our second flower, let's push it close so that it appears as though these two are overlapping. By having some flowers close and others farther away, we allow the cluster to flow as it would in nature.

Step 6c.

For the third flower, on the bottom right side, I painted some of the petals quite larger and the ones on the edges with gestural stroke (page 32). *Remember:* It's okay to leave some flowers *very* simple; we are going to be adding details soon, which will give much more character to them.

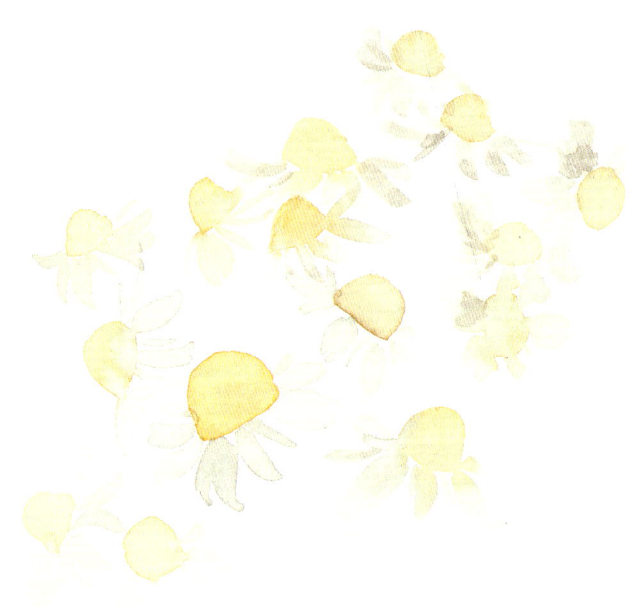

Step 7.

I'm going to give you free rein now to fill in the cluster as you like. We've walked through many options, and now I'd like you to use your intuition to guide you as you move along. Variety, variety, variety. Flowers should be big, medium and small. Some should have complex petals, others very simple.

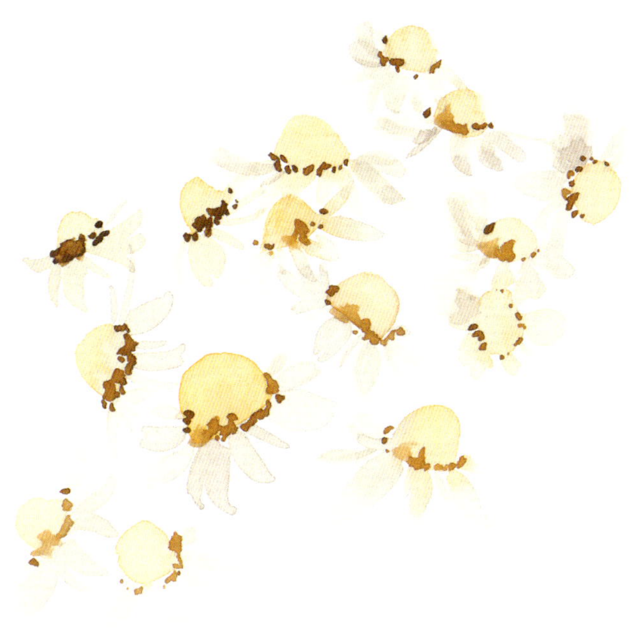

STEP 8.

Be sure your media is fully dry. Then, using your size 2 brush, mix together Van Dyke Brown and Cadmium-Free Yellow to CSC. Add in the details along the perimeter by using the tip of the brush to make dots on the paper.

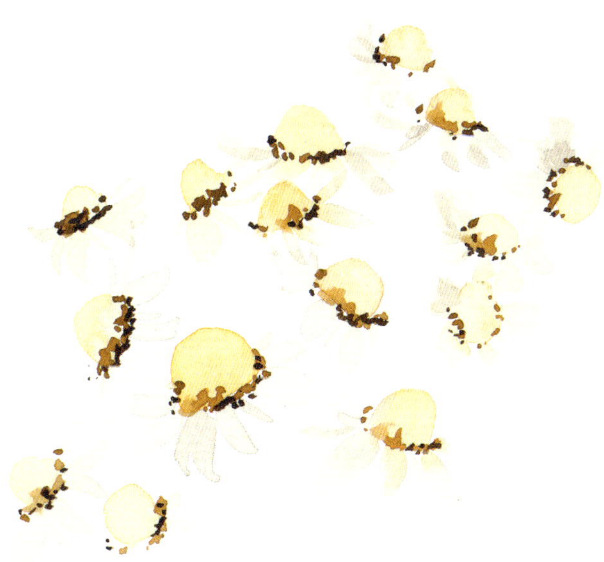

STEP 9.

Rinse your size 2 brush, load it with Lamp Black and Van Dyke Brown in CSC and create one more layer of dotting. Be sure the media is fully dry before proceeding. Try to implement variety here, allowing some flowers to have heavy dark dotting and others to have very little.

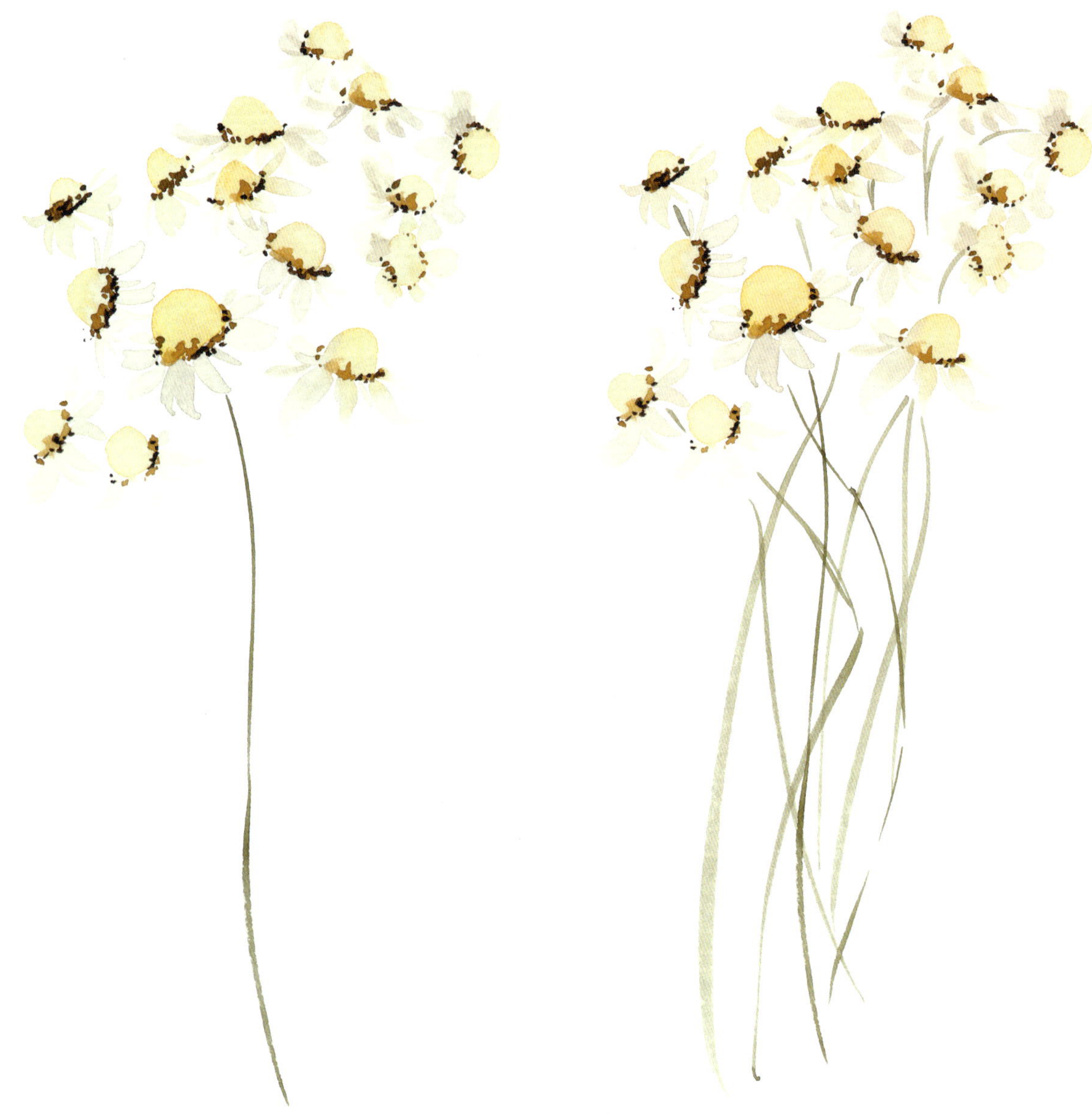

STEP 10.

Rinse your size 6 brush and load it with Undersea Green in BC. Attach the anchor stem to the first flower we painted so that you have a clear idea of where your stems should land at the bottom of the page.

STEP 11.

Continue to attach stems that don't feel too overthought. Utilize the toe of the brush for thin lines, or come down on the belly for some thickness. Allow some stems to be straight and others to curve slightly.

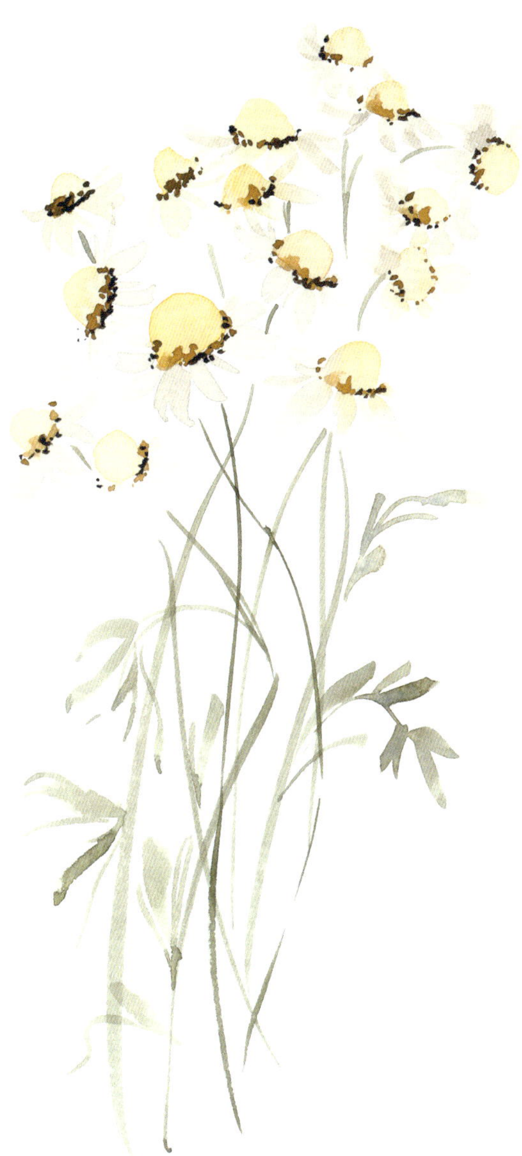

STEP 12.

Using the size 6 brush with Undersea Green in BC, add small gestural leaves to some of the stems.

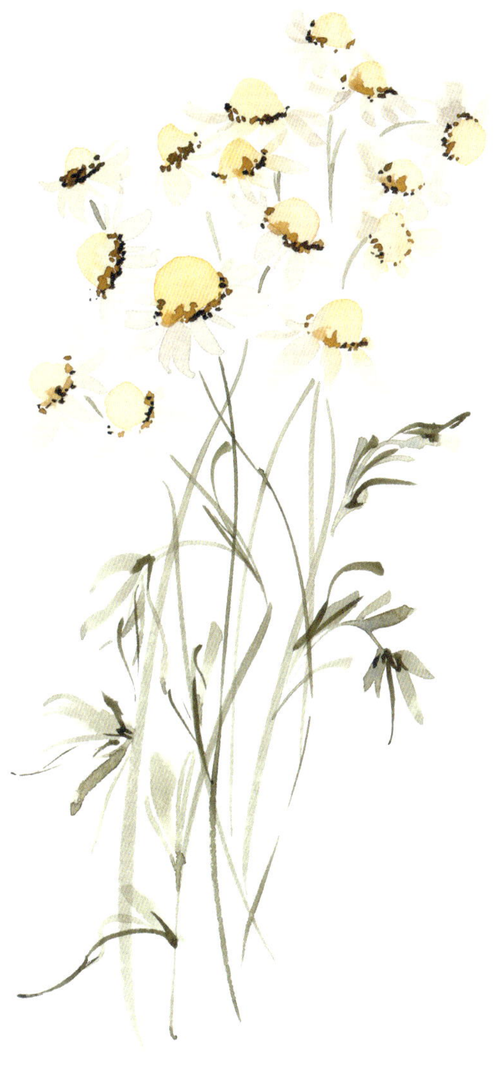

STEP 13.

For a more ornate feel, create one more layer over the leaves, using the same mixture in CSC. You don't have to include this step if you like your painting as it is! I also used the size 6 brush to create darker gestural leaves in CSC on top of the first layer once it was dry. This is achieved by using the toe of the brush and making quick, flicking motions in the direction I want the lines to end. Remember to rotate your paper around as you work to secure the most comfortable angle.

White Gerbera Daisy

Perhaps one of the simplest but sweetest flowers in existence is the white daisy. I can remember making daisy chains at recess as a young girl, and to this day I love to reinvent this flower in new ways to include in my work. We're going to add some really fun touches and embellishments to this tried-and-true flower to make it stand out. Let's get to it!

Supplies

Three size 6 round brushes

Two size 2 round brushes

Canson 140-lb (300-gsm) cold-press paper

Palette

Payne's Gray (petals)

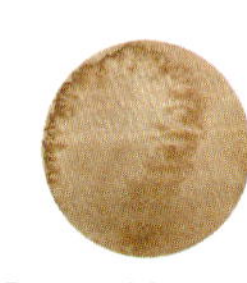

Raw Umber (petals)

Cadmium-Free Yellow (center)

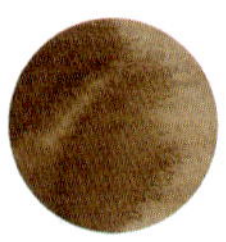

Sepia (center details & outlining)

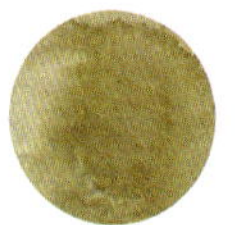

Undersea Green (leaves)

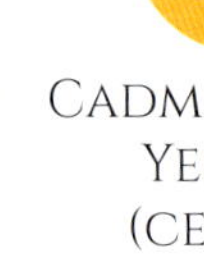

Payne's Gray + Raw Umber

Cadmium-Free Yellow + Raw Umber

Preparing the Palette

Using a size 6 brush, mix Payne's Gray and Raw Umber to BC (page 16). Dip the brush into water and begin a new pile, decreasing the value to LC, 95 percent water and 5 percent paint. (See page 16 for a refresh on consistencies.) There should now be two versions of the same color. Load the other size 6 brush with LC and set it off to the side

Step 1.

Using a clean size 6 brush, mix Cadmium-Free Yellow in BC and paint a quarter-sized (1-inch [2.5-cm]-diameter) imperfect circle, as if a lemon were on its side.

Step 2a.

Reload your size 6 brush with the Payne's Gray and Raw Umber mixture in BC. Your other size 6 brush should also already have this mixture on it at LC.

Step 2b.

Begin painting the first four petals by using the simple stroke technique (page 30). Paint the first petal on the left with the lightest color and paint the one beside it smaller with the darker color. For the third and fourth petals, don't reload the brushes with paint. This will result in lighter petals. Although we are not using a different ratio, applying only what is left on the brush is another way to use color value to our advantage and bring immense interest to your painting.

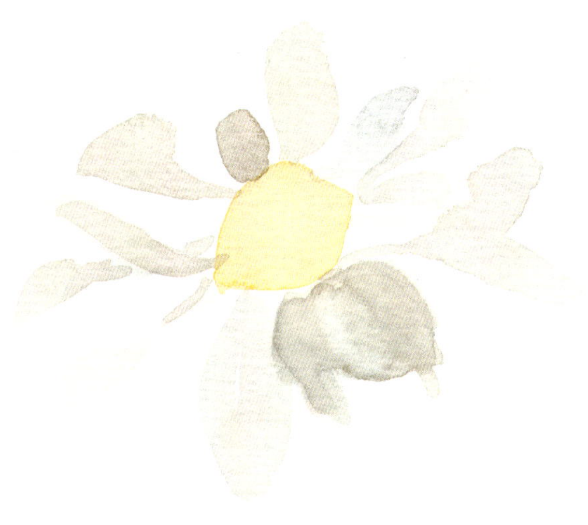

Note: For your petal shape, be sure to play with movement and variety (page 32). Specifically, try not to make them all the same shape and size. Remember, even a gestural stroke counts as structure and lends itself to creating movement in the flower.

Step 3.

Finish the flower by following the instructions in Step 2.

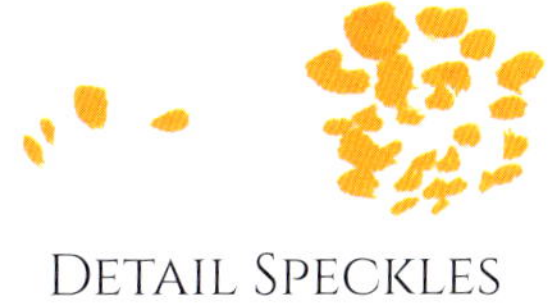

Detail Speckles

Step 4.

Mix your Cadmium-Free Yellow to CSC (page 16) and add details to the circle, using your size 2 brush. To do this, you will gently sweep the toe of the brush around the circle until it has a splotchy, speckled appearance. Refer to "Detail Speckles" to see a step-by-step progression.

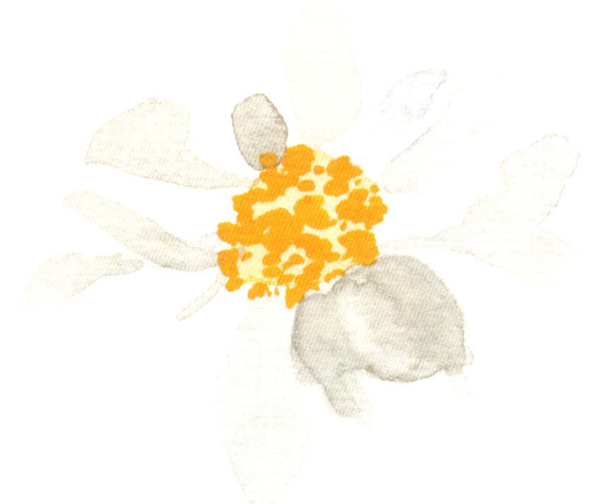

Step 5.

Still using your size 2 brush, mix together Cadmium-Free Yellow and Raw Umber in CSC and add it to the middle of the flower for another layer of interest.

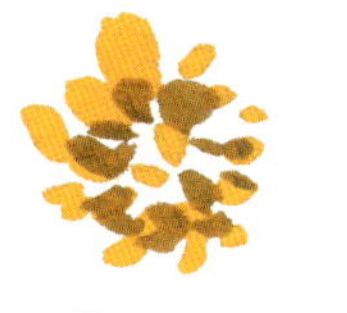

Adding Cadmium-Free Yellow + Raw Umber on top

Note: *For this technique, I'd like you to have another size 2 brush on hand to use as a softening tool. Make sure it's moist with clean water. As you add the detail speckles, gently smear the color with the clean size 2 brush so that it runs into the yellow. Some areas should be darker than others to create shadows within the center.*

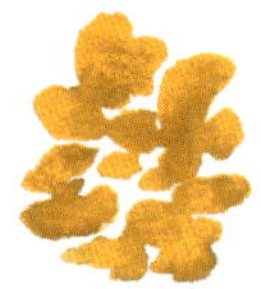

Smearing the center with a clean size 2 brush

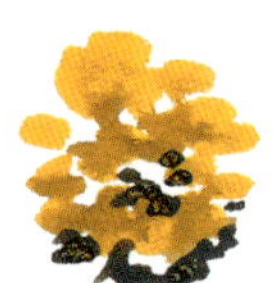

Sepia on top

Step 6.

Rinse your size 2 brush and mix Sepia to CSC. Darken the outside edges of the center using gestural marking, small lines and dots.

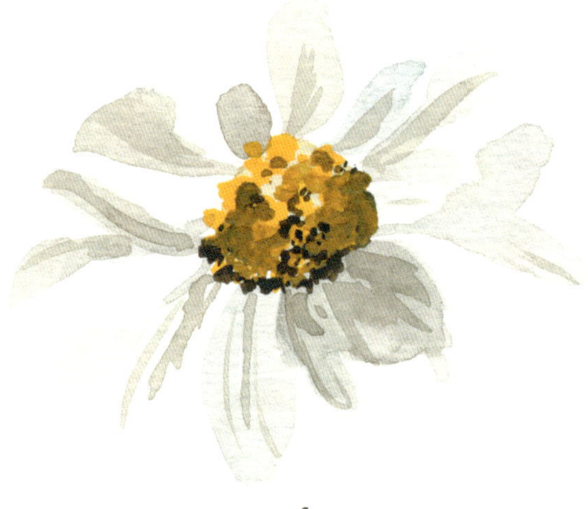

Step 7a.

Rinse the size 2 brush and reload it with Sepia in BC. Paint a few gestural strokes in the middle of the petals to serve as veins and shadows.

Step 7b.

We'll now draw out the structure of the petals by making some loose gestural marks around the edges. Using your size 6 brush, you'll come up on the tippy toe and apply very light pressure to make fine lines around the petals. You can take liberties here or follow along with my exact progress by studying each petal and applying the same strokes. For a quick refresh on gestural outlining, see page 41.

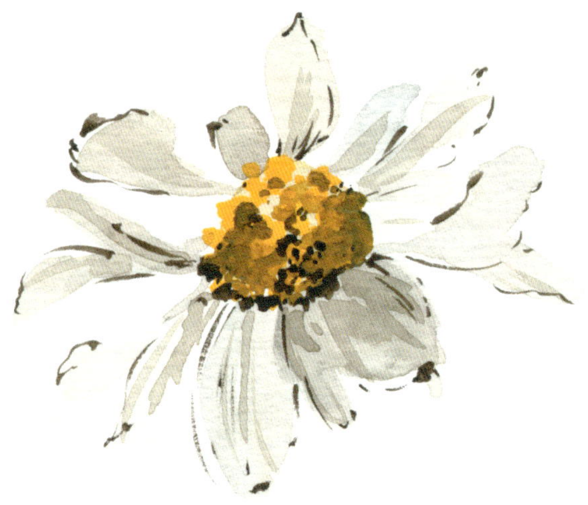

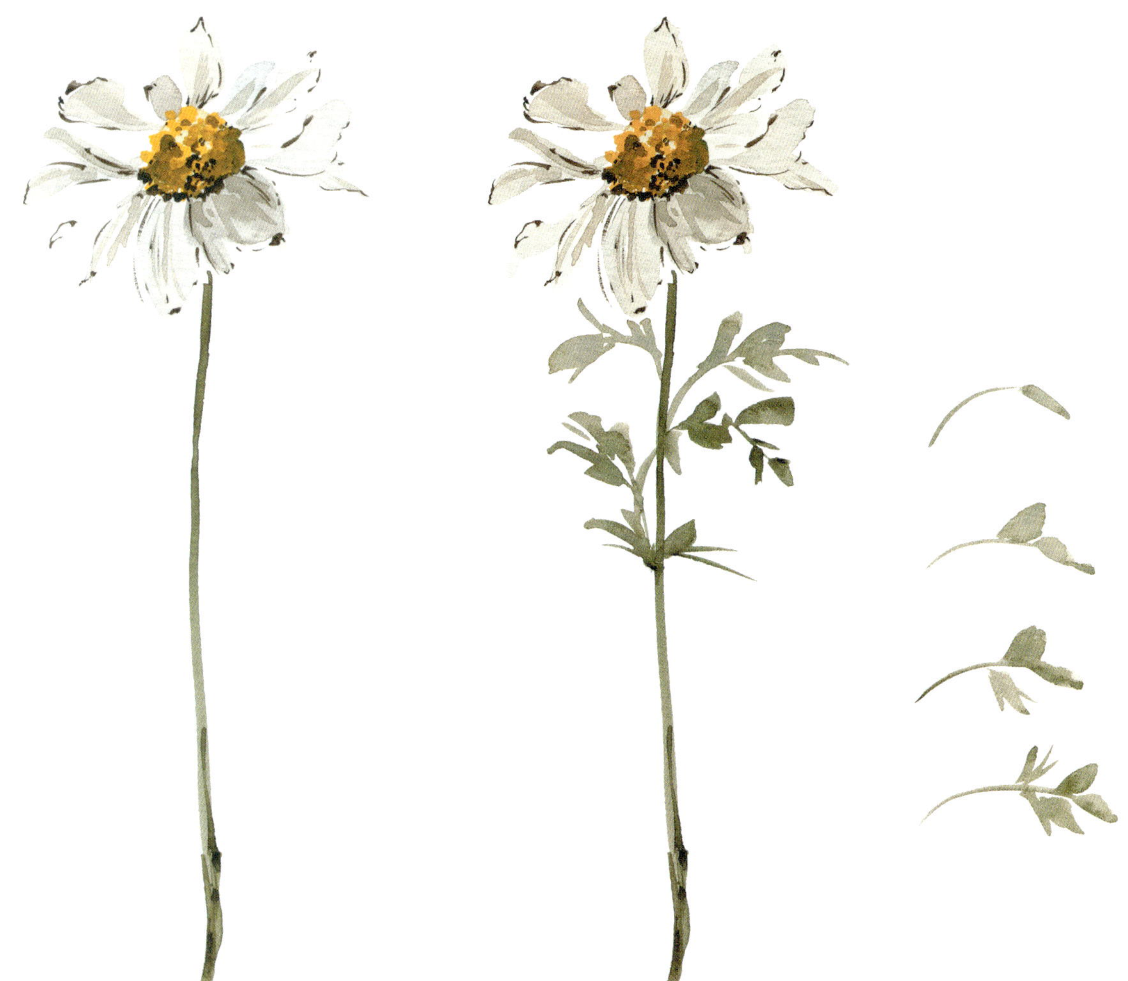

Step 8.

Using your size 6 brush, mix Undersea Green to CSC and paint a stem. To do this, you'll begin just below the bottom petal with the toe of your brush. Pull the brush down toward you using light pressure until you reach the bottom. Not lifting up, apply a bit more pressure to thicken the very end of the stem.

Step 9a.

Still using your size 6 brush, this time decrease the value of Undersea Green until it's BC. Next, you'll attach leaves to your main stem, using the same technique we used to give leaves to our pinwheel flowers (page 41). Refer to the diagram to see how these steps progress.

Step 9b.

Wait for the leaves to dry, and then, using your size 6 brush and Undersea Green in CSC, apply darker gestural strokes on top of the first layer. This will help create contrast and indicate veins in the leaves.

Ivory Garden Rose

When I was just learning how to use watercolors, one of the most daunting flowers for me to learn were roses. I thought they were so beautiful, yet each time I tried to paint one, it either felt overworked or so loose as to be indistinguishable from a blob. I set off on a journey then to figure out how to paint roses that felt right to me, tracking down that elusive balance between botanical and loose.

Nearly three giant pads of watercolor paper later, I had done it!

I want to share that process with you now, inviting you to study my techniques to learn my rose, and then feeling liberated to make it your own in the future. That part will take time, naturally, which is a beautiful aspect of the artist's evolution and not to be rushed. Let's begin by preparing our palette.

Supplies

One size 6 round brush
One size 10 round brush
Canson 140-lb (300-gsm) cold-press paper

Palette

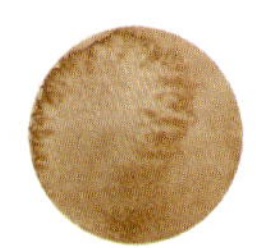
Raw Umber (Petals)

Lamp Black (Petals)

Undersea Green (Leaves)

Raw Umber + Lamp Black (LC)

Raw Umber + Lamp Black (BC)

Preparing the Palette

Mix together Raw Umber and Lamp Black to BC (page 16). Load the size 6 brush and set it off to the side.

Using the size 10 brush, swirl it through and load it with BC and then create a new pile on the palette. This ratio is lightest consistency (LC): 95 percent water to 5 percent paint. (More info on consistencies can be found on page 16.)

Step 1.

Using the Raw Umber and Lamp Black mixture in BC and your size 6 brush, come up on the toe to create a small vortex to serve as the center of the rose. For a refresh on how to create the vortex, see page 45.

Step 2.

Using your size 10 brush loaded with LC, create the next series of petals the same way we did in our rose exercise (page 45). They should cuddle. Use both the toe and belly of the brush to play with the size and shape to add variation to the flower.

Note: *Remember to look for the place where the end of two petals meet to create the next petal. See page 46 for further clarification.*

Step 3a.

Reload both the size 6 and size 10 brushes with their respective consistencies. We'll place the bottom right petal in the same place as we did on page 45, first painting the thin line with the size 6 brush in the BC mixture, and then immediately using our size 10 brush to fill in the petals with the LC mixture. This will create a natural progression of color.

Step 3b.

Create the next two petals using the same technique.

Step 4.

Finish off the flower with the final series of petals, using the same technique as above: size 6 brush for the fine line, size 10 brush to fill in. This time, you will use the up-and-down stroke we learned in our practice lesson (page 47) to create a different shape for the outermost petals. No need to rinse the brush before moving on.

Step 5.

Using your size 10 brush, mix Undersea Green to BC and CSC. Paint three leaves extending from the left and two leaves on the right side of the rose, using the compound stroke technique. See page 31 for a refresh on compound strokes, if necessary. So you'll follow along exactly with me, I painted the leaves on the left in BC, and waited until they were dry to add the gestural veins in Undersea Green in CSC. For the leaves on the right, I began with BC and then, while wet, I added CSC at the base, heaviest on the bottom leaf which then merged with the top. Again, I waited until the leaves were fully dry to add the gestural veins. The size 10 brush was used for each step.

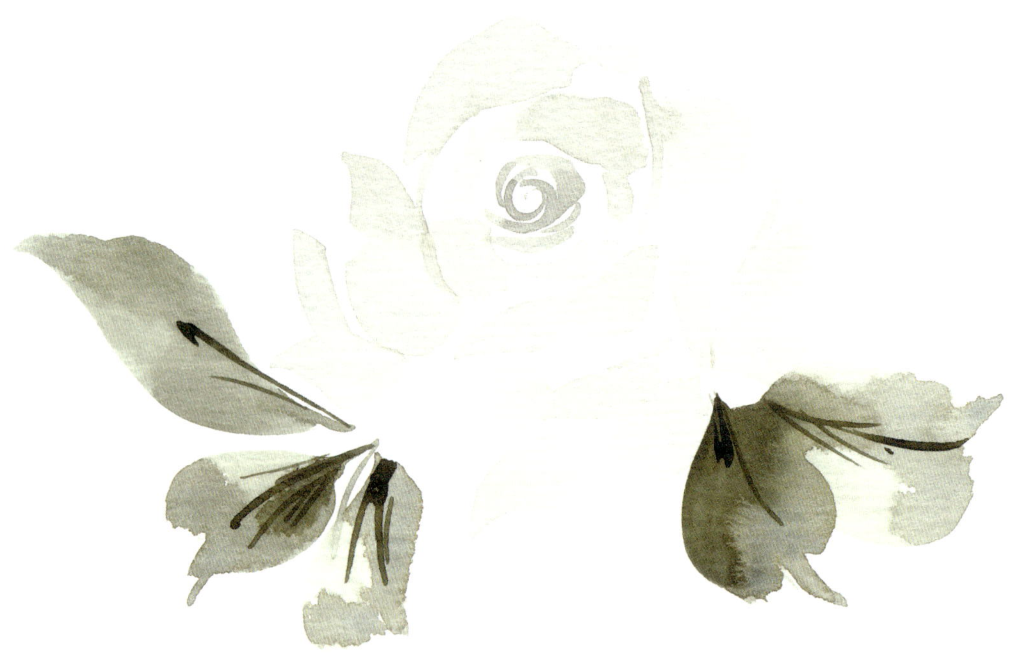

Hyacinth

This is another one of those flowers that's a real treat to have in the house because it smells amazing. Similar in structure to our forget-me-nots, these flowers have petals that are a bit longer and thinner (almost like a starfish) with a body that remains tubular. We can quickly lose the array of colors if we're not careful, so to avoid that we will be using a variety of white tones to help each flower stand apart. We'll help aid the clustering structure by painting flowers that give the impression some petals are facing out, on their sides, or peeking out from behind frontal flowers. As always, variety is KEY!

Supplies

Three size 4 round brushes

One size 2 round brush

One size 6 round brush

One size 10 round brush

Canson 140 lb (300-gsm) cold-press paper

Palette

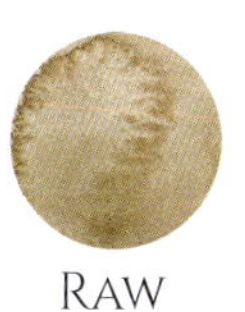
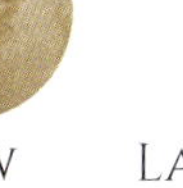
Raw Umber

Lamp Black

Sepia

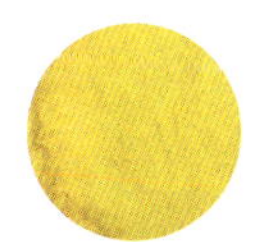
Green Gold

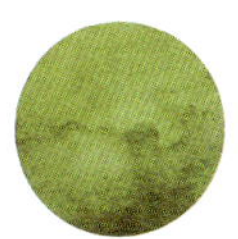
Sap Green

Lamp Black + Raw Umber

Sap Green + Sepia

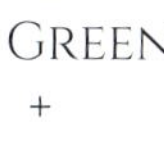
Sepia + Green Gold

Preparing the Palette

Mix together Lamp Black and Raw Umber to BC (page 16) and load a size 4 brush. Set it off to the side.

Using another size 4 brush, swirl it through the Lamp Black and Raw Umber mixture in BC to create a new pile on the palette. This ratio is lightest consistency (LC): 95 percent water to 5 percent paint.

Mix together Sepia and Green Gold to BC.

Step 1A.

We'll begin the same way as we did in the Delphinium project (page 92), starting with a cluster of flowers in the middle of the page. Use your size 4 brush loaded with Lamp Black and Raw Umber in BC to paint the first three open-faced pinwheel flowers. These should be about the size of a macadamia nut and form a small zigzag shape. Be sure to leave a tiny amount of open space in the center of the flowers, where we will later add the yellow middles.

Step 1B.

Using the size 4 brush loaded with LC, paint a few sideways pinwheels peeking out from the main open-faced flowers and in bud formation at the very top. These should be slightly smaller than the open-faced flowers. To achieve a range of color, don't reload your brush, but allow some of the paint to come off onto the paper so that some flowers are lighter than others. Additional info on pinwheel positions can be found on page 39.

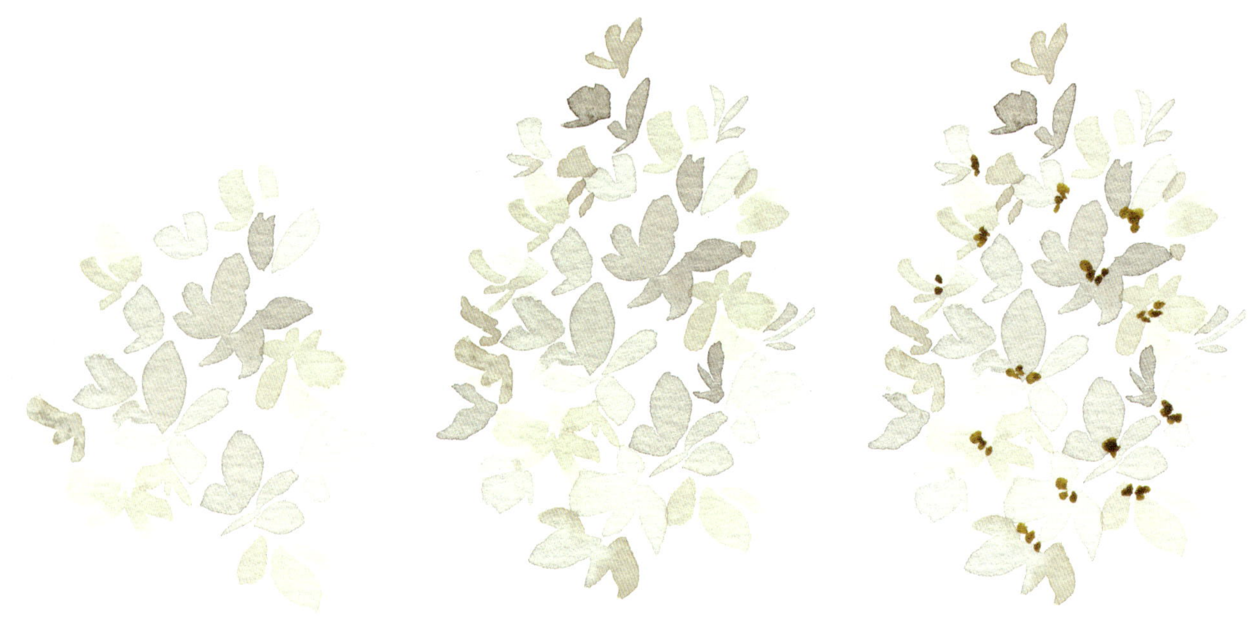

Tip: Remember, not all flowers need to look like flowers; a small gestural stroke can serve as a flower and add looseness to the composition.

Step 2.

Using your size 4 brush loaded with Sepia and Green Gold, continue to add pinwheel flowers in a variety of positions and sizes. For a review on pinwheel position possibilities, see page 39.

Step 3.

Continue in this fashion, using both mixtures, until you have achieved the general shape of the flower as a whole. Use the toe of your brush to create a few fine strokes along the edges to act as petals curling under.

Step 4.

Using your size 2 brush, mix together Green Gold to CSC (page 16). Add a small dot in the center of the open-faced flowers and those on their side that might appear to have some of the centers visible.

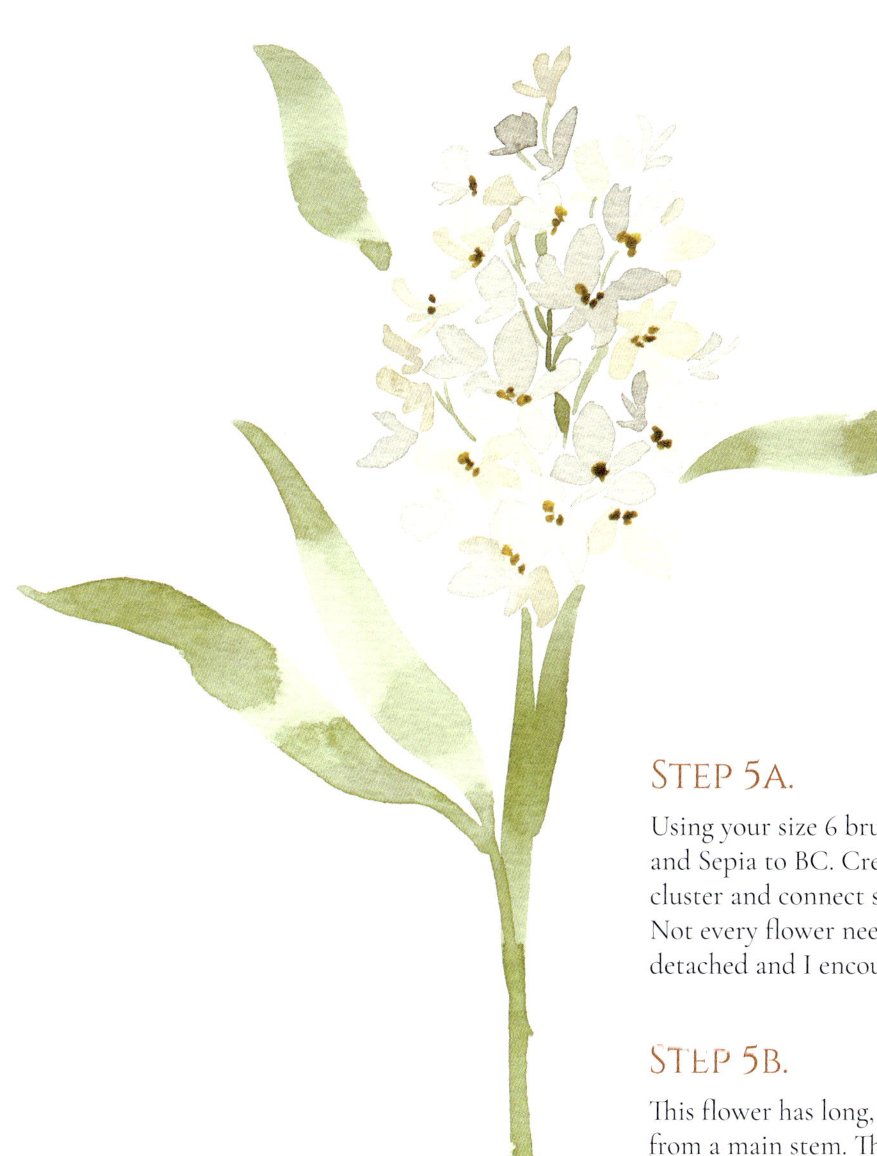

Step 5a.

Using your size 6 brush, mix together Sap Green and Sepia to BC. Create a stem at the bottom of the cluster and connect smaller stems to the flowers. Not every flower needs a stem; some will look best detached and I encourage you to keep it loose.

Step 5b.

This flower has long, swordlike leaves that protrude from a main stem. These are nothing more complicated than elongated simple strokes. Using your size 10 brush, load it with the Sap Green and Sepia mixture in BC and create two leaves on the left side that point slightly upward, then curve down. See page 32 for a refresh on movement. Be sure to lean into the belly toward the middle of stroke and ease up on the pressure as you reach the end of the leaf. Consider adding another leaf at the top and on the right, using the same technique.

African Daisy

I've grown up with African daisies my entire life. They are indigenous to where I live in Southern California and can be found blooming in nearly every neighborhood. Still, African daisies possess what can only be described as an exotic look, boasting a center with utterly intricate details. Although the gerbera daisy and African daisy share a name, they are completely different in appearance, and I'm so excited to draw out the nuances that make this particular flower so special. We'll also be using our filbert brush once again to give our petals a whole different feel!

Supplies

One size 4 filbert brush

One size 6 round brush

One size 2 round brush

Canson 140-lb (300-gsm) cold-press paper

Palette

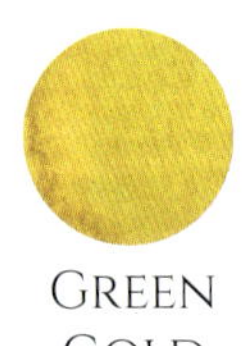

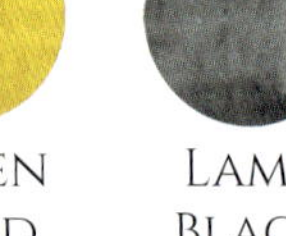

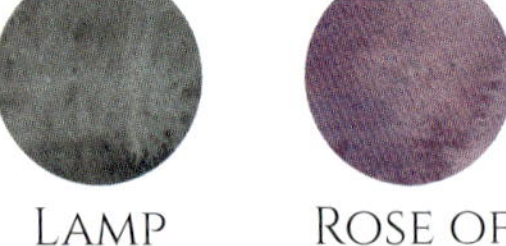

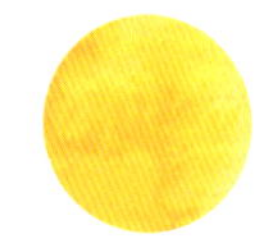

Green Gold (Petals) | Lamp Black (Petals) | Rose of Ultramarine (Center) | Cadmium-Free Yellow (Center)

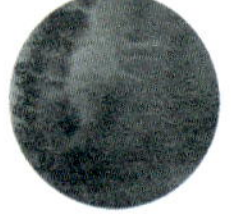

Greenish Umber (Leaves) | Sepia | Rose of Ultramarine + Sepia | Lamp Black + Green Gold

Preparing the Palette

Load your size 4 filbert brush with a Lamp Black and Green Gold in BC (page 16).

Load your size 6 round brush in Rose of Ultramarine and Sepia in BC.

Step 1a.

Using your size 6 round brush, make a small ring about the size of a quarter (1 inch [2.5 cm] in diameter), using small strokes in the Rose of Ultramarine and Sepia mixture. Be sure to leave a dime-sized (scant ¾-inch (1.8-cm)-diameter) open space in the middle.

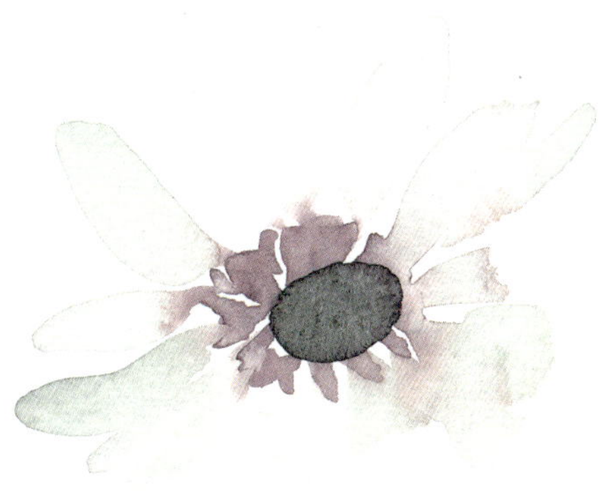

STEP 1B.

Using your size 4 filbert brush and the Lamp Black and Green Gold mixture in BC, immediately touch the end of your filbert brush to the edge of the purple ring and create petals around the ring. Remember to use the side of the brush for thinner petals, as well as the wide side, bristles flat, for thicker petals. For a closer look at this process, refer to page 43.

STEP 2.

Be sure the purple is fully dry, and then, using your size 6 brush, load it with Lamp Black in BC and add a center to the flower.

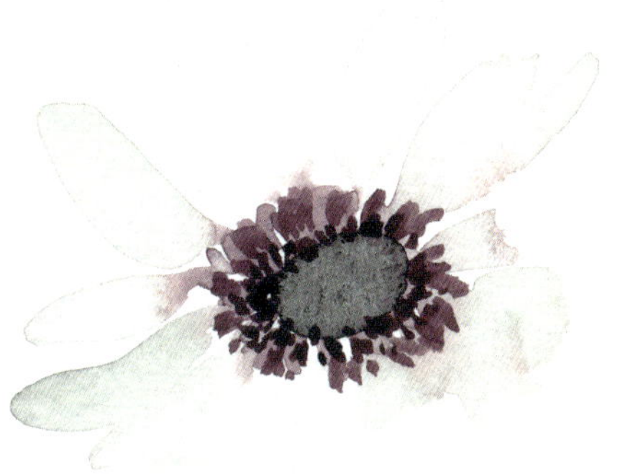

STEP 3.

Wait until the center is fully dry and then, using your size 6 brush in Rose of Ultramarine and Sepia in HRC (page 16), darken the inside with a series of small strokes to outline the black center.

STEP 4A.

Using the size 2 round brush, load it with Lamp Black in CSC (page 16) and add a speckled center. This is achieved by pressing the toe of the brush gently on the paper.

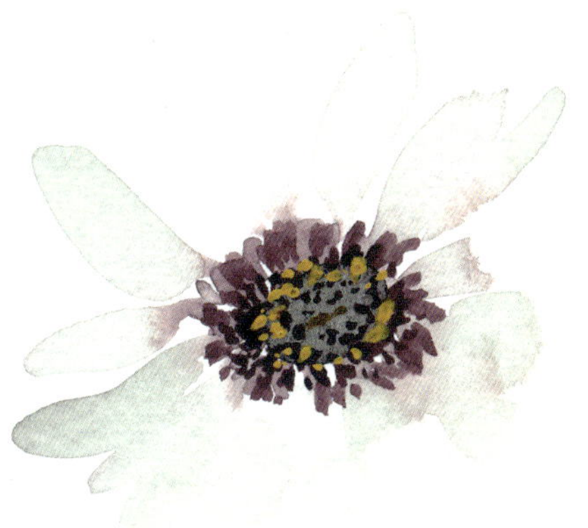

STEP 4B.

Wait until the black has dried and then rinse and reload the size 2 brush with Cadmium-Free Yellow in CSC to paint speckles on top of the black. The same technique as described in 4a applies, using slightly firmer pressure to create larger dots.

STEP 5.

Using your size 6 brush loaded with the Lamp Black and Green Gold mixture in BC, add a few thin strokes to serve as veins running the length of the petals. No need to rinse your brush before moving on.

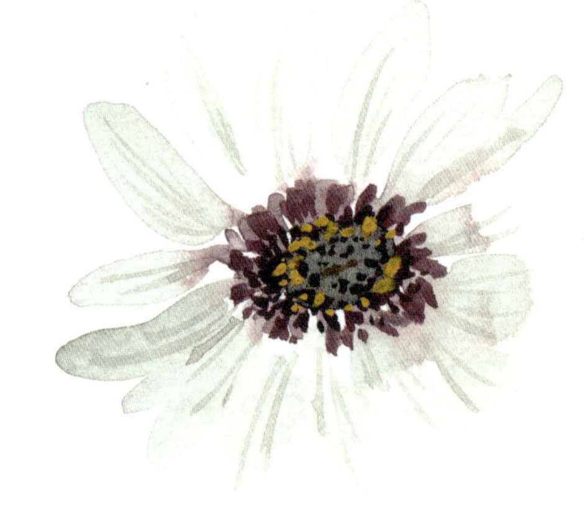

STEP 6A.

Using your size 6 brush loaded with Greenish Umber in BC, paint a stem that extends from the right side of the flower. Give it a moment to dry and then load the brush with Greenish Umber in CSC and repaint the stem so that some areas are darker.

STEP 6B.

Add the leaves, using the gestural branch technique shown on page 36. You can choose to create the leaves using your filbert or your size 6 brush, or a combination of both, which is what I did. I painted the branch and leaves using Greenish Umber in BC with my filbert brush. I waited until they were dry and then painted over them with the same color in CSC. Next, I used my size 6 round brush for gestural outlining. Please take liberties here, as always, and create leaves that give YOU joy.

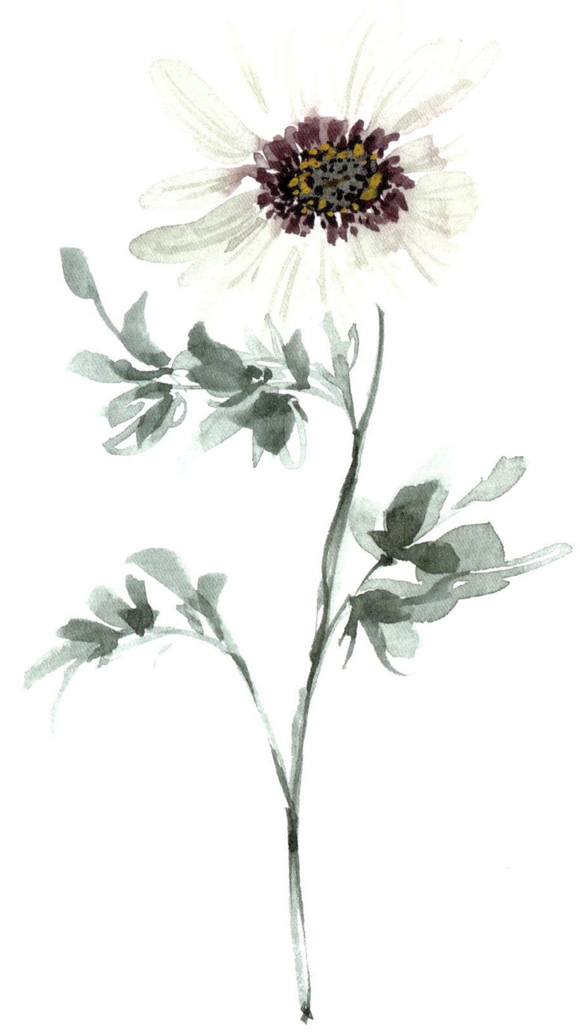

White Magnolia

For our finale of white flowers, we are going to take on the majestic magnolia. This is one of my favorite flowers, not only for its regal beauty, but for the memories it evokes. When she was younger, my eldest daughter and I would take daily walks through our community to visit with the magnolia trees, and her favorite part was to gently scrape out the seeds left behind after the flower had bloomed. Also, that lemony scent can't be beat!

I'd like you to know before we get started that this lesson will be a challenge. The goal, we must always remember, is not perfection, but to strengthen our muscles and give us something to keep working on after we have mastered some of the easier lessons. In my professional career I've painted three versions of magnolias because I always learn something new. Above all else, enjoy the process!

Supplies

One size 10 round brush
Two size 8 round brushes
Canson 140-lb (300-gsm) cold-press paper
HB pencil
Dust-free eraser

Palette

Sap Green (petals)

Sepia (petals, center & leaves)

Undersea Green (leaves)

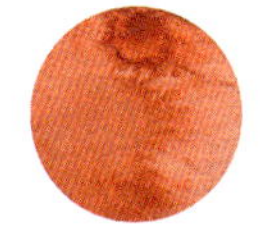

Quinacridone Burnt Scarlet (center)

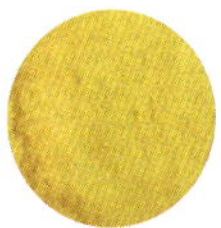

Green Gold (center)

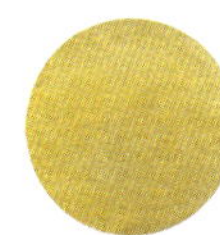

Green Gold + Sepia

Quinacridone Burnt Scarlet + Sepia

Sap Green + Sepia

Undersea Green + Sepia

Preparing the Palette

Mix together Sap Green and Sepia to BC (page 16).

Mix together Undersea Green to BC.

Mix together Undersea Green and Sepia to BC and CSC (page 16).

Step 1A.

Using an HB pencil, trace my drawing or sketch a similar flower onto a piece of watercolor paper. Once you're happy with it, go over the lines with a dust-free eraser to make them fainter. This will ensure they don't show through at the very end.

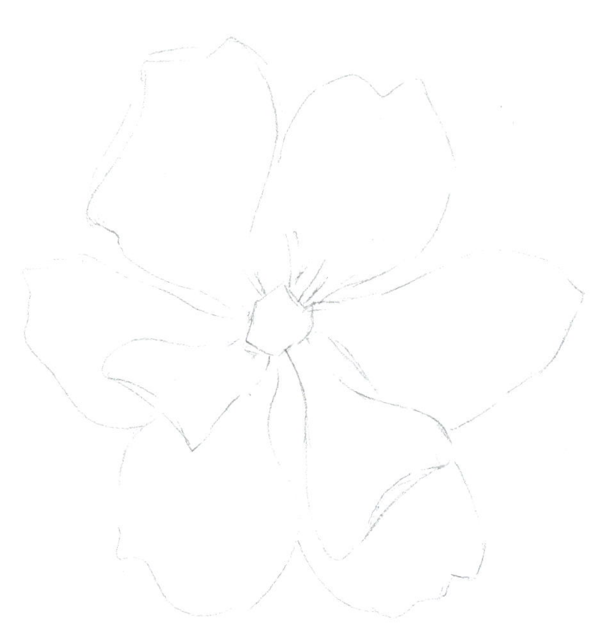

Step 1B.

Dip your size 10 brush into a cup of clean water and prime it (see page 16 for a refresh). Carefully glaze all the petals until they are moistened with an even coating of clean water. More info on glazing can be found on page 28. If you're unsure your paper is ready to accept paint, get down to bring it to eye level. There should be neither pools of water nor dry pockets.

Tip: If you find step 1B a bit daunting and haven't quite mastered the timing, you can break it down and do one petal at a time. Glaze one petal, drop in the color and so on until all the petals are completed.

Step 2.

Using a size 8 brush loaded with the Sap Green and Sepia BC mixture, quickly coat all the petals so they are an even color. For a wet-into-wet review, see page 29. If a petal dries up, simply prime the brush and load it with more of the mixture and guide the color to the edges of the petal. Some discoloration is normal and not a problem.

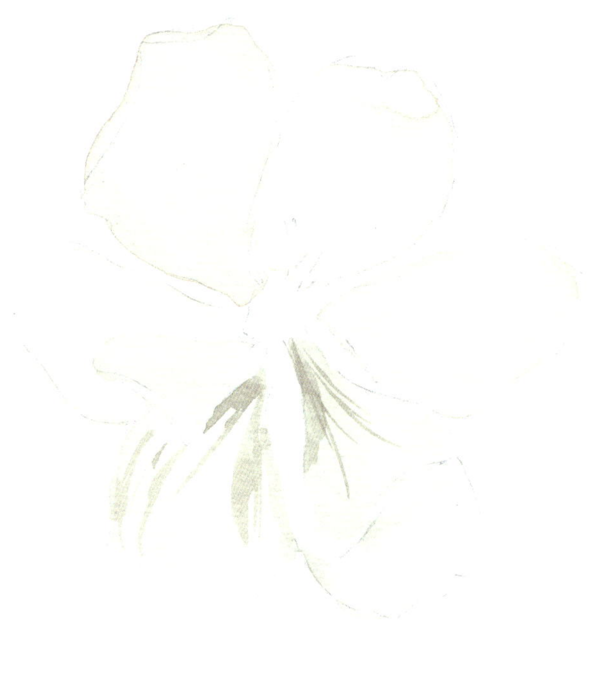

STEP 3.

Using your size 8 brush and the Undersea Green and Sepia mixture in BC, add a shadow where the top petal covers the bottom petal. Allow it to dry for about 30 seconds and then, using the toe of the brush, paint fine, gestural strokes (page 32) on top of the shadows.

STEP 4A.

Rinse and then load the other size 8 brush with Undersea Green and Sepia in CSC. Using your other size 8 brush loaded with Undersea Green and Sepia in BC, paint a few gestural strokes to serve as veins in the petals. Play with the level of thickness here so that not all the strokes are exactly the same. Use the belly of the brush loaded with BC to paint the wider strokes. Allow it to dry for 30 seconds, then use the other size 8 brush loaded with CSC to paint thinner strokes.

STEP 4B.

Repeat Steps 3 and 4a until all the petals have been completed with this technique. Be sure all media is dry before proceeding to the next step.

Step 5a.

Rinse a size 8 brush and load it with Quinacridone Burnt Scarlet and Sepia in BC.

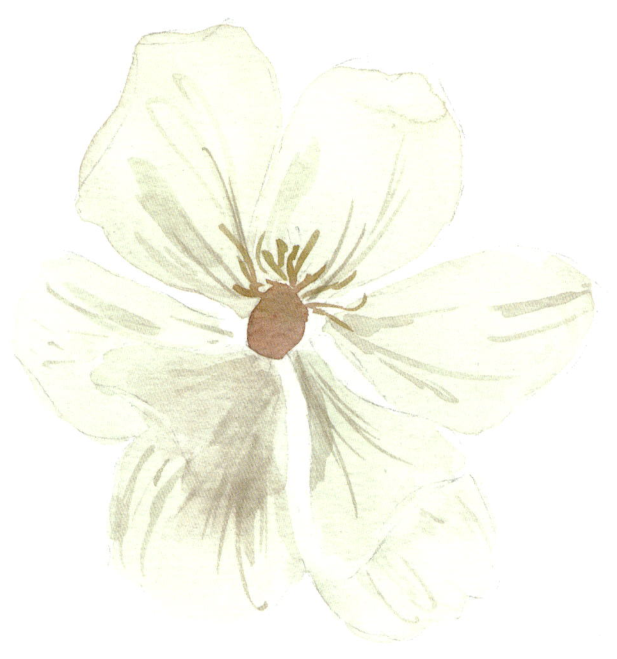

Step 5b.

Paint the center. It should occupy most of the empty space you left in the middle and be roughly the diameter of a thimble (about ¾ inch [2 cm]). No need to wait until the media is dry.

Step 5c.

Using your other size 8 brush, load it with Green Gold and Sepia in BC and paint the stamen using the gestural technique. Vary the thickness and length of the strokes for a more natural representation. For a refresh on strokes, have a look at "Pressure" on page 24.

Step 5d.

Use the same mixture, this time at CSC, and go over the stamen once more.

Step 6.

Be sure the media is fully dry. Still using your size 8 brush, load it with the Quinacridone Burnt Scarlet and Sepia mixture in CSC and darken the center by adding a few small strokes on top.

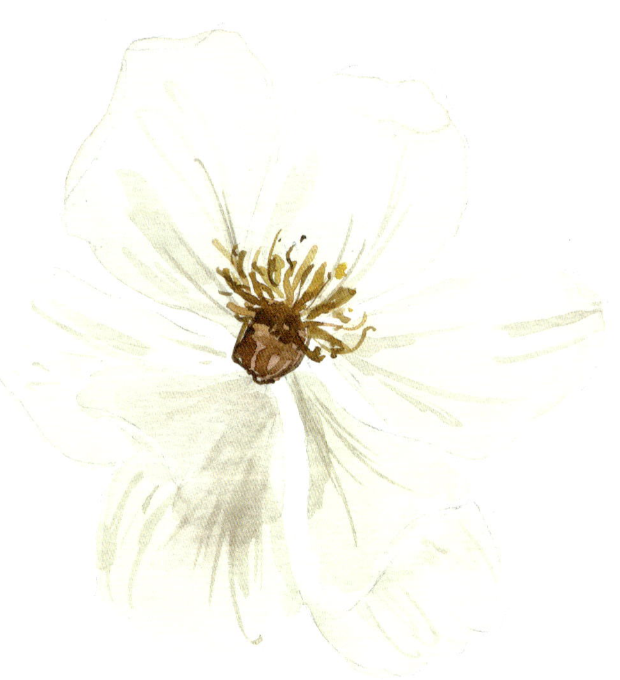

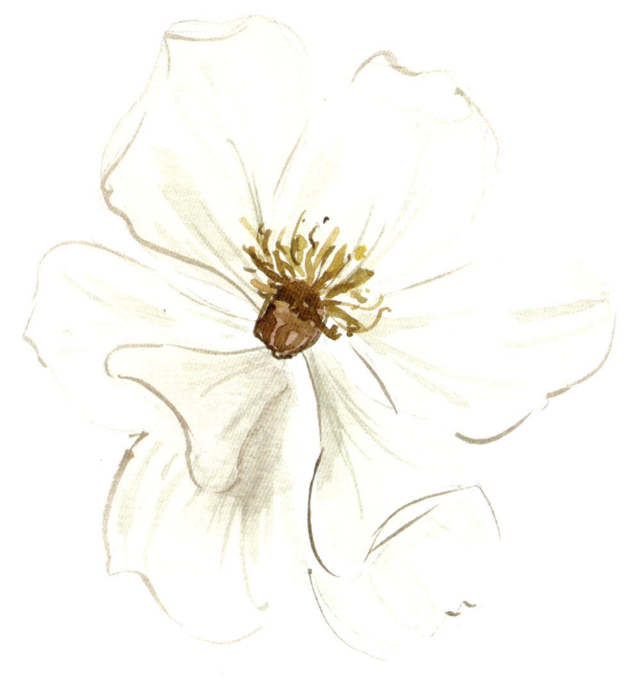

STEP 7.

Rinse your size 8 brush and reload it with Sepia in CSC. Give each petal a loose gestural outline. For a refresh on how to do this, see page 41.

STEP 8A.

Using your size 10 brush, load it with Undersea Green and Sepia in CSC and paint three leaves using the compound stroke leaf technique (page 33). I would also encourage you to take liberties here with the leaves, and if you would prefer to place them elsewhere, please do so!

STEP 8B.

While wet, use your size 8 brush to drop in a bit of this mixture at CSC to create a bleed.

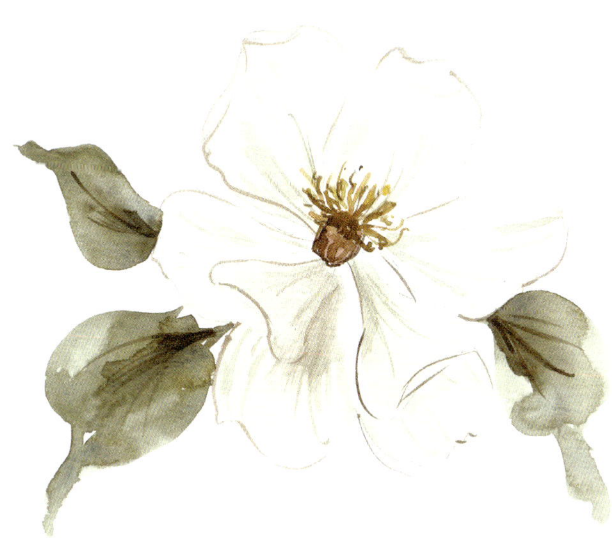

STEP 8C.

Once the leaves are dry, use your size 8 brush in Sepia BC and paint a few fine lines running the length of the leaves to act as veins.

STEP 8D.

Repeat this step using Sepia in CSC so that there are two consistencies of veins.

STEP 8E.

Erase the pencil lines once everything is completely dry.

Acknowledgments

A book is a strange and wondrous thing. It tells a story, of course, which is its own inimitable magic. Though beyond this—the telling of what and when and how—a book, when whittled down to its simplest form, is about people . . . specifically, the people without whom the book would be not in existence.

This book, for example, is not just my own, but belongs to a small but incredibly special network of benevolent souls who created space and paved the way for everything written on these pages.

I would like to thank those people now.

To my one and only Savior, Jesus Christ, who continues to be positively reckless with generosity and supplying me with endless amounts of grace.

If ever there was a champion for my cause, someone who relentlessly cheered me on to the point of annoyance, believing in my work so thoroughly until this venture became "our" dream instead of just my own, that person would be you, Michael. Your love, your unswerving faithfulness in me is a magic carpet, carrying me to heights I may only have ever imagined. You have made this *real*, giving not only your time and expertise to the less glamorous side of running a business, but most important, creating precious and sacred space amid baby-raising for me to claim this call upon my life. Thank you, my love, for every little thing, and the big things, too; i.e., showing up as though on cue with tasty libations and lavish hugs.

To my daughters, Hazel and Violet: My treasures, you are just four and one at the moment, too young to really understand what Mama has been doing up there in her studio all these months. Still, when I start to doubt myself, when I worry I am not enough for this big dream, it is YOUR faces I see. You keep me kind and gentle with myself. I love you with my every breath. Thank you for choosing me to be your Mama.

To the parents of me and this book, Mike, Debi, Nancy and Susan. Let's be real. You are the real heroes. The ones who looked after our children, so we could get something—maybe even two somethings!—done. There would be nothing at all if not for your generous and consistent willingness to love our babies.

To the vast and ruthlessly supportive community on Instagram: what a crazy world indeed to be thanking people I have never met but who have without a doubt altered the course of my career and poured into my creative journey. Thank you for staying by my side through all the transitions over the last ten years. You know who you are, and I love you.

Jenna and Lauren, my editors, thank you for your keen eyes and pursuit toward making this book the best it could be. To Meg and the design team for allowing us to take a few liberties with the cover. This was so special to us! Iris, my copy editor, you are to this book what a dentist is to the mouth. I owe you a debt of gratitude for making every page sparkle! A heartfelt thanks to everyone at Page Street Publishing; words fall short for helping us achieve a lifelong goal.

Last but certainly not least, to you, dear readers. You are perhaps the most important of all; for without you I would have no one to share my knowledge and experience. This book is a gift to you, but it's a gift to me as well, having been able to nurture your creative spark. Thank you for the honor and privilege of teaching you. I pray I have served you well, and I look forward to seeing your projects in the years to come!

About the Author

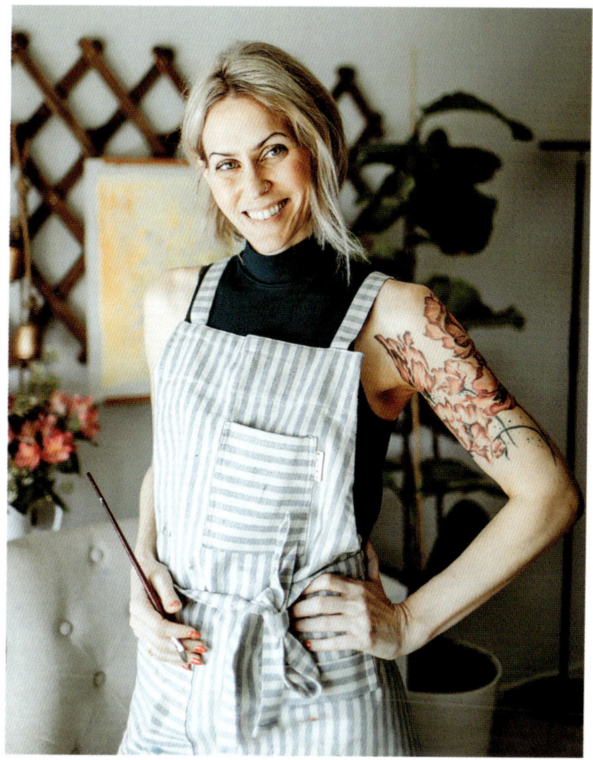

Cara Rosalie Olsen is a fine artist specializing in watercolor and gouache floral design. She is also an art educator, teaching both beginner and intermediate workshops held in Southern California, as well as online, via the learning platform Skillshare. Cara currently spends the majority of her day caring for her two girls, Hazel and Violet, who are her greatest blessings. When she's not covered in glitter glue or sitting on the floor attending high-society tea parties, she can be found painting nature in her studio.

For more information you can visit Cara's website RosalieGwenPaperie.com.

Index